NO MOTHERS WE!

Italian Women Writers and Their Revolt Against Maternity

Alba Amoia

University Press of America, Inc.
Lanham · New York · Oxford

Copyright © 2000 by
University Press of America, ® Inc.
4720 Boston Way
Lanham, Maryland 20706

12 Hid's Copse Rd.
Cumnor Hill, Oxford OX2 9JJ

Library of Congress Cataloging-in-Publication Data

Amoia, Alba della Fazia.
No mothers we! : Italian women writers and their revold against maternity /
Alba Amoia.
p.   cm.
Includes bibliographical references and index.
1. Italian literature—Women authors—History and criticism. 2. Motherhood
in literature. 3. Mother and child in literature. 4. Childbirth in literature.
5. Pregnancy in literature. 6. Mothers—Italy—Folklore. I. Title.
PQ4063 .A49 2000   850.9'353—dc21   00-036401 CIP

ISBN 0-7618-1717-4 (cloth: alk. ppr)
ISBN 0-7618-1718-2 (pbk: alk. ppr.)

Why do we idealise sacrifice in mothers? Who gave us this inhuman idea that mothers should negate their own wishes and desires? The acceptance of servitude has been handed down from mother to daughter for so many centuries that it is now a monstrous chain which fetters them.

—Sibilla Aleramo, *A Woman* (1906), 193.

Contents

An Italian Chronology vii

Preface xiii

Chapter I
Ancient Fertility Goddesses 1

Chapter II
The Mutations of Madonna Worship and the Mutability
of Motherhood 27

Chapter III
Literary Manifestations of the Changing Social Scene:
The Nineteenth Century and Beyond 59

Chapter IV
The Twentieth-Century Revolt against Maternity 71

Conclusion
Italy Awaits the New Woman 137

Notes 143

Bibliography 153

Index 163

An Italian Chronology

Paleolithic: Humans appear in Italy; rock cave drawings and incisions interpreted today as containing fertility symbolism; small population in delicate demographic balance with forests and plains.

Upper Paleolithic: Production of anthropomorphic stone and bone statuettes of females—so-called "Paleolithic Venuses"—examples of which will be found near Lake Trasimene, at Savignano, Chiozza, Grimaldi, etc. (Paolo Graziosi, *L'arte preistorica in Italia*, 15-23).

Neolithic (ca. 5000-ca. 2000 B.C.E. in Italy): Farmers, shepherds, and fishermen replace earlier hunters; pristine rural cults are based on fertility-fecundity relationship with the sacred earth; pottery includes terracotta statuettes of steatopygous females with prominent breasts and rounded abdomens, such as one that will be found in the so-called "milk fountain" near Arezzo (Vittorio Dini, *Il potere delle antiche madri*, 57).

Aenolithic (transitional): Siculan culture in Sicily: archeological finds in a necropolis will include similar female figures (Graziosi, 23).

Bronze Age (ca. 1800 B.C.E.-ca. 1000 in Italy): Northern peoples are in the main stock farmers and agriculturists; seminomadic pastoral people of the so-called "Apennine culture" will practice some agriculture by the twelfth century B.C.E. (M. Cary and H.H. Scullard, *A History of Rome Down to the Reign of Constantine*, 8); more and more hands are needed to plough and plant; fertility figures, signs, and references will increase.

Iron Age and Villanovan culture (after 1000 B.C.E.): Village settlements grow; self-contained agricultural Italic peoples practice *ver sacrum* (sacred spring, the marking of newborns who, when grown, will be banished to borderlands to found new colonies); Villanovan culture gradually absorbed by Etruscans, Celts, and Romans (Cary and Scullard, 13, 15; *Enciclopedia italiana di scienze, lettere ed arti,* vol. 28, 241).

ca. 800 B.C.E.: Contacts between Italic peoples and Carthaginians and Greeks; Etruscan city-states begin to emerge; shrines later dedicated to Hera (Greek goddess of, inter alia, marriage and women in childbed) at Etruscan city of Tarquinii; and to Uni (Etruscan corruption of Juno)/Astarte (Phoenician goddess of fertility and reproduction) at Etruscan city of Caere (Cary and Scullard, 48, 578, 579).

6th century B.C.E.: Height of Etruscan civilization; mineral wealth exploited and commerce developed, but basis of life remains agriculture, the fertile land supporting a large population; *Etrusca disciplina* (ritual books) define religious practice (Cary and Scullard, 24).

509 B.C.E.: Dedication under Etruscan king at Rome of Jupiter Optimus Maximus' temple on Capitoline hill; Juno Regina (Queen of Heaven, identified with the Greek Hera) forms part of the triad (trinity) Jupiter-Juno-Minerva; increasing numbers of springs and fountains are dedicated to fertility goddesses (Juturna, Egeria, etc.) (Ernesto Bignami, *Manuale di storia romana*, 71).

ca. 500 B.C.E.: End of Etruscan rule in Rome and Latium, where pastoral-agricultural society is based on *familia* in which the *paterfamilias* or eldest living male holds almost absolute dominion; religious usage clearly reflects the agricultural basis of life; rain and abundance evoked through a proliferation of fertility goddesses including Venus, Feronia, Fortuna, Maia, Flora, Dea Dia, Ops Mater, Bona Dea, and Mater Matuta; institution of the state cult dedicated to Ceres (identified with the Greek mother-goddess Demeter) (Cary and Scullard, 32, 44, 65, 109, 621).

ca. 400 B.C.E.: Celtic invasion brings the great earth mother Dana (or Danu, the Celtic Artemis) to Italy, where she is worshiped as goddess of animal and vegetable fecundity; Greek Artemis will later be identified with the Roman Diana, goddess, inter alia, of childbirth

(Dini, 28); Roman territory expands to ca. 4,500 sq.mi. with a population of at least one million (Michael Grant, *History of Rome*, 57-8) .

202 B.C.E.: Cult of Phrygian nature-goddess Cybele, or Magna Mater, officially brought to Rome together with the black fetish-stone from her sanctuary at Pessinus (Asia Minor) (Cary and Scullard, 198).

1st century B.C.E.: Official cults lose hold on Roman people; mystery cults multiply, notably those of Isis (mother, life-giver), Attis (offshoot of cult of Magna Mater), and Mithra (which excludes women) (Cary and Scullard, 483; Grant, 333).

1st to 4th centuries C.E.: Christianity spreads, but among the old-established cults the "religion of the peasant" remains deeply rooted in the countryside; Christian polemicists seek to extirpate pristine rural cults (Cary and Scullard, 545).

325 C.E.: Council of Nicaea prohibits, inter alia, presence of unmarried women in houses of clergy, and unsuccessfully attempts to enforce clerical celibacy.

391 and 393 C.E.: ultimate victory of Christianity having been assured in the Roman world, Emperor Theodosius I forbids all pagan worship, public or private (Bignami, 403).

431 C.E.: Council of Ephesus proclaims Mary the Mother of God, thus favoring proliferation of cults dedicated to her.

494 C.E.: Pope Gelasius I institutes the Feast of the Purification of Mary (Candelora), subrogating the ancient Roman Lupercalia festival in which, inter alia, priests (*luperci*) who had previously been cleansed with milk (the food of infancy) and who were obliged to smile (signifying the fullness of life) struck with a leather thong those women who offered to be smitten in order to obtain fecundity (*Enciclopedia italiana*, vol. 21, 668).

5th century C.E.: Dissolution of the western Roman empire; agricultural labor scarce (Grant, 444).

553 C.E.: Council at Constantinople further defines devotion to the Mother of God.

6th to 8th centuries C.E.: Archaic sacred places in northern and central Italy which had been dedicated to ancient cults of fecundity are now placed under protection of so-called "milk Madonnas" as guardians of maternity and infancy; sanctuaries of pre-Christian fertility and fecundity divinities begin to be dedicated to protective Catholic women saints (Dini, 63, 82).

6th century C.E.: Roman Catholic Church institutes Major Rogation (*litania maior*) to replace pagan procession (Robigalia) for fertility of the fields (*Enciclopedia italiana*, vol. 29, 516).

ca. 800 C.E.: Pope Leo III institutes Minor Rogations (*litaniae minores*), subrogating three-day pagan processions with prayer to Ceres for abundant crops (Ambarvalia) (Bignami, 70, 77).

ca. 1000 C.E.: Church transforms ancient Roman harvest feasts into ember days for spiritual renewal and thanksgiving for agricultural crops; Church concedes that a rational spirit may be attributed to women.

14th to 20th centuries: Proliferation of artistic representations of pregnant Madonna, of Madonna and Child, and scenes of maternity serve to feed the fantasy of bliss and plenitude in mother-child fusion.

mid-15th century: Piero della Francesca's famous painting "Madonna del Parto" (pregnant Mary, or Our Lady of Expectation) reinforces religious theme of maternity but also identifies the Virgin with the fruit-bearing earth (Elly Cassee, "La Madonna del Parto," 96; Dini, 37-9).

15th to 18th centuries: Various popes (Sixtus IV, Paul III, Pius V, Gregory XIII, Clement VIII, Paul V, Urban VII, Innocent X, Innocent XI, Innocent XIII) confer special privileges on the so-called "milk fountain" sanctuary at Lucignano (Arezzo) dedicated to the Madonna but where pagan divinities had previously been invoked; waters of the spring still used today as a cure for sterility and hypolactation (Dini, 76-7).

1543-1563: Council of Trent, while affirming the sacramental character of matrimony for the *propagationem humani generis*, condemns representations of *"Maria in exspectatione"* as unorthodox (Cassee, 95).

1614: First edition of Pope Paul V's *Rituale romanum*, containing ceremonial procedures for postpartum "Churching of Women."

17th to 19th centuries: Over one-half of Italy's employed population engaged in agriculture; high average density of population on agricultural land.

1892: Cesare Lombroso and T.L. Ferrero publish *La donna delinquente* arguing that so-called "born prostitutes" are without maternal feelings and are often sterile, while the loving mother type is endowed with sex organs that are not so much genital as maternal (Isabella Nardi, "Le 'cattive madri'," 81, 89).

1906: Sibilla Aleramo publishes *Una donna*, the foundation stone of 20th-century Italian feminism.

Early 20th century: Mass emigration from overpopulated areas; Futurist women authors attempt to desacralize the womb and create a new female archetype.

1925-1943: Mussolini's dictatorship inculcates Fascist ideals of male virility and female fecundity; hails "sacred maternity" in the name of the Fatherland (Papinio Pennato, *Sacra maternità*, 160).

1929: Lateran Treaty recognizes Roman Catholicism as "the sole religion of the state"; treaty confirmed by the 1948 Italian constitution.

1930s: Large-scale textile industry employs mainly female labor; increasing industrial employment of women in the north.

1945: Women obtain the vote; ideological commitment to idealized maternity is maintained by Italians during the post-World War II period.

1961: Birthrate at 1.84 continues to decline steadily.

1962: By law, "paternal" authority is replaced by "parental" authority within the family.

1967 and 1975: New legislation regarding child adoption and recognition of children born out of wedlock leads to a "debiologization" of family relationships (Amedeo Santosuosso, "Paternità e nuove tecniche di riproduzione," 125).

1968: Students' and workers' so-called "revolutions" give impetus to female emancipation movements which proliferate in the 1970s; women writers, finding support from French theorists such as Simone de Beauvoir, Hélène Cixous and Luce Irigaray, attack the patriarchy and vindicate release from their conditioned duty to bear children.

1970: Divorce authorized by Italian law for the first time.

1978: Voluntary interruption of pregnancy is legalized, although full application of the law is still lacking today mainly because of Church opposition.

1980s: Some women writers continue to express hostility to marriage and maternity.

1982: Law permits surgery for change of sex (Santosuosso, 135).

1987: Supreme Court legalizes voluntary sterilization (Santosuosso, 136).

1990s: Italian birthrate maintained at zero (-0.2 during 1990-1994); statistics indicate further significant reductions in agriculture (6.4% decrease in the number of farms, and 9.8% decrease in number of agricultural workers between 1990-1993) (*1994 DemographicYearbook*, 130; Istituto Nazionale di Statistica, 53). Some women writers openly condemn Church teachings on maternity, birth control, and abortion.

Preface

Italy, long hailed (or reprobated) as the poster child of human fecundity, now suddenly boasts the lowest fertility rate in the world. Once known as an agricultural land with an insatiable need for farm labor, the Italian peninsula during the past 150 years was disastrously plagued by overpopulation and unemployment, particularly in the impoverished regions of the South which fed the mass emigrations of the twentieth century.

Now, as that century nears its end, Italy has emerged as a technologically advanced country, and its fertility level has been dramatically reduced as the result of changing attitudes and practices and increased awareness of the limitations on viable population growth that are set by environmental, economic and psychological factors. With the number of rural workers continuing to decline at a steady rate,[1] by the years 1990-94 the country had actually achieved a negative population growth rate of -0.2 per cent (*1994 Demographic Yearbook*, 130).

This trend seems doubly remarkable in a land whose soil is littered with vestiges of the fertility goddesses who were worshiped throughout Antiquity and even into the Common Era; a country whose women—and men, too—long cherished the concept of a divine earth mother embodying the principle of fecundity in plants and animals, from the lowest to the highest; a nation whose dominant Roman Catholic cult has traditionally drawn its strength from the glorification of motherhood as idealized in the Virgin/Child dyad, and which has continued to condemn or restrict virtually every alternative to natural and abundant childbirth.

It goes without saying that the women of Italy, as those most immediately concerned with the phenomena of motherhood, have played a decisive part in this seismic change. Such a reversal, indeed, would have been inconceivable without the participation, even the leadership, of the female part of the Italian population. Confined for centuries in a subordinate position in which the functions of childbearing and child-rearing were looked upon as the essential elements of matrimony, thus taking precedence over every other component of personality, Italian women over the past hundred years have gradually become aware of the anomalous nature of their plight and, in recent decades, have shown a resolute determination to correct it.

A number of gifted women writers have played a leading part in this transformation, in works that in some cases have echoed the despairing cry of repressed femininity, and in others have critically examined the feminine condition and its possible alternatives. The role of these writers within the wider evolution of feminine consciousness will be the particular concern of the present book. The magnitude of their accomplishment will become increasingly apparent as we widen our view of motherhood to embrace the sweep of human development in the Mediterranean basin since prehistoric times.

The early Italic peoples, in passing from the life of hunters in the unconquered wilderness to the more non-migratory stages of a pastoral and agricultural existence, were much given to the worship of all-seeing and all-knowing fertility goddesses identified with sacred or consecrated places in the bosom of nature. Women invoked the female divinities for aid in conception and delivery; men called upon them to protect their flocks, their herds, and their crops. Known in their oriental-Greek-Roman syncretistic form as "Magna Mater" or Great Mother, the fertility goddess peculiar to each locality or population became a symbol of universal motherhood, the dynamic source and animator of wild nature, the parent of gods and men and of the lower orders of creation.

Passive, immanent, childbearing women, pliant to society's needs and vulnerable to the fear of losing their offspring, worked the fertile fields and endlessly repeated the cycle of their own bodily functions. Their role was to perpetuate life while men transcended it through their encroachments on nature's domain. Woman's traditional occupations became the all-sufficient justification for her existence. The wild haunts and shadowy groves associated with the fertility goddesses may have represented for her an ultimately impossible escape from the human condition.

Models of sexually differentiated comportment persisted through the millennia, each sex conforming conscientiously to its own pattern lest the individual be marginalized by a society quick to castigate the diverse or alien (Giani Gallino, 3). Witness the durability of the primitive mother-infant-household triptych, in which, as we now can see, the submissive and self-denigrating woman was all too likely to suffocate under the stifling effects of her own fertility and the asphyxiating sterility of the family hearth.

With the advent of Christianity, the fertility cult acquired mystical and theological content. Images of the Holy Family became a paradigm of the Italian family itself. In the centuries of Madonna worship, the idea of the sanctity of motherhood was so inculcated by the Church that women unable to conform to the maternal ideal were overwhelmed by feelings of sin and guilt. Their very reflexes were conditioned by religious art and by the ceremonial forms of Marian devotion. The material Madonna image became deeply embedded in the Catholic woman's psychocultural life.

In more recent times, Italy's new industrial society provided hitherto unknown opportunities for work outside the home, but did not essentially change the woman's role from what it had been previously (*Maria, Medea e le altre*, 220). In practice, the problematic separation/connection between public and private remained. Incorrigibly patriarchal in its outlook, Italian society recognized the existence of a huge "socio-familistic" problem but found only palliatives with which to combat it.

Thus it required years of feminist struggle in our century before Italian women in 1978 belatedly won the right to terminate an unwanted pregnancy. In theory, a phase of equilibrium between the sexes was thus established; an "equality in difference" or "equality in symmetry" began to undermine patriarchal power and to encroach on traditional male prerogatives (Guicciardi, 26). Yet even after the 1970s, Italian reality fell far short of equality of the sexes. Women, if no longer driven, continued to be gently nudged toward the basically affective role of the wife/mother.

Such ultramodern inventions as the artificial uterus and the purported "male womb" may some day free at least some women from the burdens of pregnancy, though this will not relieve them of the postnatal tasks of motherhood and childrearing. Already, advances in applied biology have brought about a change in ways of thinking about maternity, destroying at least some of the stereotypes that for millennia have regulated the laws governing reproduction and filiation.

But ecclesiastical opposition to advances in biotechnology continues, as a practical matter, to inhibit progress in these directions, even while contraception and abortion remain almost totally prohibited. Thus there has been no substantial change in the paradoxical situation in which the Church stands equally firm against the wishes of those women desiring abortion, for whatever reason, and the aspirations of those women whose desire for a child has led them to consider the option of artificial insemination.

Casual observation tells us that Italian women generally desire children, though it is difficult to know how far this desire is biologically implanted and how far it is the result of cultural conditioning. There has, in any event, been a visible shift of emphasis from quantity to quality in motherhood, from brute procreation to a selective fecundity that respects the right of both mothers and children to a more fruitful, less harassed relationship.

Italian women may thus be said to have passed from the first stage of maternal development—the so-called "instinctive maternity," characterized by a unity of interests and desires in mother and child—to what has been called "civilized maternity," in which the presence of divergent interests is frankly recognized.[2] Few if any Italian women now look upon childbirth as "miraculous," or believe the milk in their breasts to be a "magical" gift to their child from an all-important goddess. The Italian mother is gradually becoming aware that *compenetrazione*—intense intimacy and unconscious communication between mother and baby—fosters a dependency on others and implies the woman's own regression to her "baby-self" and to a state of childhood. She realizes that motherhood needs to be relieved of all manner of disabilities and encumbrances if it is to redound to the mutual benefit of mothers and children.

Pregnancy itself has come to be seen by many as a profoundly contradictory state, an enrichment but at the same time an injury, a benefit and a deprivation. For the traditional nineteenth-century woman, the act of procreation, the state of pregnancy, and the obligations of motherhood were hallmarks of femininity achieved. But many twentieth-century women, as will be seen in the writings analyzed in this volume, are not only repelled by the physical aspects of pregnancy but decline to look on wifehood and motherhood as forms of innate femininity (Parker, 155). How many men, they ask, would want to have children at the price of pregnancy and breastfeeding to the detriment of their masculinity?

Drawn to, and, at the same time, deeply discomfited by the myth of the maternal ideal, many women are now making efforts to reframe it, deconstruct it, demystify it, or even dismiss it. If on the one hand they desire to have children, on the other they desire to escape them. In the works we are about to examine, the female protagonists are typically concerned to lift the constricting, anxious sense of responsibility that binds them to their children. In attempting to reestablish their own boundaries and regain a coherent sense of their own identity, they invariably come to realize that they are simply not cut out to be wives and mothers.

The more skeptical among Italian women writers have broached the subject of maternity in a variety of ways: mysteriously, mockingly, jokingly, satirically, or sarcastically. They seem to imply that they are overcoming and exorcising, through a well-known mechanism of depth psychology, the anxiety inseparable from the birth process. As had been foretold in the Hebrew scriptures, woman's relationship to her anatomy has not been a happy one. Sibilla Aleramo, as we shall see, was among the first Italian women writers to have listened to her own body, its organs, its psyche, and to have described her aspiration to see beyond motherhood.

Fertility statistics are but one indicator of the change that is now taking place in the constitution of the Italian woman, led by the writers whose works we are about to examine. Rather than trying to explain away the maternal love/hate ambivalence, Italian women writers are now more prone to express open revolt against the conditions that have prevented their sisters from setting themselves higher goals appropriate to their talents. Nor do they any longer shy away from such sensitive topics as maternal violence against children or even infanticide.

Paradoxically, in the very country where the Church of Rome sacramentalized marriage and conferred its bureaucratic sanction on Mother Mary's innumerable roles and titles, women now raise their voices in defiant protest against conventional views not only of motherhood but even of matrimony itself. A poll of Italian women conducted in September 1997 revealed that four out of ten respondents would not again marry their husbands in view of the difficulties of leading a shared life.

Gods, goddesses, and divine earth mothers evolve and die. Once they have been fully exploited as symbols of human aspiration, they give way to other archetypes. The notion of the Great Mother of the Gods, concretized in full-breasted steatopygous female form, has long since disappeared from Italian culture. The once popular concept of the Madonna, submissively receiving Gabriel's Annunciation and later fondling her Divine Child, has dimmed in its turn.

Maternity and motherhood were obviously ripe for demythologization. What remains surprising is that Italian women, shaped by so long and intense a history of mothering, should have seized a foremost place among the demythologizers of our time. Perhaps a new myth is now needed to guide the mind and the body-in-the-making of a new, resolute type of woman, one who will assert her rational free will in matters of fertility and fecundity as in other matters. Although we need not adopt the all-or-nothing formula reported by Lidia Ravera—"In order to create, I must not procreate" (*Bambino mio*, 147), what is undoubtedly required is a more enlightened concept of motherhood that harmonizes and balances the needs of mothers, fathers, children and the encompassing society in ways appropriate to the demands of a new century and a new millennium.

Chapter I

ഇറ

Ancient Fertility Goddesses

A mother is supposed to be a milky mammal, an oozing sack of moisture. Reduced to pure matter. Mater.

—Linda Anderson, *Jocasta*

Fertility and Birth in Prehistoric Times

Since their earliest beginnings, human beings have been obsessed by the problems relating to the life, death, and reproduction of their kind and of any other life forms that are thought likely to promote or threaten their well-being. The importance always and everywhere attached to the gestation and nurture of living organisms is unmistakably apparent if we look back from our present-day preoccupation with the so-called rights to choose, to live, to die, and to enjoy freedom from hunger, clean air and water, and the like, and consider the profusion of divinities and rites that have been involved with comparable concerns since before the dawn of recorded history.

"Back to the Stone Age"

This intimate concern is above all evident in connection with the mysteries of biological reproduction and their bearing on the welfare of humankind. From early Paleolithic times, symbols of fertility and rebirth have appeared and reappeared in rites and rituals closely geared to the elemental processes of gestation. Conclusive Paleolithic remains show how the sacred tended to define the real, and all important realities of life participated in the sacred. Abstract designs on the walls of caves have been read in terms of sexual symbolism, and some experts have postulated the performance of highly complex fertility rites in cave sanctuaries (Gombrich, 10). The underground chambers themselves, with their rock fissures and cleavages, have been seen as representing the body and the uterus of the female, while the red-ochre wounds appearing on the bodies of the animals carved or painted on the walls have similarly been taken as female symbols (Giani Gallino, 31).

There are signs, too, of sexual rivalries and jealousies originating in very early times and subject, in some cases, to surprising interpretations in our own day. The mother-goddess symbol, so prevalent among the artifacts of the earliest preliterate civilizations, has been seen as a product of male anguish mingled with admiration, fear, and envy of female procreative capability. The female biological archetypes of reproduction and of menstruation, it is said, gave women the enviable advantage of apparent immortality and cyclic contact with the moon and the universe (Giani Gallino, 6).

Cyclicality is simulated artificially and culturally in the primitive practice of couvade: the father goes through the motions of motherhood at the time of a child's birth, reflecting a strong male desire to take possession of female prerogatives. In Minoan religious thought, since dying vegetation was thought of as male, the vegetation-goddess Ariadne was honored, on the island of Cyprus, in a sacred dance involving a young male dressed as a woman who feigned labor pains, demonstrating that he was a man/mother (Giani Gallino, 106). Cannibalism has similarly been explained as an attempt on the part of the male to take possession of the product of maternity by introducing it into his own body, symbolically replicating maternal gestation (Grasso, 15, 108).

The hunter, it has also been said, could claim the leadership of magic rituals by virtue of his physical and metaphysical power, and yet might be ignorant of the mysteries of actual reproduction. To such unenlightened males has been imputed a belief that animals derived directly from the womb of the mother-goddess, and that the latter could assure the continuation of the species by parthenogenesis, the reproductive process in which the female produces young alone and unaided. Thus early there arose a concept that Christianity would later appropriate—though in disguised form—in hailing the virginity and chastity of a new mother-goddess (Warner, 72).

This supposed Paleolithic equilibrium between female procreative power and male physical/metaphysical power was upset to female advantage with the passage from a subsistence economy based on the hunt to an economy that was predominantly agricultural. As farmers, shepherds and fishermen replaced the earlier hunters, women's prestige increased in parallel with that of the female goddess who, already revered as the creator of all life, now became associated specifically with the fertility of the soil and the burgeoning of plant life. Agricultural lore held that it was actually in the mother's body that the grain was sown (Van Buren, 27). Nurturing and maternal women could thus be seen as embodying the principle of the fertility of the entire earth, viewed as the divine source of terrestrial life.

Where Paleolithic man's art—his recording of observed phenomena and his symbolizing of unseen forces in formal patterns and abstract designs—appears to our eyes as veristic and naturalistic, his successor, Neolithic man, gave expression to the invisible forces and hidden inner substances as he perceived them in semi-naturalistic, schematic, and severe geometrical design (Graziosi, 1973, 75). Abstract and obscurely symbolic stylizations may have stood for such capricious forces as the fertility of domestic animals, the alternation of sunshine and rain, threats of drought and flood, storm and wind. The stylized signs and symbols of Neolithic geometrism were consistent with a world in which plenty and scarcity alternated and which therefore did not lend itself to realistic treatment.

The discovery of a sacred element in the life of plants, coupled with the domestication of animals, speeded the growth of a new religious structure strongly grounded in sexuality and fertility. Pastoral-agricultural peoples depended for their subsistence on flocks and herds, fields and orchards. To provide their cattle with grass and water, to ensure their fecundity and an abundance of milk, and to guard them from the depredations of wild beasts were objects of prime importance to shepherds and herdsmen (Frazer, II: 324). Cycles of agricultural production, and of human and animal reproduction, buttressed a maternal mystique in which pregnant women, children, crops, farm animals, and particularly milk-producing animals were considered especially valuable. And, since they were also highly vulnerable, measures had also to be taken to protect them from the evil eye by magic rites and rituals.

The Cult of Fertility

Dependence on the fertility of the earth and its creatures brought into play a host of imaginary beings, mainly female, whose business it was to accept the homage of their human clientele and watch over the latter's interests in the field of human, animal, and vegetable reproduction and growth. Such patronesses of fertility and fecundity were themselves involved in a dynamic of proliferation and frequently duplicated or competed with one another in the exercise of responsibilities too important to be entrusted to a single supernatural supporter. In most preliterate societies, such beings were worshiped through magic religious rituals reflecting ancient concepts of a life-creating force whose source and symbol was the womb. The process of reproduction, associated as it was with impulses of primitive biological need and cosmic force, was seen in essence as a repetition of the primordial act of creation.

Generous and powerful figures, fertility goddesses thus were called upon in both prehistoric and later times to promote and protect the entire reproductive process. The precariousness of women's condition before, during and after childbirth, subject as it has always been to such hazards as infantile and puerperal illness, mortality, and insufficient lactation, spelled a need in every epoch for protective systems involving a dependence on mythical forces to minimize the inescapable risks. All members of the group were affected when a mother unexpectedly failed to produce the milk on which a newborn's life depended; but it was principally the woman herself who implored and relied on supernatural intervention and support from the day of conception and even before. From the Paleolithic era to our own day, an uninterrupted chain of emotions has linked together women who have thus sought reassurance in the recourse to magic and religious ritual (Dini, 153–54).

Divine Mothers

By the close of the Neolithic period, this profusion of local and regional fertility deities was beginning to crystallize in the emergence of a type of superior female being, a generalized embodiment of the earth's fertility and the maternal tamer of wild nature, who could claim recognition by some such title as Great Mother of the Gods. The worship of such a being, under a variety of names and attributes and with the inclusion of any number of subordinate and satellite deities, was diffused throughout the Near and Middle East, the Mediterranean region, and beyond. The reign of such a complex and powerful divinity would form the center of culture and civilization through thousands of years of human experience (Van Buren, 127).

It would be futile to attempt to catalog the specific qualities and functions or even the names of this proliferating, shifting, kaleidoscopic array of goddesses and supergoddesses, each of them more or less identified with the creation of the universe and all of its life forms. Ishtar (Sumerian Inanna), the herdsmen's goddess of the Sumerian pantheon, is a prime example of these numinous females who were seen as the focus and guarantor of all vital processes. Known also as the "Lady of Heaven," Ishtar may have been the universal, all-purpose goddess par excellence, but one who has identifiable counterparts in numerous other Near Eastern and European cultures. As goddess of love identified with the morning star, she was thought to delight in bodily love, including prostitution, which was part of her cult.

Ninsun, another Sumerian deity who embodies and activates all the qualities the cowherd desires in his bovines, was herself known as the "good cow," a "mother of good offspring," which she was thought to love. As her name of "Lady Wild Cow" indicated, she was originally imagined in bovine form, but in her human shape she could also bear human offspring. The good cow that loves its offspring became, in the cowherds' pantheon, the very type of the mother—"the good cow in its [form as] woman."

Still other denizens of the Sumerian pantheon are Dumuzi-abzu, the power for fertility and new life that dwells in the marshes and lakes—her name means "the Quickener [of] the Young [in the mother's womb] of the Deep"—and the mother-goddess Gula, who was addressed in Assyrian prayers as "the lady who dwells in the pure heavens, merciful, restorer of life, whose command heals."

With the Sumerian lady Ishtar we meet again when we come to consider her counterpart in the Semitic pantheon, the great goddess Astarte, to whom she is closely related in name and attributes. As Astarte, her cult as goddess of fertility and reproduction was notably widespread, for she came to be identified also with the wifehood of Isis, the Egyptian deity whose husband Osiris, as his ritual at Abydos shows, represented the fertilized grain. Astarte was also identified with Isis's motherhood, a function in which the Egyptian goddess was commonly represented with the child Horus (Harpocrates) on her lap. (The later subrogation of this convention by Christian art makes it difficult at times to distinguish between pagan and Christian versions of the mother-child duo, as will be noted below).[1] Astarte would be assimilated by the Greek world to Aphrodite and Artemis.

Egypt's Great Mother, often represented as a sacred and heavenly Cow, creator of the entire universe (Cosmocrates), wears around her neck the *menat*, symbol of life and reproduction; her eye (*utchat*) has the shape of that of a cow. She is identified with the goddess Nut, "celestial vault" and the moon, who had generated the Sun from her flesh, and who is represented with the key indicating the power of fertility. Nut's key has been said to open the doors of the uterus and of the chthonic world, of death and of rebirth. The Egyptian Great Mother is identified also with the goddess Hathor, represented with the horns of a cow which support the globe of the sun (Giani Gallino, 47, 55).

The Phrygian goddess Cybele, whose cult arose in Asia Minor and later spread to Greece and Rome, was known as Great Mother of the Gods (*Mater Deum Magna* or *Mater Deum Magna Idœa*, a reference to Mount Ida in Phrygia). She stands unrivaled as the universal mother and embodiment of the earth's fertility. Especially celebrated was her maternal dominion over wild nature, as manifested in the orgiastic character of her worship and the frenzied excitement of her half-demonic mythical attendants, the Corybants. Cybele's notoriously profligate rites were conducted by self-castrated priests (Galli) attired in female garb, their long hair smeared with ointment, who joined her priestesses in wild music and dancing that found its culmination in self-scourging, self-laceration and exhaustion. (A series of marble sculptures representing the Galli and their activities may be seen in the Museum of Ostia Antica.)

On another side, the myth of Cybele offers some notable affinities with the personality of the Christian Madonna. Traceable in her worship are certain aspects of the so-called myth of the triple goddess, a composite of the archetypal Virgin Mary, the "Loving Mother," and the "Terrifying Mother" (Neiger, 11). Cybele's sanctuaries, moreover, were usually located upon mountains and in caves—symbols of maternity, together with forests and waters. The one on Mount Sipylus (Greece) is a water sanctuary in which the goddess was believed to issue from bare cliffs beside fresh water—a parallel to certain later apparitions of the Virgin Mary.

The Greek Pantheon

The personality of Cybele was associated at an early date with that of the Sicilian goddess Ibla (Birnbaum, 104) as well as with Rhea, the wife of Cronos and mother of Zeus. That goddess's originally primitive and barbaric cult was spiritualized in course of time into the worship of a divine, tender mother who cared for and won a ready response from her children, rather like the Sumerian "good cow" Ninsun. More directly than some other divinities, Rhea embodies an ancient archetypal religious concept that would eventually provide a basis for the emergence of the Mediterranean Mariolatry.

Here again, however, we find that the role of earth mother and fertility goddess is too manysided and too demanding to be filled for any length of time by a single divinity. A better known member of the Greek Pantheon is Rhea's daughter Demeter (the Roman Ceres), who functioned also as goddess of health, birth, and marriage and may have been associated with the Phrygian fertility powers called the Cabeiri. Demeter, in addition, filled still another important role as a divinity of the underworld; as such she is chthonia (earth goddess) at Sparta and at Hermione in Argolis.[2]

To Demeter were sacrificed pregnant sows[3] and, at the festival of Chthonia in Argolis, a cow. Both Greek and, later, Roman fertility rites usually involved some form of blood sacrifice of pregnant victims. Intended to establish a beneficial relationship with the sacred earth, the blood sacrifice amounted to a replay of the primordial act of creation and thus a renewal of vegetational life. In some sacrifices at planting time, the blood of the victim was allowed to sink into the ground and its flesh was buried in the soil in order to fertilize the earth and recharge its potencies.[4]

Those joining in Demeter's chthonic festival procession wore garlands of the ancient flower hyakinthos, botanically unrelated to our modern hyacinth but identified by some with the lily, the flower later associated with the Virgin Mary (below). Similar in some respects was the worship of Hecate, goddess of magic and spells and a chthonic deity closely associated with Demeter. To Hecate were sacrificed black puppies and she-lambs for a variety of purposes, including earth fertility. She was also the patroness of the herm-like pillars called Hecatæa that stood at crossroads and in doorways, perhaps to ward off evil spirits. They have left a pale reflection in Italy's "Madonnelle" or "Edicole sacre"—lighted images of the Madonna placed on house corners, between windows, or under arches.[5]

Demeter had a consort called Iasion who, according to Homer, "lay with her in a thrice-plowed field," and to whom she bore Plutus, the god of wealth—i.e., of abundant produce of the soil. The story is likened by Frazer to a West Prussian custom involving the mock birth of a child on the harvest field to ensure a plentiful crop in the following year (Frazer, I: 139). In another ancient Nordic ceremony held in the month of May, a young couple copulated on the freshly plowed and planted earth, in a magic solicitation of nature's fertility (Giani Gallino, 111).

Aristophanes took note of the cult of Demeter in what may be his funniest comedy, *Thesmophorizusæ* ("Women celebrating the *Thesmophoria*, or Feast of Demeter," 411 B.C.E.). This was a three-day Athenian festival featuring women who prayed for their own fertility and that of the land. Among the numerous other agrarian festivals held in honor of this indispensable goddess were the *Haloa* (a religious harvest festival), *Chloia* (festival of the sprouting corn), *Proerosia* (prayers for an abundant harvest), *Thalusia* (a thanksgiving festival), *Skirophoria* (a midsummer companion festival), and an obscure ceremony, the *Demetria*, in which the participants beat each other with whips of twisted bark, a well-known fertility charm (Encyc. Brit. VII: 213).

In our absorption in the Demeter legend, we must not forget the important role of those other well-known Greek goddesses, Aphrodite and Artemis, in promoting the fruitfulness of animate and perhaps also of inanimate nature. Aphrodite, who early became identified with the obscure Italian goddess Venus, bears many resemblances to the Near Eastern Great Mother whose worship she absorbed. Goddess of beauty and sexual love, to whom were dedicated phallic symbols appropriate to fertility worship, she is thought by some to have played a secondary role in promoting vegetable fertility as well.

The easing of childbirth was among Aphrodite's primary functions. On Mount Hymettus, near one of her temples, gushed a spring (known in ancient times as Kyllou Pera) where women drank who wished to conceive or to ensure an easy childbirth. Elsewhere in Greece, the women of Hermione sacrificed to Aphrodite before marriage, perhaps in hope of satisfactory sexual relations but more probably to ensure their own fecundity. Spartan mothers, upon the betrothal of their daughters and doubtless for similar reasons, sacrificed to "Aphrodite Hera," a fusion of Aphrodite with Hera, the marriage goddess and consort of Zeus, who served also as protectress of women in childbed.

Titled "birth-goddess" at Argos and at Athens, Hera was patroness in the former place of a markedly agricultural ritual where sprouting ears of corn were called "Flowers of Hera." Especially sacred to her was the cow; and the practice of sacrificing cows to Hera has been said to explain Homer's references to her as *boopis*, meaning either "cow-faced" or "large-eyed" (like a cow) (Encyc. Brit. XI: 385).

In Attica, Aphrodite was associated with the Moirai (Fates) and the Genetyllides, goddesses who presided over birth and immediately determined the newborn's future career; while in Corinth, Cyprus, and Eryx in Sicily, the "Paphian goddess," as she was sometimes called, was worshiped by religious prostitution, intended, as in other ancient cults, to promote fertility.

The primitive vegetation-goddess Ariadne of pre-Greek Minoan Crete, Cyprus, and Naxos came to be associated first with Aphrodite and later with the Ariadne of Greek mythology. In the latter role, her incorrupt body was assumed into heaven, where her bridal crown was set among the stars. Her assumption, like that of the Greek moon-goddess Semele, passed into Catholic iconography and literature, in which Mary is often depicted with the crescent moon under her feet and on her head a crown of stars (Giani Gallino, 103).

Of Cretan origin were Persephone, daughter of Demeter and goddess of agriculture; Britomartis ("sweet maiden"), goddess of birth and health; and Eileithyia, the goddess of childbirth who was worshiped in a cave at Amnisos (the port of Knossos) continuously from Neolithic to Roman times. (In Homer, Eileithyia appears sometimes in the plural as a personification of birth pangs [Encyc. Brit. VIII:95].) Both Britomartis and Eileithyia tended to be identified in later times with Hera or Artemis.

Artemis, goddess of wild animals, of vegetation, of chastity and the hunt, embodied the wild life of nature in all its fertility and profusion. Later identified by the Romans with their own goddess Diana (see below), in her Greek incarnation as goddess of prolific maternity she was occasionally offered the clothes of women who had died in childbirth. To the Western classical tradition she is known mainly as a virginal huntress; but to the ancient world she was also the many-breasted Artemis of Ephesus and the Artemis Lochia who aided women in labor.

Several of the mythological love goddesses—Artemis, Aphrodite, Ishtar, Astarte, Anat—are referred to as "virgins" despite their many loves. Their sacred virginity had no moral connotations such as would come to be the case in Christianity, but simply symbolized their autonomy and freedom of choice in lovers. Ishtar, for example, each year married the young shepherd Dumuzi, but her image, like the purified Madonna after birth, was that of a virgin divinity (Giani Gallino, 89). The Christian religion, in developing the ideas of asceticism, celibacy and continence, would inherit from the classical world a concept of virginity that was not so much an ethical ideal as a powerful form of magic that conferred on the woman both purity and potency (Warner, 72-73).

We shall shortly have the opportunity to look more closely at the phenomenology of motherhood in the context of ancient Italy, the matrix in which the cult of the Madonna originated and flourished. In the meantime, it will be useful to remember that the worship of fertility and its divine patronesses had gradually become a worldwide rather than a merely tribal or regional phenomenon—that maternal power was seen as a universal force that had created the very universe together with all of its life forms (Van Buren, 127).

In Celtic mythology, for example, the goddess Dana or Danu is known as the great earth mother or female principle, sovereign of the fruitful earth and all animal creation (Dini, 28); two hills with rounded summits in Kerry County, Ireland, still today bear a Gaelic name meaning "nipples of the goddess Anu," perhaps referring to Danu (whose name appears also in the river Danube) (Giani Gallino, 144).

Germanic mythology gives us Nerthus, a demanding Mother Earth who prescribed human sacrifice to ensure the yearly rhythm of the crops. Her veiled statue was moved from place to place by sacred cows and, after the performance of the rituals in her honor, her image, vestments and vehicle were bathed in a lake. Nehalennia, in Germanic mythology, was the protectress of the family (Dini, 28).

Frey (Freyr) in Scandinavian mythology was son of the fertility god Njörðr and himself ruler of peace and fertility, rain and sunshine. The Vikings worshiped him and his sister and female counterpart, Freyja, as gods of fecundity and fertility.

Shakti, the Hindu mother goddess, stands for nature in all its aspects, and is credited with having given birth to the universe through a sort of cosmic union with her transcendent spouse, Shiva (Encyc. Brit. XI: 509-10). Siddieka, a Buddhist goddess of fertility, whose image in the rock caves of Ajanta shows her sitting on the right of Matanga, the god of wealth, holds a child in her left arm and closely resembles certain artistic renditions of the Madonna and Child. (We may note, however, that the Buddha himself was no family man and named his own son "Ruhala" or "Impediment," in other words, an obstacle to the father's search for wisdom and a nonworldly life.)

In China we have, among others, the Princess of the Streaked Clouds, also called the Holy Mother, protectress of women and children and usually present at births. Her Buddhist counterpart is the androgynous goddess Kuan Yin, represented in a draping white veil, seated on a lotus flower, and again holding a child in her arms. Amaterasu, the Japanese sun goddess, became the progenetrix of Japan's imperial line and, by extension, of the entire race.

Amid this profusion of fertility goddesses, we may note that there is no goddess of *in*fertility in the pantheons of either East or West. In cultures so overwhelmingly dedicated to the fertility principle, the power to inhibit birth and growth was rarely ascribed to any supernatural being, and then only as a momentary deviation in exceptional circumstances. Thus the rather obscure Mesopotamian goddess Ninhursaga (or Belitili), though primarily known as a goddess of birth and "mother of all children," was sometimes invoked, in curses on evil rulers, to stop all birthgiving in the land (Encyc. Brit. II: 975). Lamaštou, the dethroned daughter of the supreme god in the Akkadian pantheon, was thought to aim her angry darts against newborn babies and their mothers (Saadé, 191). Legend describes how Hera attempted to prevent the births of her enemies Heracles, Apollo, and Artemis, by hindering the work of Eileithyia, the Cretan goddess of childbirth (Encyc.Brit. VIII:95). Similarly, Plutarch reports that the trees were made barren and the fruits of the earth were blighted by the very sight of the image of Artemis at Pellene in Achaea (Frazer, I: 15).

Even Demeter allowed the land temporarily to become sterile in protest against the kidnapping of her daughter Persephone. But these were clearly exceptional manifestations on the part of deities who, as we have seen, are most frequently associated with marriage, midwifery, and the nurturing of life, not its destruction. The woman of antiquity who may have wished to invoke a goddess of *in*fertility in order to be spared another draining pregnancy perhaps found herself in a situation not unlike the contemporary one in countries where contraception is forbidden through, in Marina Warner's words, "the collusion of Church and state" (*Sola fra le donne*, 330).[6]

Mamma Italia

Little has been said thus far about the country that in modern times has been thought of as unique in its appreciation of maternity and the mother figure. The roots of this maternal ideal in Italy extend deep into the past. From very early times, a generic cult of the Great Mother (*Dea Mater*) embodied the fertility aspect of the archaic hunting and agro-pastoral cultures. Certain religious rites and magical functions which operated through images had the threefold aim of maintaining the fertility of the earth, facilitating childbirth, and procuring offspring for the barren woman. Archeological finds in a single sacred space show statuettes and votive offerings in stone or bone made by Etruscans, Romans, and other peoples. The artifacts include terracotta breasts, uteruses, female and male genital organs, and so forth, which reveal a continuity in artifice that changes only in its stylistic iconography (Graziosi, 1973, 108).

Archeological evidence from the Upper Paleolithic provides us with samplings of Italian prehistoric mothers. So-called "Paleolithic Venuses" have risen in large numbers from the Italian soil, among them the Venus of Savignano near Modena, the Venus of Chiozza di Scandanio in Reggio Emilia, and the Venus found near Lake Trasimene in Tuscany.

A two-dimensional bone statuette of a female, found at Riparo Gaban near Trento, continues the evolution of the Paleolithic archetype. This woman has no arms and a very small head in proportion to her body, while her belly, wide hips, and legs form a single triangular unit without any indication of feet. An elongated cavity incised in the abdominal region represents the vulva, topped by incisions in fishbone form which have been interpreted as pubic hairs. With its full hips and wide vaginal slit, the statuette eschews all ambiguity in its symbolization of the fecund female (Graziosi, 1973, 103–5).

Similar characteristics are found in later, Neolithic female figurines from the caves of Balzi Rossi di Grimaldi near Ventimiglia (see illustration), the so-called Grotto of the Venuses near Parabita (Lecce), and the Aenolithic necropolis of Cozzo Busonè near Agrigento, Sicily. In Sardinia, marble figurines found in tombs and cult places, as well as a basalt one found in a grotto near Nuoro—the so-called Venus of Macomer—continue the iconography. Voluminous breasts (except for the last-named Venus), bloated bellies, adipose thighs, hips, and gluteal regions (Graziosi, 1973, 16, 106, 107) give the entire body the appearance of a single sexual organ.

Expressing female fecundity and maternity in a full and absolute sense, these steatopygous figurines encapsulate a primitive belief in the woman pervaded by "the powerful breath of life" (Graziosi, 1965, 52). With no personal identity or subject status whatsoever, the woman as such is erased by her all-encompassing role (Neiger, 157). If the pubic region is exaggerated and in some cases monstrous, the heads of the figures are pitifully small (suggestive of mindless childbearing?). Some figures stand with arms folded and stare into space; others have eyes but no mouth scooped out. Sometimes the heads of the figures amount to nothing more than a cone-shaped addition repeating the geometry of the lower extremities, joined legs with no indication of feet. Such incompleteness seems to hint at a swaddling or binding up of the woman's movement, with no promise of future development. With their big bodies, ample breasts, and small heads, these female figures vaguely suggest the whole history of mothering.

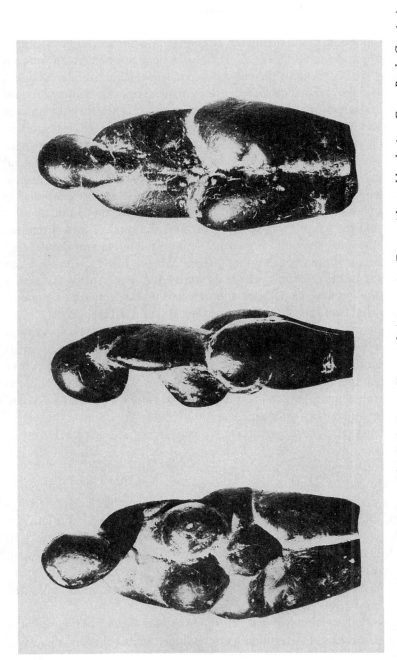

So-called "Paleolithic Venus of Grimaldi" (Balzi Rossi, Ventimiglia) in steatite. Front, side, and back view. From Paolo Graziosi, L'arte dell'antica età della pietra, Figure 4a.

(Courtesy of Biblioteca Nazionale Centrale di Roma)

Sacred Places

The well-being of the shepherds, fishermen and farmers of the Neolithic era (beginning about 5,000 B.C.E. in Italy) depended upon a well-ordered fecundity-fertility relationship with nature, one in which the mother goddess stood forth as the creator and sacred ground of all beings. Agriculture brought with it a non-migratory life style and the veneration of specific geographical places as sanctuaries whose holiness was believed contagious (Encyc. Brit. XIX: 111). From the new patterns of more permanent settlement there emerged hierophantic areas well suited to harbor contact with terrestrial and chthonic forces. In these orographic, hydrographic, and hypogeal places, an archetypal *imago templi* took gynemorphic shape, as, for example, in Sardinia's Nuraghic sanctuaries[7] (similar in layout to the megalithic temples of Malta and the temple well at Yazilikaya in Anatolia). These structures have been seen as symbolic representations of the vulva and the descent into the uterus of the Great Mother (Giani Gallino, 130-31; 136-7). Even the structure of the dolmen has been interpreted as representing the triadic nature of the Female, its door, as entrance and uterus, constituting one of the primordial symbols of the Great Mother (Giani Gallino, 186).

In spots of natural fertility, by fountains and riverbanks, in groves, thickets and mountain glades, simple rustics could feel the presence of spirits and of an indwelling divinity. The fascination exerted by such sacred or consecrated spots would reach beyond primitive humanity and make its influence felt at many successive stages of civilization, Phœnician, Syrian, Hebrew, Egyptian, Greek, Roman, Germanic, and Irish. Spirits of the waters were seen and felt as beneficent beings, dispensers of life and the fertility of women and animals, whether such blessings descended as rain from heaven or welled up as springs of bubbling water (Frazer II: 159).

In Italy, places inhabited by water-spirits with the power of bestowing offspring on barren women and cattle provided sanctuaries for fertility worship. The warm waters near Sinuessa (formerly Sinope) in Latium, for example, were believed to bless childless wives with offspring (Frazer II: 161), while near Arezzo in Etruscan territory the so-called "milk fountain of San Leolino" (below) has yielded a terra-cotta statuette, probably an ex-voto of Neolithic times, with huge conspicuous breasts and accentuated gluteal prominences (Dini, 57, and plate 11).

In grottos containing within their deepest recesses waters of high calcium content, stalactites and stalagmites formed white rounded clusters suggestive of huge dripping breasts.[8] At Toirano in Liguria, such a grotto, known as

"Grotta della Bàsura" [of the witch], was the theatre of cults and liturgies going back to the Neolithic and perhaps even the Paleolithic. Recently the name of Cybele was given to one of the rooms in the grotto because of the clusters of "breasts" adorning its walls (Giani Gallino, 152).

To water rites and ablutions were ascribed magic and thaumaturgic powers, as well as valences of purification, regeneration, and rebirth—ancient baptismal rituals which Christianity would subrogate to permit accession to the womb of Mother Church. Water as a cosmogonic element and source of life acquired symbolic value as the universal matrix which reduced to a common standard waters hidden in Great Mother Earth's womb and woman's amniotic waters (Giani Gallino, 147-9).

Ver sacrum (sacred spring) was the name of a ritual practiced by the self-contained Italic peoples during Italy's Iron Age after 1,000 B.C.E., when the utilization of iron for weapons put arms in the hands of men and set off folk movements that changed the face of the territory. Originally it involved the marking of firstlings (male children and cattle) to be sent out to new settlements when grown.[9]

Later, *ver sacrum* took the form of a public vow in the name of the Roman people to the effect that specified newborns reaching maturity, rather than being killed like sacrificial animals, would be assigned to the borderlands to support the foundation of new colonies and enlarge their living space to accommodate the increasing population.[10]

During the Iron Age, when the use of arms conferred on men a new source of strength, it may be assumed that male gods appeared next to the goddesses, taking over some of their powers. Their appearance on the scene was marked by the same cyclicality of birth and rebirth as that of the woman who was reborn in her offspring. The blood of Adonis and of Attis, for example, from which vegetation sprang, became symbolic of fecundity. Osiris, Dumuzi, and Baal each year died and each year resurrected, just as a later male god, Jesus, would do each spring at Easter time (Giani Gallino, 35-6).

The Etruscan Connection

The primitive divinities and rites of the Italic peoples began to assume a more cosmopolitan air thanks to increasing interaction with the Carthaginians and Greeks on one hand and with the expanding Etruscan civilization on the other. Local mother goddesses began to assume the names of Hera and Juno, and to centralize their shrines at such Etruscan sites as

Graviscae, the port of Tarquinii, where a Greek shrine was dedicated to Hera, and at Pyrgi, the port of Caere, site of a fifth-century Etruscan temple dedicated to Uni (the Etruscan equivalent of Juno) and Astarte.

The Etruscan goddess Uni had earlier been associated with an Etruscan mother goddess called Thalna, who appears on the decorative back of a mirror found in Arezzo[11] as a protective divinity attending the birth of Minerva from the head of Tinia (Jupiter) (Dini, 94). Uni herself appears on the decorative back of a well-known third century B.C.E. bronze Etruscan mirror (now in the Archeological Museum of Florence) where she ritually suckles Hercle (Hercules) on that hero's final introduction into Olympus. "*Hercle Unial clan*" (Hercules son of Uni), the inscription reads. (Hercules, whose name means "Glorious gift of Hera," would be capable, mythology tells us, of engendering fifty children in a single night.)

The Etruscan Uni was later identified with the Roman Juno,[12] queen of the Roman pantheon, and assumed the latter's epithet of "Lucina" (light-bringing)[13]—a title Juno shared with Diana, goddess of the moon, but to which she herself could exert a primary claim in her capacity as protectress of the life of women, especially in childbed. Terra-cotta figures dedicated to the protectress of pregnant women and childhood, some of them representing newborns, have been found in fertility-fecundity sanctuaries of Juno Lucina in Etruscan territory (Dini, 89, n. 4).

Lucina's functions as goddess of moonlight, and hence as controller of the menses, expanded to encompass the entire birth cycle—fertility, conception, pregnancy, nourishment of the fetus, labor, delivery, and lactation. In her role as female comforter, she assumed various epithets. As Sospita, she originally was the savior of women but eventually became savior of the state itself. As Interduca, she takes the bride to her new home. As Cinxia, she is the patroness of the unfastening of the bride's girdle.[14] As Opigena, she brings aid to the woman in labor; and finally, as Lucina, she brings the child to light.

Under Rome's Etruscan kings, Juno Regina (Queen of Heaven, later an appellation of the Virgin Mary) appears as part of the trinity of Jupiter, Juno, and Minerva. On coins she is represented as a matron holding a flower in her right hand and, in her left, a baby in swaddling clothes resting against her bosom. Both images are symbols of fertility, whose iconography foreshadows that of Mary of Nazareth (Dini, 45).

At the temple of Juno Lucina on the Esquiline Hill, Roman matrons swore an oath (Eiuno!) every March first in the cult known as the Matronalia. In another significant festival, the Nonæ Caprotinae (Nones of the Wild

Fig, held beneath a wild fig tree in the Campus Martius), the goddess was worshiped by female slaves in an old fertility rite involving a mock fight and mutual beatings—again, a well-known fertility charm.

Juno Lucina's other attributes are the lily of fecundity and the delivery scissors. Myths of birth, breastfeeding, fecundity and maternal protection are conflated in her various representations, making for a maternal mystique that would perpetuate itself beyond the deculturization of the Etruscan tribes and their acculturation in the Roman ethos. In time, the supremacy of Christianity would result in the cultural disintegration of the Etruscans, but Juno Lucina and her attributes would survive to serve the new religion. Her lily of fecundity, for example, would be held in Saint Gabriel's hand in paintings that represented the Annunciation of Mary's maternity.

In many Christian feasts of pagan origin the lily appears in its ancient connection with fertility. To this day, during the Feast of the Lilies in Nola (Campania), young men ritually carry eight lilies (seen as phalluses) behind a boat (representing the uterus) through the narrow, winding streets (vulva-vagina) of the old city (Giani Gallino, 170).

Roman Fertility Goddesses and Their Agrarian Cults

Among the most important of Rome's own fertility goddesses was the earth goddess Terra or Tellus Mater, probably the holder of the numen, or divine will, that was thought necessary to make the Roman territory productive. She would later be associated with Maia (or Maiesta), the cult partner of Vulcan and a minor goddess of fertility, water, and springs. Unrelated to the eponymous Greek mythological figure, Maia would give her name to the month of May, which not only was dedicated to her but came to be celebrated in the Christian calendar as the Marian month.

Mater Matuta, a deity of the ripening of the grain (her second name means early morning), is associated with Ino or Leucothea (white goddess), the daughter of Cadmus, as well as with Aurora, the morning goddess. She too was venerated as the protectress of women in childbirth. Her annual feast (Matralia) was celebrated in her own temple in Rome's Forum Boarium on June 11. Participation was limited to free women of a first marriage, who are said to have prayed not for their own children but for those of their sisters. As a fertility charm, they drove out by whiplash a slave woman introduced for that purpose.

Mater Matuta may also have been the dedicatee of some hundred ancient tufa statues, found in the territory of ancient Capua and now housed in the so-called "mother museum," where a writer of the Fascist period described their rigid pose and the fixed gaze which he ascribed to "ecstasy" (Magaldi, 6-7). Some of the statues represent a woman in the act of breastfeeding a child; others show seated women holding in their laps or outstretched arms one, two, four, six, or even up to twelve babies in swaddling clothes.

The tutelary goddess of Roman herds and shepherds was Pales, whose festival (Palila), with all its superstitious rites, was dedicated each April 21[15] to the welfare and increase of flocks and herds. The day's activities probably began at the temple of Vesta, where the Vestal Virgins distributed ashes of unborn calves—snatched, we are told, from previously sacrificed pregnant cows—as well as blood dripped from the tail of a sacrificed horse. These delicacies were thought to exert a fertilizing and cleansing influence and to quicken the wombs of women, as well as of cows and ewes. After offering baskets of millet, millet cakes, and pails of warm milk, the shepherd prayed to the goddess for, inter alia, milk-filled udders of his female domestic animals; lusty rams and prolific ewes; the birth of many lambs; and protection of the flock from witches and wolves (Frazer, II: 326–27).

The Syrian goddess Atargatis, who was kin to Astarte, Cybele, and Aphrodite, was also adopted by the Romans as the Dea Syria, a fecundity goddess venerated, in addition, as the creator of all things (*omnipotens et omniparens*, all-powerful and all-producing, in the words of Apuleius). Her cult, later briefly embraced by Nero, was carried by Roman soldiers throughout the Empire. Processions and rituals in her honor, led by priests and "fanatics" (devotees), were similar to the pronouncedly orgiastic rites of Cybele (above). A votive relief in Rome's Capitoline Museum depicts the goddess as holding a sheaf of grain while the lions that support her throne declare her strength and power over all nature.

The Italic and Umbrian mother goddess and agricultural divinity known to the Romans as Cerfia was originally identified with the dual terrestrial-chthonic nature of the Greek goddess Demeter (Dini, 41). From her name derives Cerfone, a river in Etruscan territory that retained its sacredness until very recent times (Dini, 43, 89 n. 3). Unfecund cows were led to bathe in its waters, and on its banks sterile women were wont to lie with their husbands (below).

Cerfia was later associated with Ceres, Demeter's Roman equivalent and goddess of the growth of food plants, to whom offerings were made of cakes, honey, flour, broad beans and wheat kernels, while piglets were sacrificed to her on feast days. The worship of Ceres, who was usually represented holding ears of wheat, extended over a great part of the Italian territory.

Processions about the land to purify and protect the crops and ensure the fertility of the fields were known in pagan times as Robigalia, from Robus, the deity invoked by the Romans to preserve their grain from mildew. The Church would later throw its cloak over this old heathen festival. Major Rogation (from Latin *rogare*, to beseech) or *litania maior*,[16] in which priests beseeched God's blessing on the lands for the ensuing harvest, was instituted in the sixth century. The pagan procession used to leave Rome by the Flaminian Gate, proceed by way of the Milvian Bridge to a sanctuary at the fifth milestone of the Via Claudia, and there, each April 25, a dog and sheep were sacrificed to avert blight from the crops. The later Christian procession would follow the same route as far as the Milvian Bridge but would then turn off and return to Saint Peter's for a celebration of the mass. The thaumaturgic value of the Robigalia celebrations would continue to be defended against "the derision of the incredulous" until as late as 1897 (Rusconi, 21).

Another peripatetic ceremony dedicated to the assurance of an abundant harvest was the Ambarvalia, a three-day processional event celebrated by the Fratres Arvales or Brothers of the Tilled Fields, a college of twelve priests charged with the *lustratio agrorum*, the purification of the fields. The victims for the annual public sacrifice—oxen, sheep, and pigs—were conducted around the boundaries of the ager Romanus, the Arval brothers being assisted by four boy choristers wearing wreaths of ears of corn, a white fillet, and the *praetexta*, a characteristic garment of prepubertal boys (Frazer, II: 122; Encyc. Brit. II: 557).

At a shrine in a sacred grove near Rome, the Arval brothers worshiped a rather obscure Dea Dia (divine goddess), a deity of the fields and of fecundation. Almost forgotten in republican times, her annual festival was revived by Augustus (Cary and Scullard, 329), only to be Christianized by Pope Leo III in about the year 800 as Minor Rogations (*litaniae minores*), held annually on the three days preceding the Feast of the Ascension.

In a somewhat similar rite, the priests responsible for the ancient Roman festival known as Lupercalia—and themselves known as Luperci—ran around the base of the Palatine hill, where stood the temple of Magna Mater, striking with a thong those women who sought to obtain fecundity. Both the Ambarvalia and the Lupercalia were public rites in which a magic circle was traced to keep out evil and to radiate blessings—especially fertility— inward (Encyc. Brit. XIV: 436). The Lupercalia began with the sacrifice by the priests of goats and a dog, after which two of the Luperci were led to the altar, their foreheads were touched with a bloody knife, and the blood was wiped off with wool dipped in milk.

This last detail highlights the extraordinary and far-reaching significance of milk, not merely as an element in the Lupercalia but as part of an ancient and complex symbolic language in which it served as the central metaphor of the gift of life.[17] The Roman myth of the creation of the Milky Way, for example, is based on the overflowing of Juno's milk into the heavens as she was suckling Hercules (Warner, 229). A mother's milk, associated both with the food of infancy and with the eternity of the heavens, became for Christianity the sublime symbol of the eternal mystery of the human soul nourished by grace (Warner, 227).[18]

In the further course of the Lupercalia, new adepts in the corporation of the Luperci were cleansed with milk to assimilate them with the resurrection of the sacrificial victims. The Lupercalia rites also required that the two young men at the altar exhibit a smile, ritually signifying fullness of life— a symbolism discernible also in the beatific smile often seen on the faces of the Virgin, the Child, and the Saints.

Although the Lupercalia continued as a pagan rite until long after the establishment of Christianity, it was subrogated in 494 C.E. by Pope Gelasius I as the Feast of the Purification (Candlemas). The Christian feast commemorates the occasion when Mary, in obedience to Jewish law, went to Jerusalem to be purified, forty days after giving birth to a son, and to present her first-born to God in a ritual involving the sacrifice of a pair of turtledoves or two young pigeons (Luke 2: 22–38).

Shortly after the Feast of the Purification, the Sardinians of Oristano still today perform a pagan magic ceremony connected with fertility rites and cycles of vegetation. Their celebration of the feast of "La Sartiglia" ("The Star" or "The Magic Spell") engages the Purified Madonna as protectress of an androgynous hero (Giani Gallino, 103). A galloping horseman, carrying a spear and wearing a mask representing the face of a woman, must perform the feat of piercing the center of a suspended star, thereby assuring fecundity of the earth and an abundant harvest of grain. (The ceremony has been interpreted as an annunciation of male fertility, in which a man proclaims his capacity to reproduce [Giani Gallino, 76–96].)

Christianity would also effect a makeover of the pagan Diana, the "virgin goddess" of woodlands and groves, goddess of the moon, and counterpart of the Greek goddess Artemis. As a personification of the teeming life of nature, both animal and vegetable, she had absorbed also the connections of Artemis with Selene (i.e. Luna) and with Hecate of the underworld. Her strong association as a fertility deity led to her invocation by Roman women to aid conception and delivery.

The Church, however, would downplay the chthonic aspects of Diana's myth, endowing her instead with typically Christian feminine virtues (Warner, 730). Her annual festival, previously celebrated all over Italy on August 13 with illuminations and bonfires, was "adroitly" converted by the Church into the feast of the Assumption of the Blessed Virgin, celebrated on August 15 (Frazer, I:14) with illuminated processions that continue to this day.

Bona Dea (good goddess), the old Roman deity of fruitfulness in the earth and in women, was identified on the one hand with Fauna (the female counterpart of Faunus, bestower of fruitfulness on fields and cattle) and on the other with the goddess Anguitia (from the Latin *anguis* meaning snake or serpent, the symbol in antiquity of life, death and rebirth, and a sign of the power of regeneration. Christianity would stress the death aspect of the serpent, rendering it a symbol of evil.) The plebeian clan of the Marcii called the goddess Magna Mater Anguitia and dedicated to her temples in which domestic animals and nonpoisonous reptiles were raised.[19] This chaste and immaculate deity was worshiped on May 1 in nocturnal and daytime rituals involving the sacrifice of pregnant sows as in other fertility-goddess cults. Later, by syncretism, she became identified with Maia as well as with Ops, an obscure goddess perhaps originally occupied with the earth's fertility. In a sculptural representation in a temple on Rome's Aventine hill which was cared for and attended only by women, Bona Dea is accompanied by a serpent, frequently associated with fertility in primitive religions (Giani Gallino, 125).

If celebrations in honor of Bona Dea and of Maia were decorous and proper, those in honor of Flora—goddess of the flowering plants, of crops and fertility—were accompanied by much licentiousness. Her cult, known as the Floralia, was celebrated from April 28 to May 3, a time when offerings of ears of wheat were made to her by women eager to attain fecundity. Her temple on the Aventine hill was situated near the Circus Maximus, where games were held in her honor; and since harlots considered the Floralia their special season, the games are known to have included lewd mimes.

As queen of spring and of nature, Flora's head was invariably distinguished by a floral crown not unlike those traditionally set on the head of the Virgin Mary. Specifically connected with the cult of the Floralia were the favorite pink and white blossoms of the hawthorn—flowers whose aroma is said to produce an erotic effect and to which are attributed magical qualities believed due to the plant's intoxicating properties. In Catholic tradition, the hawthorn is sacred to the Virgin Mary in many of her sanctuaries in Ireland (Warner, 324).

Throughout medieval Europe it was customary on May first to crown a May Queen, a figure who was sometimes wedded to a Green Man in an ancient fertility rite that had survived up to that time. The Church, reacting against the perceived immorality of such festivities, managed to draw the sting by transforming the May Queen into the Virgin Mary. Thus, in Catholic countries, on the first of May a statue of the Virgin is decorated and crowned with flowers and carried in procession along flower-strewn streets (Warner, 324).

Another curious ceremony deriving from the Floralia was celebrated in Rome at Easter and survived up to the eleventh century. Beneficed clergymen (*mansionarii*), crowned wirth cherry blossoms, shaking a tintinnabulary copper instrument and preceded by a parish priest, led the populace to the square in front of the Lateran palace to receive the papal benediction. Then began a strange ritual in which each *mansionarius*, accompanied by the rhythmic sound of his instrument, solemnly danced a circle around his parish priest, who was mounted backward on a donkey facing the animal's tail[20] while a papal chamberlain held over its head a small dish filled with copper coins. After a turn on the donkey, the priest set garlands of flowers at the feet of the pope, while one of the parish priests let a live fox out of a sack in a manner reminiscent of the Hebrew scapegoat.

There followed a ceremony of baptism by immersion of all the unbaptized Romans present in the baptistery of Saint John Lateran.[21] The people then returned home bearing holy water from the baptistery as well as branches of laurel and cone-shaped sweet wafers not unlike those sold on the same square by today's ice-cream vendors (Costanzi, 4).

The ancient Romans, to make the union of couples fruitful, had prescribed the *confarreatio*, a solemn form of the marriage ceremony in which the spouses ate *panis farreus* made of flour, water, and salt—the precursor of the modern wedding cake—while the bride held three ears of wheat, symbol of plenty. In the Middle Ages, the wheat ears would be worn or carried by the bride, and it was customary for young girls to assemble outside the church to throw grains of wheat over the bride. Similarly, the modern custom of casting rice is symbolic of the wish that the bride be fruitful.

In the *flammeum* (large flaming-yellow veil, perhaps symbolic of fields of wheat), which completely covered Greek and Roman brides, may be found the origin of the modern bridal veil. Such fertility rites as the accompaniment of the bride by a little child, the sprinkling of fruit or grain over the newly wedded couple or on and around the nuptial bed, and the offering of prayers and sacrifices to the divinities were all intended to make the marriage teem with offspring.

The list of lesser Roman goddesses responsible for the protection of fecundity, fertility, fetuses and mothers, against whom Saint Augustine so eloquently inveighed (*The City of God*, 127), is lengthy indeed. While fathers uttered ardent vows and supplications for the fertility of their wives, sacrifice was made to Feronia, the incarnation of fecundity and the reawakening of the spring, and to Fortuna Primigenia, considered queen of heaven and earth and represented at Praeneste as a mother goddess suckling the newborn Jupiter (Dini, 95). Alemona, goddess of the prenatal phase, nourished the fetus and favored lactation. Nona and Decima were invoked for the care and protection of both the fetus and the gravid woman in the final months of pregnancy. Fluoria's task was to interrupt the menstrual flow and stop hemorrhages during the months of pregnancy and postpartum.

Various divinities were available for assistance at the delicate moment of delivery: Partula, Diespiter (Jupiter), Juno Lucina, Diana, and Mater Matuta as divinities of light to favor the newborn's entrance into the world. The ancient Italic goddess Ilithyia, represented with torches (symbolizing life), scissors (childbirth), and sometimes a fruit (fertility), was also called upon to help the woman with her childbearing. For births in which the child was abnormally positioned in the mother's birth canal, there was Carmenta, goddess mother of the legendary Evander, in her epiphanies as Antevorta and Postvorta (or Porrima). A protectress of all waters, Carmenta had a special relationship to the uterine bag of waters (Dini, 113).

Other maternal goddesses connected with the cult of waters were Giuturna, wife of Janus and mother of Fontus, and goddess of springs and fountains; the Umbrian goddess Cupra, to whom were consecrated springs propitious to human and animal fecundity, protection during the childbirth process, abundant lactation, and protection of the mother and the newborn; and Egeria, nymph spirit of a stream near Rome, who shared Diana's functions of triggering and easing childbirth.

Once the child was born, Nundina would preside over the *lustratio* and naming of the infant; Rumina, to whom milk rather than wine libations were offered, would protect the suckling until it was weaned; Geneta Mana (perhaps a reflection of Aphrodite's Genetyllides) and Fata Scribunda determined and recorded its destiny; Levana was first to help it stand on its feet; Educa was charged with stimulating its appetite and growth; Potina taught it to drink and helped it to swallow; Cunina protected its sleep, warding off the evil eye.

Ossipagina and Carna (or Carda, Cardna, or Carra) superintended the healthy development of the child's body, the former concentrating on the bone and joint structure and the latter on the flesh. Abeona and Adeona respectively protected the child in its first steps away from home and back again. Mens was the goddess of understanding; Volumna of good will (Magaldi, 3-6; Dini, 94–114).

Thus the child in antiquity was entrusted to an extraordinary assortment of local, native divinities and to the superstitions and magical practices surrounding their cult in each region. As magical rites and rituals spread, miraculous healings by pagan divinities were widely and unquestioningly accepted.

Roman Mystery Religions

By the first century B.C.E., the women then alive in the nascent Roman Empire had given life to between seventy and one hundred million human beings, although the vast majority—the inhabitants of the villages and rural areas—lived generally at a bare subsistence level with no pretension to mental or spiritual cultivation (Grant, 247, 267). Among the more educated classes, increasing numbers throughout the empire, weary of this world's evils and hopeful of a better life beyond the grave, were by then embracing the spreading mystery cults, some of which featured the elaborate secret rituals of Demeter and Cybele (Grant, 332–33). Perhaps because these newer cults made greater demands and offered proportionately higher rewards, they continued to win new adherents from the last pre-Christian century onward.

Cybele's mysteries had first obtained a foothold in Rome in 204 B.C.E. when, by advice of the Sybilline oracles, the cult of the Great Mother of the Gods was imported from Pessinus in Asia Minor. To Cybele was dedicated in 111 B.C.E. a temple on the Palatine hill, where rites performed each spring by eunuch priests were accompanied by stirring ritual dramas. Hopes of immortality were stimulated by the enactment of such mythic events as the resurrection of Cybele's consort, Attis, amid scenes of resplendent pageantry connected with fertility rituals (Grant, 333). Interestingly enough, in the space today considered the center of Roman Catholicism (Saint Peter's Square), initiation rites following ceremonies in honor of Cybele and Attis were performed up to the fourth century in the area adjacent to the Circus of Caligula. During the rites, the faithful emasculated themselves in imitation of the gesture made in Phrygia by Attis, who by his self-mutilation, death, and resurrection represents the fruitfulness of the earth (Giani Gallino, 175).

Under the early Roman emperors, Isis, the ancient Egyptian nature goddess, was transformed into an essentially cosmopolitan deity, a universal mother benevolent toward all of humankind. Propagated at every Mediterranean port, her cult spread rapidly through Campania to Rome (Cary and Scullard, 400). Believers thought that she repaid her worship and the observation of a few simple rules of life—such as an occasional fast—with happiness in this world and the next.

Accompanying Isis in the liturgical drama was her mate Osiris, who, like Attis, stood for all that annually grows and dies, the birth and death of the year. Osiris combined with Sokaris, the mummified hawk-god, and Apis the sacred bull, to form the composite figure of Sarapis, whose cult also flourished in Rome during the second and third centuries, when temples in his honor were built on the Campus Martius and the Quirinal.

During Isis's major festivals, penitents roamed the city streets intoning hymns, competing in acts of piety and self-mortification, or contemplating the magnificent images of the goddess and meditating upon her countenance. Among the worshipers were great numbers of women, to whom the Isis cult made a direct and powerful appeal (Grant, 333).

Isis, however, was fated to lose much of her primacy to another oriental deity, this one a male, the Persian Mithra, who was gradually transformed at the end of the pre-Christian period into the central figure of a Roman mystery cult. The moral urgency and emotional force of his worship, with its baptisms, sacrifices, and communal meals, offered resemblances to Christian rituals and sacraments and approximated Christianity also in advocating active well-doing rather than mere abstinence from sin (Cary and Scullard, 483). But Mithraism excluded women, who, as the cults of Cybele, Isis—and Mary—made clear, provided the largest numerical support for successful faiths of this character.

The Coming of Christianity

Cybele/Attis, Isis/Osiris, and Mithra worship, at once rivals to Christianity and stepping-stones toward it, slowly yielded to the Christian cult that was gradually emerging as the predominant faith of the Roman Empire and achieved official status in the fourth century C.E. The new religion would continue to elaborate magical practices such as purported to bring the practitioner into direct contact with the deity. Worshipers would continue to seek a beneficial relationship with a sacred female force in the hope of making her power present and efficacious, and fecundity would continue to be supremely valued on the vast estates (*latifundia*) that grew up in the late Empire and were chronically short of agricultural labor. Urban property, too, would require masses of nonservile labor for private and public works, so that a high birthrate was everywhere esteemed.

The woman's role was to supply the ever-growing families of Italy's agro-artisanal society, subordinating all other capabilities to her procreative responsibility. Passively and self-sacrificingly, she nurtured children and saw to their physical needs (*Maria, Medea e le altre*, 220). Reduced to an implement of nature, she lived out and waited upon her biological rhythms—menstruation, pregnancy, delivery, menopause—waiting, as the earth awaits the cycles of the seasons. She was assumed to "be" the earth, while man, in contrast, exerted his dominance over nature, intervening, exploiting, reworking it through his cognitive and operative processes (*Maria, Medea*, 185).

Thus the woman not only produced the means of life through her work in the fields; she also perpetuated life itself by reproducing sexually, like an animal, to augment the size and wealth of families, tribes, and lineages. What of the pain and sacrifice connected with childbirth and motherhood? Theoretically, and we must stress the word, they could be alleviated through sacrifice to some goddess of fertility and fecundity and the appropriate use of magic rites and rituals. How effective such expedients proved in practice, we shall probably never know.

Chapter 2

ℰᴏᴄᴙ

The Mutations of Madonna Worship and the Mutability of Motherhood

S uch was the world in which Christianity grew up and ultimately triumphed. The primeval mother goddesses, driven almost completely underground, would still leave traces of their presence and power. Christianity, confronted by the old religions in which female divinities held a central place, would use the figure of Mary in ways that repudiated yet at the same time reaffirmed the very concerns the pagan goddesses had symbolized (Pelikan, 220).

It is true that there are differing opinions as to how directly the ancient fertility cults are reflected in some of the later, nominally Christian practices. Marina Warner (*Sola fra le donne*, 242) stresses the parallels between pagan and Christian mythology in the cult of the Virgin, as well as the psychological analogies between the Middle Eastern cult of the *Magna Mater* and the Mariolatry so widely encountered in Mediterranean lands. Jaroslav Pelikan, on the other hand (*Mary Through the Centuries*, 58), insists that "the history does not in any direct way corroborate the facile modern theories about the 'mother goddesses' of Graeco-Roman paganism and their supposed significance for the development of Christian Mariology." E.O. James strikes a balance, writing that Mary hardly could escape taking on the aspects of Magna Mater, but that to regard the Mary cult as merely the Christianized version of its pagan prototype would be an oversimplification (*The Cult of the Mother-Goddesses*, 202). What does at any rate seem clear is that Christianity offers no clear dissent from Erik Erikson's dictum that all religions seek to gratify "the simple and fervent wish for a hallucinatory sense of unity with the maternal matrix" (*Young Man Luther*, cited in Parker, 35).

Pagan Survivals

The ancient fertility goddesses had been seen as reenacting primordial biological processes pervaded with cosmic force. If these archaic mothers had projected what was on the whole a dark and fearsome image, Mary on the other hand was to assume the character of a benign presence whose maternal power would come to be associated with the Church itself (Van Buren, 132). Recourse to Mary would, by extension, reinforce the strength and authority of the fledgling religion as well.

Pastoral localities that had previously been dedicated to nymphs and tutelary goddesses were to become Mary's new homes. Etruscan, Roman, and Longobardic acculturation in central Italy produced bewildering syncretisms of myths, divinities and rites (Dini, 68). As late as the sixteenth century, Italy would exhibit a superimposition and intermixture of heathen idols and church-sanctified figures as pagan and Christian cults cross-fertilized and mutually contaminated one another. The miraculous waters of the sacred cave at Lilibeo (Marsala), for example, where a sibyl of yore had prophesied, would give way to a sanctuary for the cult of Saint John the Baptist. In Sardinia, Neolithic sacred wells (above) took the names of Santa Anastasia di Sàrdara, Santa Cristina, and Santa Vittoria di Serri, from the names of the small churches built on or near them in Christian times (Giani Gallino, 154). Nor did the ruins of Etruscan and Roman temples on which many Roman Catholic churches were built ever completely lose their original associations and significance. The names of Etruscan and Roman divinities—Tigna, Faflon, Turanna—were invoked in Tuscan litanies recited to obtain divine protection for crops even as late as the end of the nineteenth century.

In a hierophantic continuity, Christian figures of the Virgin and protective saints replaced the former salutary divinities, especially in the Etruscan territory (Dini, 48), where rituals for fecundity and lactation were probably directed by augurs (from *augere*, "to increase"). Sanctuaries formerly dedicated to the pre-Christian deities of fertility and fecundity yielded their sacredness to Mary, who by the early eighth century had assumed all of the obstetric functions of the classical goddesses Hera and Demeter (*supra*; Warner, 317). "Black Madonna" sanctuaries, located on or near sites that yelded archeological evidence of ancient worship, metaphorically suggest Mary as the dark and fruitful Mother Earth, who offered hope for the poor and the oppressed (Birnbaum, 3, 12). Other archaic sacred places would later be dedicated to Saint Margaret, placater of birth pangs; to Saint Filomena, protectress of maternity and infancy; or to the virgin martyr Saint Agatha, protectress of delivery and lactation.[1] To staunch bleeding in the delivery process, up to quite recent times a key dipped in a spring dedicated to Saint Agatha was used in various regions of central Italy. The key, associated with many ancient goddesses of fertility—Hecate, Artemis, Diana, Eileithyia—has been interpreted as the device that "unlocks" the uterus and facilitates the exit of the child from the maternal womb (Giani Gallino, 168-69).

Connections between the moon and fertility, as with the cosmic associations of milk, are prominent in the iconography of the Virgin Mary—who, like the goddesses before her, became the lady of the lunar cycles, of waters and tides, of nature's protective divinities and, above all, of pregnant women (Warner, 299, 300). Particularly associated with fertility and fecundity are certain springs in archaic sacred places in central Italy whose whitish waters may be attributable to rich deposits of calcium bicarbonate. Protected by images of the so-called "Milk Madonnas," [2] the sites were used in the past by pregnant women and wet nurses to promote lactation (Dini, 74). Even up to recent times, women in childbirth continued to seek the miraculous milk-producing waters of the so-called "Milk Fountain of San Leolino" near Arezzo (Dini, 57). Also in the province of Arezzo is the sanctuary of the "Milk Madonna of Sestino," successor to a Stone Age cult of fecundity and lactation that had been transformed into a cult of maternity and infancy during the Longobardic era (Dini, 63).

A typical "milk fountain" ritual, with all its pagan overtones, would unfold as follows: at the entrance to the sacred area, the pregnant woman or wet nurse, customarily bearing two bottles, one filled with cow's or goat's milk, the other empty, would recite an "oration" or "ejaculation." Then, filling the empty bottle from the fountain and addressing a prayer to the Virgin Mary, she would drink the contents of both bottles in alternating sips designed to ensure abundant lactation. The beneficent effect of the waters was thought to extend even to the child (Dini, 74).

Where such miraculous springs have dried up, pregnant women and wet nurses are said to have grated flakes of calcium and lime from the calcinated earth before such images as the "Milk Madonna of Taragnano" in order to spinkle them on their food. At an earlier date, these powders were also used to prevent the nausea associated with pregnancy (Dini, 80).

Other sacred waters—streams, in this case—have been dedicated to the overcoming of female sterility and male impotence, lending their waters for bathing and drinking and their banks for outright sexual encounters, preferably by night. One ritual requires that a woman desirous of gravidity should lie face downward with her abdomen pressed flat against a certain plant or against the holy ground itself (Dini, 65). "Relief from childlessness," as one writer calls it (Campione, 203), has been sought in other ways by not a few Italian women even in the enlightened 1990s. In the northern district of Friuli, a black chicken may be slaughtered as a precautionary measure during the actual birth process (Neiger, 19), while in the Abruzzi region a sterile woman may have recourse to a fetish in the form of a pregnancy-provoking black pig (a symbol of regeneration). These traditions obviously are vague derivatives of the ancient Greek sacrifice of black pregnant sows to the earth mother Demeter, or of black puppies and she-lambs to Hecate, her close associate.

An attempt to root out these pagan cults in Italy was undertaken as long ago as the fifteenth century by San Bernardino of Siena, the Franciscan theologian and preacher; but the call of ancient sacred places continued to stir "practicing" believers, some of whom performed their rituals in the presence of such images, nailed perhaps to a tree trunk, as a Madonna holding a child to her breast (Dini, 60). Such images can have differed little from paintings of Isis, the goddess of birth and nursing, breastfeeding the child Harpocrates (Horus)—or of the Etruscan goddess Uni ritually suckling Hercle (Hercules) (*supra*).

The story of the "Milk Fountain of Lucignano" in Tuscany illustrates the way in which the protective figures and sacred sites of the Etruscan and Roman goddesses have dissolved into Christian counterparts. Here, after an unspecified "miracle," a chapel was built on the site of a sanctuary formerly dedicated to an obscure local prehistoric divinity. Popes Sixtus IV, Paul III, Pius V, Gregory XIII, Clement VIII, and Paul V, a series of pontiffs extending from 1471 to 1621, all bestowed special privileges on this Marian sanctuary of pagan origin (Dini, 73, 76).

In other Tuscan places, Mary, like Juno Lucina before her (*supra*), still receives gifts of the lily (symbol of fecundity), milk, ears of wheat, and various offerings for the protection of delivery, lactation, and other female requirements (Dini, 117). To this day, gravid women in Friuli, especially in

Ambrogio Lorenzetti's "Madonna del Latte" (fourteenth century).
From La Madonna Benois di Leonardo da Vinci a Firenze.
Il capolavoro dell'Ermitage in mostra agli Uffizi, *Figure 4.*
(Courtesy of Biblioteca Nazionale Centrale di Roma)

the last stages of pregnancy, wear scapulars and other religious objects around their necks and light candles in honor of the Madonna (Neiger, 20). Sardinians seek therapeutic benefit from the waters of their Nuraghic sacred wells, imploring not a pagan divinity but "Santa Maria de is aguas" (Giani Gallino, 154), while in Sicily some precocious children, apparently aware of possible abuses in the veneration of the saints, recently petitioned the Pope to restrict their parents' injudicious spending on charms and amulets.

Early Christianity

It is well known that the festivals of Christmas and Epiphany, commemorating respectively the birth of Christ and his manifestation to the Gentiles in the persons of the Magi, reincarnate pagan celebrations of the winter solstice and are attended with secular customs connected with pagan agriculture and solar observances of the midwinter season (*supra*). In the Roman world, the Saturnalia (December 17-24) was a time of merrymaking and exchange of presents, while December 25, according to the Roman calendar, was the date of a pagan festival introduced by the Emperor Aurelian in 274 C.E. as the *natalis solis invicti* (birthday of the unconquered sun). Since it is at this season that the sun begins to show an increase of light, Christian liturgy could readily equate the birth of the new sun with that of the Savior himself.

This Christianization of pagan custom was of course immensely stimulated by Constantine the Great's recognition of the new religion in 313 and by the determination of Theodosius I in 380 to establish Catholicism as the state religion of the empire. It was Theodosius who ordered all the peoples of his realm to subscribe to the dogmas of the ecumenical council of Nicaea (325), whose canons among other things forbade the clergy to have unmarried women in their houses, apparently even as housekeepers—although the same Council failed in its attempt to enforce a rule of celibacy upon all bishops, priests and deacons.

Another telltale indication of the direction in which organized Christianity was already moving was the Nicene Council's ambivalent treatment of the Virgin Mary. The Nicene Creed declared that Jesus was "incarnate from the Holy Spirit and the Virgin Mary," but Elaine Pagels demonstrates that refusal of a female godhead lies at the very origins of Christianity (*I Vangeli gnostici*, 101-21). Bettina L. Knapp (*Women in Myth*, 13-14) points out that Mary's exclusion from the all-male Trinity of Father, Son, and Holy Ghost was an indignity not unlike that suffered earlier by the

Egyptian goddess Isis.

During the fourth and fifth centuries, Mary was much thought of as the Human Mother of the One Who Is God, and her cult was beginning to burgeon in all of its ambivalence. Her appellation of *Theotokos*, usually rendered in Latin as *Mater Dei* (Mother of God), was given official status by the Council of Ephesus in 431. Possibly of Christian origin (Pelikan, 55), this term is more plausibly derived from the pagan *Mater Deum Magna* (Great Mother of the Gods, *supra*). It promptly achieved artistic expression in the celebrated fifth-century mosaic of the Annunciation and Epiphany in the church of Santa Maria Maggiore, the largest of the eighty Roman churches dedicated to the Virgin (Pelikan, 56).

Through Mary's parturition "in a fleshly way of the Word of God become flesh" (Council of Ephesus, cited in Pelikan, 56), the female procreative capacity was directly linked to the supreme objective of human salvation. Her consent to divine motherhood made her a *mater omnium* who could at the same time be approached as a human mother brimming over with a mother's love. Her accessibility and her immediate power to effect good were there for the invoking. All humans were her children through her Son. Prefiguring and symbolizing all other mothers, from Byzantine times, the Holy Mother emerged as a maternal figure whose love of humankind was like that of a mother for her child.

Piety toward the Mother of God having by this time become articulate and institutionalized, the Second Council of Constantinople (553) further defined the forms of Marian devotion which would continue to develop in the West during the following centuries. Doctrine and devotion availed themselves of the language needed to speak about her; Christian piety and theology constructed a picture that fulfilled the prediction ascribed to Mary herself in the *Magnificat* (Luke 1:46-55): "Henceforth all generations will call me blessed." This canticle of the vesper service[3] has been used since the beginning of the sixth century as part of the daily ritual of the Roman Catholic Church. Luke's own words derive from the song of Hannah (I Sam. 2:1-10) and from Genesis 21, each dealing with a distressed barren woman who at long last bore a son.

By the end of the seventh and the beginning of the eighth century, Mary's persona had entirely supplanted the pagan maternity figures and assumed an undisputed identity as the divine protectress of maternal functions (Dini, 115). The establishment of the feast of the Purification of Mary in the seventh century—another instance of the Christian takeover of a pagan ceremony, in this case a lustral procession (*supra*)—contributed to the development of her cult by celebrating her saintliness, her incandescent purity and her supremacy over the spirits of darkness (Warner, 94). Ways of thinking and speaking about her continued to be elaborated; in both East and West, various images of the Mary figure—the woman at the cross, at the marriage of Cana, and so forth—were devised to provide women with some sense of what they might be and of what, by the election of God, they could become (Pelikan, 27).

Mary had from an early date been credited with a special concern for women, a concept that left a permanent mark on Christian devotional tradition and practice. Cults grew up rapidly around the figure that symbolized the nobility of motherhood. Mary embodied the ideal of maternal altruism, unconditional love uncontaminated by self-interest. In a bitter time, she was an embodiment of love, tenderness, care and domestication. To her was sung one of the earliest Christian prayers, *Sub tuum praesidium*, invoking her help and composed before the eighth century, long before the medieval *Ave Maria*. The eleventh-century antiphones *Alma Redemptoris Mater* and Salve Regina pleaded for her intercession in obtaining the pity of God (Warner, 328).

More and more praises, titles and roles were heaped upon her: "Mother of Truth," "Mother of Christians," "Mater Gloriosa," "Mother of Peace," "Mother and Daughter of Humility," "Queen of Angels," "Ever-Virgin," "My Most Merciful Lady," and even, in an appellation reminiscent of Saint Augustine, "City of God" (Pelikan, 130). She thus became embedded in the language, the spirituality and the history of countless believers throughout the Western world (Pelikan, 99). Her cult as the Great Mother would reach extraordinary levels of fanaticism and magical-religious exaltation, especially in southern Italy.[4]

Even the symbol of the "woman" who figures as the mother of the Messiah in Revelation—and who is usually identified with the heavenly Jerusalem—lent itself to Marian interpretation: "And there appeared a great wonder in heaven; a woman clothed with the sun, and the moon under her feet, and upon her head a crown of twelve stars. And being with child, she cried travailing in birth, and was in pain to be delivered" (Rev. 12:1). Although these words were probably not intended originally as a reference to Mary, they were nicely adapted to the Marian interest that was developing in the later Christian community (Pelikan, 32).

By the tenth century, *Everywoman's* life story was fused in some way with that of Mary. Improving remarks from the pulpit assigned to women a unique role reflecting the special quality of the Virgin's exemplary saintliness and moral goodness. Mary's official role and titles combined with Marian hymnody and religious art in contributing to the formation of maternal ideas and ideals in the minds of both women and men.

Maria in partu

It was a foregone conclusion that Mary's unique experience as a virgin mother would focus attentive curiosity on the physiological aspects of her story (Warner, 382). The Gnostic teacher Valentinus (b. ca. 100 C.E.) had seen the feminine member of the divine dyad as "Grace, Silence, the Womb, and Mother of All" (cited in Pagels, 50). He and his followers, hoping perhaps to temper the association of Mary with the pagan Great Mother, asserted that Jesus had not been "born" of the Virgin in the usual sense, but had "passed through Mary as water runs through a tube."

Mary, moreover, had assertedly delivered without birth pangs, and, indeed, without involvement except in a purely passive sense (Pelikan, 47-48). The Christian artist, translating the myth into iconic form, portrayed the pregnant Mary (*Maria Gravida*) in unruffled quietude—a serene figure that could calm expectant mothers' fears of suffering and give them hope of survival in an era of devastating maternal and infant mortality. Poor, suffering, downtrodden women, in repeating Mary's act of delivering a child, might feel assured of her maternal protection and their own salvation.

Popular piety found expression in the masses of simple souls who approached God through pictures and symbols. Bible study, for them, took the form of contemplation of scenes depicted on church walls and, later, windows. Images of roses, lilies, doves and lambs created an unreal decor of hieratic light and splendor which reconciled future beatific visions and present vales of darkness (Pirotte, 80-81). Devotional images spoke softly but penetrated everywhere in the routine of daily piety, flattering the eye even while diffusing certain ideas about life and the beyond. The response to such images may in many cases have been of the same order as the response to reality, the images serving as substitutes as seen in customs and rituals throughout the world (Gombrich, 10). Fetishistic statues of Madonnas with open wombs to show the Trinity contained therein (*vierges ouvrantes*) became common devotional objects in fifteenth-century Europe (Warner, 72).[5]

A fanatic and superstitious devotion developed around pictorial representations of the mother nursing or fondling the child, images which contributed to the virtually limitless veneration of Mary as the protectress of maternity. The child itself became an object of exuberant, uncritical, and unbalanced veneration, best represented by Rome's "Sacro Bambino," a statue allegedly carved from the wood of an olive tree from the garden of Gethsemane.[6] Women in the ninth month of pregnancy, especially if primiparous, had their wombs blessed by the "Sacro Bambino" at least up to the beginning of the twentieth century; and the statue might on request be carried into the home of a pregnant woman experiencing difficult labor.

The High Middle Ages

One cannot imagine the Christian Middle Ages without the feminine presence which has stamped them for all time, in Christian iconography and in the evolution of Western thought. So prominent a place does Mary hold in the writings of that time, as well as in the visual arts, that the twelfth century has without exaggeration been called "indeed the age of the Virgin."[7] Her portraits as the *Mater Dolorosa* (Mother of Sorrows), in which she replaces Christ as the figure of redemption, hark back to the tradition of mythical fertility goddesses who wept for their sacrificial victims. At the same time she was seen as Mary Mediatrix, an intermediary between Christ and humankind. As *Maria in partu*, she figured as intercessor to Christ in an age when even "ordinary" pregnant women enjoyed such respect that they were permitted on occasion to intercede on behalf of criminals brought to court (Cassee, 96).

Particularly cherished by medieval Christians was the story of the Annunciation to Mary by the archangel Gabriel of her selection to become the mother of Christ—a subject that had inspired artists ever since the time of the Roman catacombs, and became the theme of innumerable altarpieces and paintings during the Middle Ages. In these representations, Mary appears as the Handmaid of the Lord, passive and submissive, a vessel that receives. In this pose she could be held up to women as a model of proper behavior, submissively obedient to God, to husband, and to the clergy and hierarchy of the Church (Pelikan, 83-84). "Everywoman" was expected to comport herself as handmaid, bride, vessel, mother.

As the Annunciation derived its importance from the miracle of Incarnation (Pelikan, 81), the very act of childbirth came to be seen as an extraordinary event directly manifesting divine intervention in human affairs. Women and men alike perceived the containing of unborn young within the body as "miraculous." "Are not infants already fashioned by the hands of God in the wombs of their mothers?" asked Helvidius, an opponent of Saint

Jerome (Pelikan, 118). As the iconography of the Virgin and Child evolved, theories about the mysteries of continuing life were bodied forth in images of pregnancy, birth, and infant care.[8]

To reinforce the concept of the Virgin in her most elevated state of soul and body, both art and rhetoric extolled the "mysteries" of her maternity and virginity as the source of her eternal honor and incorruptibility. If her coronation in heaven connoted the Assumption of her physically incorrupt body, her terrestrial glorification was furthered by her state of physical expectancy (Feudale, 13).[9]

Image-makers were also much concerned to represent the period of Mary's life that lay between the archangel's announcement and the actual nativity of Christ—the time when the prenatal life of Jesus was beginning in his mother's womb (Feudale, 8; Grabar, 128). Devotional images of the Madonna of Expectation combined doctrinal, symbolical and allegorical references to all of the mysteries growing out of her maternity (Feudale, 20). In iconic and devotional form, the incarnation was suggested by calling attention to the Virgin's pregnancy through the fullness of her form and the gestures of her hands (Feudale, 8-9).

Two of the earliest prototypes of this figure of *Maria Gravida* or the "Madonna del Parto" are attributed to the fourteenth-century Tuscan Master of San Martino alla Palma. One is the so-called "Madonna della Ninna" from the church of San Piero Scheraggio, now in the Academy of Florence; the other is a provincial panel that remains in Santa Maria in Campo in the same city.[10] In the latter painting, the drapery of the standing Virgin is so arranged as to reveal the fullness of her form even while an enveloping mantle partially conceals it (Feudale, 10) in what may reflect the existence of conflicting views about pregnancy at the time of its execution. Similarly, in a fourteenth-century fresco attributed to Nardo di Cione[11] in the Florentine church of San Lorenzo, the Virgin partially conceals the fullness of her body by the gesture of her hands, the left holding a book while the right draws a veil across her breast, thus firmly excluding any erotic suggestion in this depiction of Mary's fertility.

Other examples of this favorite theme include a pregnant Mary in the frescoed scenes from the life of the Virgin in Santa Croce in Florence, the work of Giotto's pupil Taddeo Gaddi, author also of a Virgin and Child dated 1355. A choirbook illuminated in 1365 in the workshop of Niccolò da Bologna shows an obviously pregnant Madonna holding in her right hand a closed book, symbol of her virginity, and resting her other hand on her belly (Cassee, 95).

Somewhat similar in concept is a Madonna del Parto represented in a fresco from ca. 1359 in the church of Santa Maria dei Servi in Bologna, attributed to Simone dei Crocefissi. Shown as a seated pregnant woman, her hands on her knees, a closed book on her lap, and a halo around her head, this Virgin is directly identified with the fertile earth that will bring forth fruit; her gaze is fixed upon a bowl filled with earth that stands on a sort of lectern placed at her side. Indeed, the bowl of earth has been seen as the supreme symbol of Mary herself, based on the words of Isaiah 45:8 (Revised Standard Version): "...let the skies rain down righteousness; let the earth open, that salvation may sprout forth."[12]

Piero della Francesca's famous fresco of the Madonna del Parto in the cemetery chapel of Monterchi—on the site of an archaic sacred spot connected with a water and fecundity-fertility cult (Dini, 38)—is marked by an increasing humanization consistent with evolving Renaissance feelings. The Virgin's posture and gestures, and the omission of the traditional mantle, strongly focus the viewer's attention on her swollen breasts and womb (Feudale, 12). These and other iconographic signs, such as the grotto-like setting and the apotropaic position of the hand on the pregnant womb, remind us of Piero's familiarity with the archaic cult of pre-Christian maternal divinities (Dini, 38, 100).

Near the chapel is a fountain where pregnant women even today draw water after having besought the grace of Piero's Madonna. Gravid women who fear Caesarian section allegedly are reassured by a mere touch of the dress or the belly of the Madonna del Parto as they prepare to leave the chapel (Dini, 198). Such belief in the power of the image seems another throwback to archaic magical practices.

But extant portrayals of a Virgin thus glorified in body by her maternity are, after all, very few in number. The growth of humanism, followed by the Protestant Reformation and its sequel in Catholic Europe, brought far-reaching reconsiderations of traditional attitudes and practices. While affirming the sacramental character of matrimony for the propagation of the human race, the Council of Trent (1545-63) at the same time withdrew its approval from representations of what it called "*Maria in exspectatione*." Such representations were henceforth to be considered unorthodox.[13] It may be assumed, moreover, that many earlier depictions were destroyed in deference to this ruling.[14] Contemporary artists were thus left free to exercise their talents on those portrayals of the Madonna and Child which had already emerged as one of the chief glories of the Italian Renaissance.

Leonardo da Vinci's "Madonna Benois." From La Madonna Benois di Leonardo da Vinci a Firenze. Il capolavoro dell'Ermitage in mostra agli Uffizi, *Figure 1.*
(*Courtesy of Biblioteca Nazionale Centrale di Roma*)

Mother and Child in the Renaissance

Concern with the details of Mary's pregnancy had never distracted attention from its happy results, or from the qualities in Mary's personality that made her an archetype of gentle, benevolent motherhood. Giotto, in the fourteenth century, had given weight and dignity to her figure and style as a delicate, serene yet concerned mother whose lovely tapering fingers lent support to a loving child. Duccio di Buoninsegna's variously depicted Virgin and Child, adored by the patrons of Siena and surrounded by saints and angels in a blissful state of union, must also have helped women to accept their burdens more or less gladly.

Domenico Veneziano's fifteenth-century "Virgin and Child with Four Saints" in the Uffizi Gallery is remarkable for the soft contours of its figures, its fresh and delicate palette, and a mastery of light that fills the viewer with a sense of comfort. Merely to mention the names of such Renaissance artists as Fra Angelico, Perugino, Botticelli, and Giovanni Bellini is to conjure up legions of Madonnas and children that combine exquisite refinement and delicacy with just sufficient human quality to convey an unmistakable message to those for whom they were painted.[15]

The gist of that message was that women, unstinting in their love, should find complete satisfaction in their role as mothers and take unalloyed pleasure in caring for their children. Self-abnegating women could dote on the child that looked deeply into the mother's face or touched it adoringly. They could read into religious art an ideal of mother-child oneness encompassing an entire world of inspiration (Parker, 24). They could see how mother and child together enjoyed peace, comfort and beauty in the shared space of Leonardo's or Raphael's or Michelangelo's painterly backgrounds.[16]

Artistic representations of a smiling Mary nursing a drowsy baby at her bared bosom, a supportive Joseph standing close by, synthesized domestic joy and subtly implied that women are endowed with an intuitive knowledge of nurturance. The rigid, concrete forms and poses of earlier paintings gave way to nestling, cuddling and nursing in intimate, affectionate relationships of a kind unknown up to the fifteenth century. More humanized representations of the Madonna and Child showed the baby as a flesh-and-blood infant, close to the mother's body and in emotional rapport with her.

The idealization of this mother-child unity is perhaps best illustrated by Leonardo da Vinci's Madonna Benois of ca. 1478 in the Hermitage Museum—the earliest among his numerous portrayals of the Madonna seated with the child in her lap. In its projection of mother-child *"compenetrazione"* or "interpenetration," it celebrates the ideal of what one writer has called an "intimate affective and emotional relationship that ties mother and child [in a symbiosis of reciprocity]" (Villa, 10). One of the mother's arms encircles the child's body; the two are in a physical contact emphasized by lines and forms conveying unity, intimacy and homeliness.[17]

Presentation of the Madonna and child as an organic unit or dyad often left room for the inclusion of additional figures, whose presence in no way diluted but frequently reinforced the basic message. The mother-child cult had itself been triply emphasized in a very early Christian mural painting, located in the church of Santa Maria Antiqua in the Roman Forum, depicting Mary's mother, Saint Anne, holding her daughter in her arms while Saint Elizabeth and her son John the Baptist flank the Madonna and child. Similar groupings were, of course, effectively employed by Leonardo da Vinci and other artists.

Later art would also produce a multitude of comforting pictures of saints surrounded by children in charming, decorative poses and with little if any emotional depth. The saints are idealized as all-giving protectresses, their qualities of mercy, gentleness and indulgence deriving directly or indirectly from maternal affection. Such representations seem to suggest that the mothers' gratification springs only from gratifying their children (Parker, 48), whose lovableness and "innocence" are taken for granted.[18]

Although some writers persist in seeing Mary as "the single feminine influence in the male-dominated religion [of Christianity]" (Van Buren, 132), other women saints from Saint Anne to Mary Magdalene to Saint Thecla "equal with the apostles" in the Greek Church (Encyc. Brit. XXI, 982), (to mention no later figures), have also carried significant weight in Catholic practice and tradition. Thecla has been called the "female rebel [who] became a model for the new religious woman," and a legend is cited of her baptizing herself in a puddle of water, thereby challenging the emergent male priestly monopoly over the ministration of the sacraments (MacCarthy, 31).

Each of the special virtues defined in the New Testament—the so-called theological virtues of faith, hope, and charity and the so-called classical virtues of temperance, prudence, justice, and fortitude—found embodiment in the female saints and in the Virgin Mary herself. These virtues were not only to be admired and cherished, but also to be imitated, and were elaborated as guides to God-pleasing behavior (Pelikan, 220-21). The glory of the Royal House of Savoy, whose dynasty ruled Italy from the eleventh century to 1946, would rest on the cult of five saints , two of whom were women: Margaret (1390-1444) and Ludovica (1463-1503) (Cabibbo, 331), while to enhance the dynamic union of religion and nationalism Saint Catherine of Siena would be declared patron saint of all Italy in 1939. The lives of Mary and the saints served also as patterns of character and models of still another Christian virtue, humility.

A Mirror for Mothers

Not only on the Italian Catholic scene but throughout Christendom, women thus came under the sway of a stereotyped, idealized mother-child construct that persists to this day. Its influence, obviously, was strongest of all in its country of origin, where religious morality and idealization colored not only the paintings and statues of the Madonna and child but the whole popular view of life and of woman's role in it. The Church's concern for *"propagationem humani generis"* (propagation of the human species) (*Rituale romanum Pauli V, PM,* 237) not only reinforced the fundamental theme of maternity but also shaped the meaning of the female in Roman Catholic society.

Through the manipulation of art and the Mary-Jesus iconography, the church restricted and idealized both mothers and children, diverting them from the processes that further coherence and individuation. The overprotectiveness of most Italian mothers, who often function as their grown children's sole life-support systems, is notorious. Emphasis on the dignity and monumentality of the mother-child relationship inevitably meant that women's individual personalities were obliterated, emaciated, or exaggerated.

Women were not expected to have any share in the spontaneity, creativity, curiosity and imagination associated with the Child archetype (Parker, 172). Roman Catholic cultural expression demanded that the mother's desires be subsumed in the child's; the fact that at least a part of a woman always remains outside the mother-child relationship was ignored or denied (Ruth de Kantor, "Becoming a Situated Daughter," cited in Parker, 234).

Pious imagery underpinned beliefs and devotion which took the mind away from the realities of life (Pirotte, 82). Painterly visions of the mother and child thus rose from the canvas to distort the reality of maternity. Delectable forms and colors obscured the pain inherent in the mother-child relationship. A part of this pain was grudgingly acknowledged when the asceticism of Paul IV (1555-59) led to the cessation of paintings of Mary suckling Jesus, just as representations of the pregnant Madonna had ceased some years earlier. The evolving doctrine of the Immaculate Conception, finally established in 1854, popularized the notion that birth pangs and breastfeeding were woman's punishment brought on by the Fall of Eve (Warner, 237-38).

Canvases depicting saintly mothers could also pull the female viewer into their painted world, inviting women to assimilate themselves in a vital vortex of domestic mythology. Religion (and religious orders) gave a sacramental polish to the world of women working together, weaving, sewing, cooking, and caring for children. Women could be persuaded that they were carrying on the work of making a world. The growing and cooking of vegetables, for example, were women's tasks reflecting nature's seasonal rhythms, and in these simple tasks simple women became trapped in an overarching domestic mythology.

Keeping pace with the proliferation of images of the Holy Mother and Child was the expansion of the Madonna cult into new realms of ecclesiastical architecture and ritual. Architects developed the first of many "Lady Chapels," dedicated to the Blessed Virgin and located in the most important position, directly behind the church's high altar. Concomitantly, linguistic formulas, rites and ceremonies continued to be elaborated together with extraliturgical forms of worship.

Ever more frequent praises were addressed to Mary. The pre-Christian devotional practice of the rosary, used also in Hinduism, Buddhism, and Islam as a mnemonic device for the recitation of prayers (Pelikan, 98), was upgraded under the name of "The Rosary of the Blessed Virgin Mary." Pope Leo X in 1520 officially approved a formal observance involving the recitation of fifteen *Pater Nosters*, fifteen sets of ten recitations each of the *Ave Maria*, and fifteen recitations of the *Gloria Patri*.

Pope Pius V in 1572 established the feast of our Lady of Victory to commemorate the victory of Christian over Turkish forces at Lepanto on 7 October 1571. (The name was changed in 1573 to Our Lady of the Rosary.) The seventeenth-century devotion of the *Angelus*, in memory of the Incarnation, was systematized on a basis of three *Ave Marias* with versicles and a collect, recited three times daily in response to the ringing of the prayer bell at about 6 a.m., noon, and 6 p.m. Another defeat of the Turks, by Prince Eugene in Hungary in 1716, prompted Pope Clement XI to order the observance of the feast of Our Lady of the Rosary throughout Christendom each October 7.

Pope Benedict XII in 1727 broadened the Church's liturgy to include the *Stabat Mater* (Latin for "The Mother was standing"), a thirteenth-century Latin hymn, composed by the Franciscan friar Jacobus de Benedictis, which recites the seven sorrows of the Virgin at the Cross.[19] Responding to the Napoleonic persecutions of the Church, Pope Pius VII ordered the observance on September 16 of the feast of the Blessed Virgin of the Seven Sorrows in 1815, when traditional religious models began to fuse with Romanticism's new forms of Marian cult (Fattorini, 13). The pontificate of Pius IX will be forever remembered for the proclamation in 1854 of the Immaculate Conception of the Virgin—i.e., the determination that from the moment of her conception, Mary was free from the taint of Original Sin— as well as the enunciation of the doctrine of Papal Infallibility at the first Vatican Council in 1870. Pius IX's successor, Leo XIII, in an 1891 encyclical proclaimed Mary's exclusive intermediary powers in her capacity as Mediatrix (Warner, 328). Full saturation of the Church calendar was achieved under Leo, during whose papacy the four Sundays of October were dedicated in many dioceses to the feasts of the Holy Rosary, of the Divine Maternity, of the Purity and of the Protection of the Virgin Mary (Evenou, 50). The month of May was consecrated to the Madonna, and with the help of Leo's nine encyclicals and seven apostolic writings, the entire month of October was dedicated to the rosary as a cult unto itself (Fattorini, 215).

Faced with the secularization of society which was marked by anticlericalism of the elite, industrialization and the formation of a working class that was slipping through its fingers, the Church sought to reposition itself. The nineteenth century saw not only new forms of devotion to the Madonna and a flourishing cult of angels, but also a plethora of historical-ecclesiastical volumes reaffirming papal primacy (Rusconi, 21-24). Much of the Catholic world's male population having become disaffected, the clergy turned mainly toward women and youth, entering with them into a lasting alliance (Fattorini, 11-12).

We shall see later in what ways the cult of Mary was further extended and exploited during the twentieth century. Meanwhile, we need not question the sincerity or the piety of either the sponsors of the cult or its adherents. Undoubtedly the adoration of the Virgin Mother conferred a grace, a sense of beauty and significance on many lives that would have been the poorer without it. Just as surely, though, it strongly reinforced the age-old limitations on the position and role of women, and at the very period when new perspectives and limitless opportunities were opening before humanity at large.

The Sexual Paradox

A striking paradox resides at the heart of our conception of the Virgin Mary, the Mother of Christ—a human female untainted by sexuality, yet capable of discharging with distinction the maternal responsibility assigned her from On High. The very expression "virgin mother" is a glaring oxymoron from the standpoint of ordinary physiology and logic, and the problems it presents have caused difficulty through the ages and into our own time.

To Bishop Irenaeus of Lyons (130-200), Mary was the Second Eve, and her virginal obedience corrected and set right the untenable condition created by the disobedience of her predecessor (Pelikan, 50; Warner, 86). Through childbirth and motherhood, Mary was seen as having expiated Eve's fault and purified or sanitized Eve's loathsome sexuality (Neiger, 155)—a trait that was symbolized by the serpent, often represented in art as a sexual symbol associated with the nude goddess of fertility. Yet despite this supposed expiation, Western women would continue to labor under a stigma and to suffer the misogynous contempt accorded to the devil's snare, whose aim was to corrupt the *vita angelica* of the ascetic or the celibate man (Pelikan, 121).

In Western Christianity, Mary would continue to play a dual role consistent with these ambivalent beginnings. As Virgin, she would be used to combat the perceived excesses of sexuality prevailing in Late Antiquity. At the same time, as Mother, she would serve as a counterpoise to the perceived excesses of Christian asceticism, whose rejection of the body seemed at times to reach such lengths as to deny that God had created it at all, while its revulsion against sexuality appeared to suggest that this God-given function was tainted with an inherent immorality (Pelikan, 121-22).

In her role as Virgin Mother, Mary effectively illustrates this fundamental paradox in the Catholic view of sexuality. Thought and contemplation by the Church led to the glorification of virginity over matrimony; yet, paradoxically, it was matrimony, not virginity, that came to be celebrated as a sacrament (Pelikan, 113). "It is good for a man not to touch a woman," Saint Paul had said. "Nevertheless, to avoid fornication, let every man have his own wife, and let every woman have her own husband" (I Cor. 7: 1-2). And again, "It is better to marry than to burn" (I Cor. 7-9).

Christianity thus was saddled with the task of at one and the same time deprecating sexuality as at best a regrettable distraction from higher things, and glorifying its results—so long as they appeared under acceptable circumstances—as woman's supreme accomplishment and responsibility.

Marriage and Morals

That the purpose of marriage is to promote the discharge of this feminine responsibility might seem evident even as a matter of etymology. Even our word matrimony"—*matrimonium*—has a female, maternal connotation. The counterpart of patrimony or *patrimonium* (the aggregate belongings of the *pater familias*), it originally signified "legal maternity" and then came to refer to its instrument or condition. Viewed principally as the function of the mother, matrimony in fourteenth-century Italy was defined as *ufficio di madre* (office, function of the mother).

Church debate on matrimony continued throughout the centuries; its sacramental nature, and its indissolubility, were finally established by the Council of Trent in 1563. From then on, sacramental and institutionalized wifehood were elevated to an oppressive degree. They could serve the pedagogical function of reinforcing both the cult of the mother and, at the same time, a virgin/bride mythology involving, for example, the Church as the Bride of Christ, the mystical marriages of various saints with Christ, and so forth. Such implicitly erotic "bridal allegories," essentially male concepts, firmly pinned both brides and consecrated virgins to their sexual natures (Jo Ann Kay McNamara, *Sisters in Arms*, quoted in MacCarthy, 31).

Marriage, in Catholic theology, endowed the woman with the highest responsibility to her husband, to their offspring, and to the Lord.[20] Her emotions and actions, however, were to be firmly channeled by the patriarchal, anti-erotic norms of Roman Catholic society, which stressed virginity prior to marriage but thereafter insisted with equal emphasis upon the obligation of fecundation for the *propagationem humani generis* ("Ritus celebrandi Matrimonij Sacramentu," in *Rituale romanum*, 237).

Various ceremonies and customs surrounded this responsibility. Women in childbirth had been classified in the Old Testament as "impure" for seven days—or for two weeks if the child happened to be a girl—and subject to rituals of "purification" (Lev. 12:5). Similarly, in sixteenth-century Florence, newborns were immediately taken from their mothers and entrusted to a wet nurse for fear of puerperal contact and infection.[21] Perhaps in part to mask the high rate of maternal mortality due to puerperal infection,[22] the Church would invite the faithful to sing *"Gaude visceribus mater in intimis"* (Rejoice, mother, in the fruit of thy womb), a hymn sung in celebration of the feast of the Assumption.

Later would come the ceremony of the feast of "Blessing of a Woman

After Childbirth," or the "Churching of Women." At the beginning of this ceremony, the mother knelt at the church door, a lighted candle in her hand; the priest sprinkled her with holy water, recited Psalm xxiii, and then led her into the church, saying in Latin, "Enter into the temple of God, adore the Son of Blessed Mary the Virgin, who has granted thee [the grace of] the birth of a child." The mother then knelt before the altar and prayed, "thanking God for the gifts given her," while the priest uttered a prayer for her temporal and eternal happiness and that of her child. Finally, he invoked upon her the abiding "peace and blessing" of the Trinity ("De benedictione mulieris post partum," in *Rituale romanum*, 237-39).

Such songs and ceremonies illustrate the Church's manner of subtly linking in the mother's mind the "grace" of childbirth as a cause for rejoicing and the promise of the "peace and blessing" of God. Undoubtedly they have been of assistance to many Catholic women attempting to navigate among the reefs and shoals of ecclesiastical doctrine.

Sexuality and procreation have remained inseparably associated in the minds of Catholic women, and cannot readily be separated without a sense of culpability. Deeply imbedded in the concept of virginity is "a revulsion from the tyranny of the flesh that is peculiar to women" (McNamara, cited in MacCarthy, 31). Overcome by the sense of their own sin, women have been compromised by male regulations. Female sexuality as such being considered intrinsically evil, maternity alone is accepted as the female counterpart of male sexuality. The dichotomous desire/refusal of maternity in many women arises from the conditioning of woman's sexuality by her "love-hate relationship" with her own body. Only through sublimation in motherhood does the repressed sexuality of many women find expression (*Maria, Medea*, 145).

And motherhood, as we cannot too often emphasize, is not only a right but a duty—if brought about in the right way. Originally formulated in the sixteenth century, the obligation to participate in the propagation of the race remained in undiminished force at least until comparatively recent times. So long as Italy remained a labor-intensive agricultural society, woman's fertility could be perceived as a positive contribution to national and personal wealth. Fruitfulness was considered an essential requisite for a young bride, especially among the lower classes. The fecund woman was esteemed, and at the same time condemned to the heaviest household work. The sterile wife was scorned and could even be repudiated; there are pathetic stories of attempts by sterile peasant wives to appear pregnant by such devices as stuffing their skirts with rags (Dini, 171). (One might also cite contemporary cases of anguished women who, having undergone several unsuccessful inseminations *in vitro*, are driven to suicidal thoughts.) In some backward Apennine areas, the fear of bringing a sterile woman into a household authorized a "test" for proof of fertility: should the woman indeed become pregnant, an immediate marriage of reparation took place (Dini, 151).

The prevailing attitude toward male sterility was at least equally harsh, in line with the biblical text: "He whose testicles are crushed or whose male member is cut off shall not enter the assembly of the Lord" (Deut. 23:1). The sterile woman or man was maligned and ridiculed, and the decline of whole civilizations would come to be linked with a decline in fertility.[23]

We have noted that childbearing has been considered a laudable function only when accomplished within the theological and legal framework of Catholic marriage. Traditionally, an unmarried girl who happened to become pregnant had few choices if she was to avoid dishonor to herself and her family. She could flee from home, commit suicide, or, if she did not fall into insanity, might seek to abort through magic brews and rituals or by piercing her uterus with a knitting needle, a procedure usually resulting in infection and death. On all levels of society, it was customary to cover up unwanted pregnancies by unwanted marriages when these could be arranged (see Sibilla Aleramo, below).

Unfeeling and intolerant as the prevailing attitudes may appear, it must be remembered that the upholders of traditional morality were heirs to a long history that reached back beyond the beginnings of Christianity. Chastity of the unmarried —especially girls—was considered a virtue even in ancient Rome, where the sacred fire was maintained by the physically and mentally perfect Vestal virgins. Their vow of chastity remained in force for a period of five years or more, and to break it was considered a capital offense punishable by entombment alive. Although nothing forbade marriage after their period of service, by custom and superstition they rarely married.

In a final paradox, we may note the insistence of Christian teaching that while childbirth passed the contagion of original sin like a venereal disease from one generation to the next, woman's childbearing function still remained her supreme glory and distinction (Armstrong, 124). Religion continued to stress the importance of the woman's fertile years—the "Child-Bearing years," in the words of one contemporary writer, "as though you stand there like a blossomed pear tree and the fruit plops off" (Jayne Anne Phillips [b. 1952], cited in Magill, 402).

Motherhood in United Italy

The attitudes and practices shaped by centuries of childbearing persisted with little change in the hundred years that followed Italy's national unification in the 1860s. In nineteenth-century bourgeois families, maternity was seen as an unquestioned social and cultural value, and the function of every *donna per bene*, or woman of good social standing, was to procreate. The responsibilities of women were those of domestic management, nurture of the young, and guardianship of morals. If they were spinsters, they might serve in charitable institutions or as teachers and religious missionaries.

The family remained frozen in the traditional pattern in which the father dispensed authority while the wife and mother fulfilled the Madonna ideal by offering unconditional love and unflagging devotion to husband and children. Strict segregation by sex-roles was still enforced, on the principle that motherhood and economic dependency went hand in hand and that to be a "good mother" a woman must stay at home. Wifehood, motherhood and "householditude" were full-time occupations. Motherhood, in accordance with the maternal mystique, was a beacon of order and an emblem of unity (Parker, 123).

In Italy's predominantly agricultural zones, women remained caught in the longstanding social patterns of rigid family structures, high birth and mortality rates, and numbers of handicapped children. Even today, the persistence of old-fashioned attitudes regarding the family, paternity, maternity and "birth chains" (continuous pregnancies) illustrates the durability of traditional stereotypes.

Although female labor was employed to some extent in Italian light industry, the marginalization of women in the nation's productive life was intensified with the post-World War I economic crisis of the 1920s. Female workers, no longer needed in the factories, were exhorted to dedicate themselves to home, children, and agricultural work. Woman's role as a demographic mechanism came in for renewed emphasis in the Fascist era that began in 1922 and was largely shaped by dictator Benito Mussolini's ambition to restore the glory of the long-dead Roman empire. Not only did the Duce's heavily subsidized agricultural projects require a large labor force; his political aims presupposed ample reserves of military manpower based on a high birthrate. Absolute devotion to the nation was touted by the Fascists as the guiding principle of education, and "sacred maternity" was held up as a supreme familial and social value. To the "August Maternity" of Her Royal Highness Princess Maria José of Piedmont was dedicated a book of

"Canti della Maternità" (Songs of Maternity) in 1937. Italy's 1939 codification of civil law described the family as basic to the organization of the State but rendered only the father/husband responsible for its "education in conformity with national fascist sentiment" (Santosuosso, 122).

The notorious slogan, "War is to the man what maternity is to the woman," encapsulated the dual mission of the Italian people. By rearing her children to adulthood, it was asserted, the Italian woman par excellence would assure Mussolini of an army of nine million men, ready to hurl themselves against any enemy under his personal direction.

The doctrine of marital responsibility for the race, the demand for *"procreazione della prole"* (procreation of children), were of course in the direct line of Roman Catholic teaching going back at least to the sixteenth century. A sacerdotal textbook published in 1939 confirmed the nullity of a marriage contract if a spouse was unable or unwilling to procreate, and, for good measure, called down execration on the impious Malthus and his doctrines (Gaspardo, 147-49). Procreation, long established as a Christian duty, was now a Fascist obligation and responsibility as well.

Another exponent of Christian motherhood, Monsignore Corrado Groeber, after expressing sympathy for the plight of unmarried women— "poor lonely vessels unable to find a safe pilot"—invited their married sisters to luxuriate in the *"dolore,"* *"grandezza,"* *"dignità,"* *"richezza,"* *"responsabilità,"* and *"spiritualità"* of "Christian maternity" (*La madre* [1927], 3-4, 149). The author of another work of the Fascist period inveighed against wet nurses and sang praises of mothers who breastfed their own offspring (Magaldi, 9–10). A writer on Euripides' dramas asserted that the Greek tragedian drew his main inspiration from the *"bimbo"* (child) and *"l'amore materno"* (mother love) (De Martino Rosarol, 7). Exhorting women to create large families, a treatise on "Sacred Maternity" praised the "sweetness," "power," and "importance" of the maternal state and invoked "the calm, radiant maternal serenity, the cheerful infantile smile in the Madonnas of Lippi, Correggio, Rubens, Giotto, Raphael!" (Pennato, 153).

Echoes of Fascist teachings continued to reverberate even after Mussolini's demise and the overthrow of his movement in 1945, the year in which Italian women gained the vote. Italy's postwar public school children were given intellectual sustenance not dissimilar to that of previous decades. The maternal imperative continued to prevail, and cultural representations of motherhood continued to equate maternity and femininity. Many Italian women to this day feel something of an obligation to society to undergo the maternal experience.

Times and attitudes were changing none the less, spurred in part by the psychological upheavals of World War II, in part by related changes in the national economy and social structure. By the early 1960s, Italy had ceased to be a predominantly agricultural nation. The brutal, chaotic transformation of the countryside, the emergence of large cities with their factories and slums, the turmoil of politics and class strife brought the nation to what has been called its "modernist rendezvous with unmediated family life with all its pains and pleasures" (Van Buren, 128).

The sudden transformation into a technically advanced society found Italy's women writhing their way through cracks in a dying order, abandoning age-old attitudes and practices, reducing their level of fertility, and thereby imposing a dramatic reduction in family size, at least in the North. Accompanying the social and political turbulence of the 1960s was the Italian woman's "upheaval from within"—a personal revolt against the "servile" nature of motherhood and the impossible task of juggling job, housework, and the "work of reproduction" (*Maria, Medea*, 220).

Caught between tumultuous cultural changes that undermined patriarchal conditions and the changing circumstances that thrust them into the workplace with its relative freedom and multiple male contacts, many women abandoned children, homes and husbands. The maternity concept faced an uncertain future.

The apparent waning of the traditional ideal of Christian motherhood was not unnoticed at the Vatican, which, however, seemed intent on bolstering the Madonna cult and even extending it into new areas. A series of popular "Libretti religiosi" published in Florence in the early twentieth century included twenty-nine books of Marian devotion which invited readers to obedience, resignation, and acceptance of the harshness of the times (Romaniello, 105). Medals, rosaries, candles, flowers, holy pictures, gonfalons, and sacramental scapulars, as well as novenas, congregational devotion to Mary, and books for the edification of young girls, gave witness at one and the same time to the greatness of the Virgin and the spiritual power of the pope (Evenou, 54). Sentimental and popular piety gave rise also to the spread of small printed holy images (*santini*) for personal protection. The heliogravures, chromolithographs, and commercialized images that served as powerful arms for the diffusion of religious ideas but which have since been seen as a regression to infantilism have now mostly disappeared from the scene and have become collectors' items (Pirotte, 67, 69, 70, 73).

Pope Pius IX in 1908 established the Feast of the Apparition of the

Immaculate Madonna to commemorate the fiftieth anniversary of the Lourdes apparitions. Pope Benedict XV beatified in 1920 a certain Anna Maria Taigi for her "feminine, domestic and family holiness" (Palma, 530), while her subsequent biographers would stress the saintliness of her daily life as a housewife, and her faithfulness to her duties of matrimony and maternity (ibid., 541-2).

The Society of the Admirable Heart of Mary and the cult of the Sacred Heart of Mary, which had been established by Saint John Eudes in the seventeenth century, were commemorated in Eudes's canonization in 1925 by Pope Pius XI, even as new canonizations attempted to combat the "plague of laicism" (Fattorini, 12). Pope Pius XII (1939-58), confronted by the crisis that brought Mussolini to power, saw fit to dedicate the entire world to the Immaculate Heart of Mary.

Under Paul VI (1963-78), Mary was given the new title of *Mater Ecclesiae*, and the Second Vatican Council (1962-65), summarizing the principal themes of the entire historical development of the doctrine of Mary, stressed her role as advocate, helper, and mediatrix and exhorted priests to imitate her (Warner, 221). In his apostolic exhortation *Cultus Marialis* of 2 February 1974, Paul VI went so far as to propose that the Virgin Mary— Virgin and mother—be taken as the model of the New Woman, a recommendation not much in harmony with the evolving outlook of gender-conscious women either in Italy or elsewhere. Nor did the eight volumes of proceedings of the most recent (1987) Mariological conference (*De cultu mariano saeculis XIX-XX*, published in 1991) suggest any restoration over the last two centuries of Mary's ineffable mystique and idealization as Mother of all. In fact, Marian cult and mystic fervor during the period of Romanticism may have been a doubled-edged sword: extreme sublimation in Mary has been seen as the cause of the "dangerous overevaluation" of women in the twentieth century (Fattorini, 213, 219).

Mary, Marriage and Motherhood Today

Despite the best efforts of the Vatican, the increasing modernization and secularization of Italian society since World War II has inevitably brought with it a progressive etiolation and impoverishment of the Madonna figure, whose subtle attraction held women—and men, too—in thrall for hundreds of years. The absolute, polarizing and renunciatory myths of the Virgin Queen, Bride, and Mother have lost their hold in Italy's secular age (Nozzoli, 31).[24] Even the word *"smadonnare"* (literally "de-Madonnize," used to express annoyance or as mild imprecation) has come into the Italian language.[25] Marian apparitions and the communication of messages, to visionaries and to the world, continue to be acknowledged by ecclesiastical authorities as worthy of pious belief; but to attribute to the Virgin Mary the performance of actual miracles has ceased to be a standard expression of piety.[26]

The denial of Mary's objective transcendence by many Italian women has further deprived her of her title of Mediatrix (Pelikan, 136). In contrast to the devotion of millions of humble medieval women who identified themselves with the figure that represented womanhood for much of Western history, external devotional observance is now dying out. Some Italian women today, perceiving a gap between the assertions of Roman Catholic dogma and what to them are the realities of life, have tended to belittle the dogma even though few of them achieve the vehemence of Edna O'Brien, whose books are banned in Ireland because of her sometimes very bitter indictments of the Church.[27]

Old attitudes change slowly, however. The sense of guilt attending sexual activity outside marriage remains deeply rooted in Italy, reinforced by the traditional *padre/padrone* influence and by the role of the matriarchy in molding female comportment, especially in the South. The debate on premarital virginity continues even while defrocked priests become fathers. Fanaticism and superstition in connection with virginity still prevail in certain villages of the deep South, where villagers will offer public proof of a bride's virginity by displaying bloodstained sheets from the nuptial bed. Reverence for maternity is still so deeply rooted in Italian society that the government protects pregnant women workers by granting conspicuously lengthy periods of paid maternity leave and giving priority to pregnant women (though not to the ill or elderly) in the notoriously long queues in Italian public offices.

Unimpressed by such cultural residues, the present generation of Italian women writers has already demystified the sexual taboos in what has been called their "phallocratic" culture, and now assert that maternity and motherhood are likewise in need of demythologizing and redefinition. Having thrown off the fetters of socio-religious authority, they see themselves as going through a process of self-liberation from the normative representations of motherhood, extricating themselves from the image of woman "pinioned in the trap of maternity" (Parker, 234), and revealing their own warlike side in the destruction of the domestic hearth.[28]

Equally outdated today are the image of the Italian husband, strutting beside his pregnant wife and using her condition to flatter his vanity and proclaim his virility, and that of the idealized mother figure which formed its counterpart. Writers now assert that "mothering" has been constructed and reconstructed to a point of intolerable difficulty. Having made known their intense dissatisfaction with married life and oppressive husbands, they are now writing about the fatigues and frustrations of maternity and the contradictory emotions that buffet mothers.

No longer hypnotized by the stereotype of "maternal happiness," Italian women in the main have ceased to view maternity as their biological and social destiny and have begun to seek an identity distinct from the maternal function. Rejecting the Church-sponsored idea that a woman's role is to be submissive and to suffer, they are increasingly distancing themselves from the religious ideology and power structure in which it is anchored. Pious attitudes toward religion, religious art and devotion to the Virgin have given way to active protest against such outmoded concepts as that of Gregory of Nyssa's (fourth century) "tender mother who joins in the inarticulate utterances of her babe" (quoted in Pelikan, 220)—that same Gregory who deliberated over whether he should call his sister Macrina, who defiantly refused to marry, a woman at all "since she has gone beyond the nature of a woman" (quoted in MacCarthy, 31).

Increasing numbers of Italian women have become neglectful, even forgetful, of the sacraments of the Church. The institution of marriage has lost its aura of sanctity and indissolubility, just as childbirth has lost its air of "miraculousness." The church's contention that women must suffer the pains of childbirth as a punishment for Eve's transgression is no longer taken seriously. Disputing the Church's rejection of contraception (Warner, 382), its female critics in turn reject what they call its "neurotic misogyny" in refusing even to consider the ordination of women (Armstrong, 124-25).

In such respects, Italian society has been moving ahead of its own laws, especially those of the Church. The structure of ecclesiastical and legal sanctions that formed the support of traditional matrimony was dealt a crippling blow with the legalization of divorce and, in 1974, the defeat by popular referendum of attempts to annul the earlier legislation. Four years later, the voluntary interruption of pregnancy was also legalized,[29] to the particular satisfaction of those abortion advocates who professed to see the termination of a pregnancy as a creative act (cf. Elvira Banotti, *La sfida femminile—Maternità e aborto*, cited in *Maria, Medea*, 166).

Public debate on women's issues during the 1970s furthered the dissolution of inhibitions and restraints. Debates concerning maternity which developed unexpectedly in Rome in 1978 resulted in the publication of innumerable and startling women's works offering fresh focus on mothers and children. The findings of a two-year workshop held in Bologna and Genoa on male control of women's sexuality was published in 1980 in a historical review under the title, *Parto e maternità: Momenti della biografia femminile* (*Maria, Medea*, 222).

Women writers of the period openly admitted their will to distance themselves from their devouring children, to free themselves from "carrying" babies and serving as their "feeders." They looked for inspiration to Virginia Woolf, Simone de Beauvoir, and the French feminist theorists Hélène Cixous and Luce Irigaray, formulators of the "maternal metaphor" (Becker, 19-21; 170-71). These French thinkers provided an enabling mythology for Italian women authors who, like de Beauvoir and Julia Kristeva, perceived the radical ambiguity of pregnancy, at once an enrichment and an injury, a deprivation and a benefit (Parker, 202-03).

Increasingly, Italian women have been ready to discuss the negative side of maternity, the discomfort, suffocation, sense of imprisonment, and moments of fear, recoil, panic, nastiness, and resentment—even hatred—of their children (*Maria, Medea*, 88, 104, 207, 211, passim). There is fierce resentment of the tendency to look on motherhood as "the ultimate personality test for women, according to which femininity [is] either admirably achieved or admirably transcended.... Drawing on their own feelings as mothers," Roszika Parker recalls, "such thinkers began to argue that to experience childbirth as an exam which their sex mysteriously required them to pass or fail contributed massively to maternal misgivings and misery" (*Mother Love/Mother Hate*, 157).

The birth of a new baby is only the beginning, moreover. Too often, the advent of a new member of the household provides a couple not with the cement of a shared love but with a catalog of grievances. The status quo is violently shaken, leaving one or both partners aggrieved, unsupported, isolated or overburdened. In such circumstances, the element of hatred in a mother's feelings toward her baby can burgeon to a point where love is almost drowned out (Parker, 12). Maternity becomes perversity; maternal abuse and cruelty come to the fore (Parker, 219 ff.).

Filled with such grievances, some women have explicitly challenged the traditional concepts of motherhood that still dominate Italian social ideology and classify any contrary views as a "deviation" and "social error." Not content with having secured the right to regulate their own fertility, such women have been demanding to know what valid biological, social or economic interest is served by the generation of still more individuals in the violent and insecure world surrounding them. The species is "already too propagated," they assert, and prolificness is no longer a social merit but a social menace.

"*E se decidessimo di non generare?*" (And suppose we should decide not to generate?), some women were demanding as far back as the late 1970s, as increasing numbers declared their outright rejection of maternity.[30] A survey conducted in 1980 revealed that 46.66 per cent of women factory workers in an area of Tuscany answered negatively the question whether they desired to have children (Dini, 161). In Italy as a whole, the rate of population growth has fallen to zero; for the years 1990-94 it reached minus 0.2; and currently the nation enjoys the lowest fertility rate in the world.

The advent of alternatives to childbearing—abstinence, contraception, abortion—has not erased the evils of infanticide and child abandonment. Such practices, however abhorrent, may find a measure of understanding or even cultural sanction[31] in circumstances when earlier births have strained the resources of a household to the breaking point; when financial and practical problems render maternity so burdensome; when the specter of unemployment looms, illegitimacy is harshly dealt with, and human body tissues, through organ transplants and embryo experimentation, tend to be treated as just another commodity (Appleyard, 7).

The regular abandonment of babies on church steps or in garbage bins and the innumerable infanticides that Italy has seen through the years are responses to economic, social and political circumstances as well as symptoms of the absence of maternal love as posited by Elizabeth Badinter or the maternal indifference described by Roszika Parker. An Italian woman may kill a child not as a manifestation of insensate cruelty but because she is still under the influence of the puerperal condition or is acting in response to external influences.

One psychoanalyst contends that "most mothers do not murder or totally reject their children, but death pervades the relationship between mother and child" (quoted in Parker, 19). There is a growing awareness among women that maternity does indeed involve an approach to death as well as the production of new life. The illusion that a child bestows some sort of "immortality" on the parents has given way to the sober realization that in outliving them the child will certify their own mortality (Cattaneo and Pisa, 52).

Like all historical developments, the transformation of motherhood in our time has brought with it both gains and losses. It is too early to assess the long-term implications of the secularization of maternity and the disparagement of the Madonna cult, but it is undoubtedly true that from an immediate and practical standpoint, release from the maternal imperative has given reassurance to many contemporary Italian women, stimulating new ideas and freeing their desires and preferences. As their professional and political visibility increases, women no longer consider motherhood a *sine qua non* for their existence or the ultimate expression and fulfillment of their femininity.

In a reappraisal of maternal subjectivity, the new Italian woman is expanding her life, bringing complex and diverse identification to herself, to her mothering or her disinclination for mothering, and even to her dis-identification as a mother. In seeking to assert her "womanness" as opposed to her "motherness," the new woman has carved out ample space between herself and her child. The filling of that space is the task to which the Italian women writers discussed below have set themselves.

Chapter 3

℘⩗

Literary Manifestations of the Changing Social Scene: The Nineteenth Century and Beyond

Contemporary writers on the "Woman Question" usually depict the female sex as more or less helpless victims of a male plot designed to keep them in permanent subjection and stifle every impulse toward independence and self-worth. Though not without a measure of validity, this concept is oversimplified to say the least. For women, often enough, have visibly served as instruments and willing accomplices of their own subjection. A student of English women writers of the Victorian period has noted that far from having suffered under "the blighting effect of the Victorian moral code,...most of these [women] authors were revealed as social tyrants rather than victims of tyranny"[1]—in other words, as active participants in formulating and enforcing the standards to which Victorian women were expected to conform.

With some honorable exceptions, we shall find that much the same was true among those Italian women writers who were beginning to gain a foothold and an audience in the century that brought to fruition Italy's dream of independent nationhood.

The Silent Years

That Italian women of the nineteenth century should be writing for publication at all marked an important innovation in a country where female literary production had hitherto been rare indeed. During the Middle Ages, women writers about maternity—or about any other subject of female or general concern—were virtually unheard-of, although one poetess felicitously known as the "Compiuta Donzella," or Perfect Damsel, did compose some verses preserved in the Vatican archives in which she deplored among other things the *mariage forcé* imposed by an unfeeling parent.

As literacy among women increased in the following centuries, so did their visibility in religious, social and intellectual life. Some early feminine humanists became conspicuous in the highest ranks of society; but their writings were directed chiefly toward maintaining the power and prestige of the autonomous, male-dominated courts to which they belonged, and in which they served as useful supporters of the rulers' cultural ambitions. The hymns to God, the Virgin, and the saints by Lucrezia Tornabuoni (1425-1482), the mother of Lorenzo the Magnificent and the grandmother of two popes, were closely tailored to Lorenzo's policy of enhancing and upgrading popular traditions and activities, a policy that gained further support from the quasi-medieval religious plays composed in the vernacular by Antonia Pulci (?1452-?).

The early decades of the sixteenth century brought with them a proliferation of lyric poetry in imitation of Petrarch, as well as a popularization of Platonic doctrines by such women poets as Veronica Gàmbara (1485-1550), Vittoria Colonna (1492-1547), and Tullia d'Aragona (1510-1556). Petrarch's well-known "Canzone alla Vergine" (Hymn to the Virgin) would also inspire "Vergine santa, immaculata e pura" (Holy, immaculate and pure Virgin) by Laura Terracina (1519-c. 1577) and a religious lyric addressed to Mary by Isabella di Morra (1520-1545), the young Renaissance poet who was beaten to death by her three brothers for having exchanged letters and poems with a married man.

Other sixteenth-century women poets, openly expressing their very personal emotions, fashioned for themselves identities charged with out-and-out erotic passion. Gaspara Stampa (1523-1554) and Veronica Franco (1546-1591) defined their diverse lyric universes in rich descriptions of the joys and pains of love.

Such intimate expression was dampened, however, as the century progressed by the new wave of moral conservatism associated with the

Counter Reformation and the publication in 1556 of the "Catechism" of the Council of Trent. Women's writings now focused on such relatively safe topics as the praise of conjugal love or the love of God in allegorical guise. Amid pious celebrations of church ceremonies, saints, the Virgin, and the nativity, actual maternity as a literary subject remained conspicuously lacking.

By the early seventeenth century, women were still producing such works as *La vita di Maria Vergine imperatrice dell'universo* (Life of the Virgin Mary, empress of the universe, 1602) and *De' gesti heroici e della vita meravigliosa della serafica Santa Caterina da Siena* (The heroic deeds and marvellous life of Saint Catherine of Siena, 1624)—in which the mystic union of Catherine with Christ is celebrated, like a mundane marriage, in the presence of the bridegroom's mother (the Virgin Mary), and is sealed by Christ's gift to his bride of a diamond ring.[2]

The neoclassic age of the later seventeenth and early eighteenth centuries was not lacking in models of feminine beauty and gentility, nor did a handful of female authors fall short in the introduction of new ideas from the rest of Europe. And, by the nineteenth century, with the strengthening calls for reform and political independence that accompanied the Risorgimento or Italian national revival, some women overtly enlisted under the banner of national unity, though their support of republican and radical causes was seldom carried beyond the semiprivate confines of their own salons. Other women, meanwhile, continued to uphold the traditional concept of what amounted to the vestal virgin tending the sacred fire on the domestic hearth. In the end, conservatism and clericalism imposed their own ideal of the Risorgimento heroine as one whose fulfillment is that of the *wife* who sacrifices herself for her husband, the *mother* who consecrates her offspring to the motherland.

Forging Their Own Chains

The achievement of Italian political unity in the 1860s did little to deflate the glorification of maternity that continued to permeate most writing by and for women throughout the century. The maternity cult and church-supported models of motherhood persisted with little change. Reproduction and rearing of the species were seen as woman's primordial function and sacred duty; marriage and maternity were felt to embody a perfect integration of biological and social laws.

This concept reached far beyond a prescription for channeling the reproductive capacity of the individual woman. *Everywoman* was called upon to be fertile and to shoulder the consequences. The literature teems with stereotyped young females whose value as potential wives is bound up with virginity and "reputation"—yet who, paradoxically enough, are expected to become prolific once the marriage frontier is passed. Prisoners of the ambiguous relationship between femininity and the reproductive function, such heroines strive to understand the man-woman dyad in terms of the idealistic notions inculcated by church and family; but when the man responds to the sensual reality of the woman, the heroine is duly shocked and disillusioned.

The Cult of Domesticity

The ideal held up before the eyes of Everywoman was that of the bourgeois family with its universal, essentialist and normative characteristics. An entire body of writing underscored the dignity of wifehood, the woman's mission as manager of the household and protectress of both matrimony and patrimony. The ideal of female domesticity spawned the concept of the "angel of the hearth," virtuous, purged of all sexual taint, disinclined to intellectual pursuits, faithful and submissive to her husband. Her "honor," unlike his, was essentially bound up with her sexual comportment. In defending it, she implicitly defended the honor of the entire family. At home a laborious housewife, on the outside her dignified obedience to her husband served as the foundation of his public esteem.

Wifehood and motherhood are thus the single aim of the nineteenth-century heroine, who typically is ushered through her season of glory with the preparation of the dowry, the sacred marriage, the birth of the eagerly awaited first child, and then of subsequent children who will guarantee her sacrificial self-annihilation.

Mothers not only nurture their offspring but serve as their refuge from the hostile outside world. Their bodies literally prefigure the house, an extension of the protective prenatal womb (Morris, 154), just as in prehistoric times the *imago templi* conformed to the shape of the female body.[3] Epigones of the mythic Demeter, mothers bring forth children to whom they remain morbidly attached all their lives, having no other raison d'être but these (Neiger, 12). Total dedication to their offspring is seen as an essential aspect of a well-ordered society, a fundamental presupposition of Italian history and literature (Camaiani, 433).

Deviations from this norm were considered unnatural and transgressive. Women who betrayed the expectation that earthly madonnas become perfect mothers, who did not passively and selflessly nurture and care for their offspring, who refused to be dominated by domestic and family ideals, risked being labeled "sinners" by, among others, the majority of outraged nineteenth-century women authors. The unfaithful wife automatically became a "bad" or "deconsecrated" mother, while the wife uninterested in maternity was perceived as a dangerous threat to the male's wife-mother-lover trinity and thus to the whole order of society.

To the nineteenth-century Italian mind and even well into the twentieth century, the sterile woman—or any woman who did not fill the maternal role—represented an element of social disorder (Nardi, 80, 81). Girls were educated to the idea that every woman must desire to become a mother, and that it was only a cruelty of fate that condemned her to become a worker, an employee, a teacher, doctor, or lawyer (Ida R. Sée, *Le devoir maternel* [1911], quoted in Badinter, 1981, 203). Even among nominally "enlightened" women, this deep-seated prejudice remained rooted in the Italian mind decade after decade. Society expected that the woman's maternal role should so absorb her mind and body that she would be unable—and would not even desire—to play any other role or to engage in any form of work outside the home.

If one does occasionally encounter in the literature an energetic and gifted woman—usually the mother of small children—who latently desires to develop her talents, one may be sure that her ambitions and abilities will be stifled in deference to her husband's determination that she remain no more than a wife and a mother. The persona of the "self-directed" female having been de-legitimized, such a woman lacked the possibility of developing an autonomous personality. Resignedly she accepted traditional society's repressive norms, smothering the anguish of her inescapable, perpetual marginalization (Dini, 151-52).

The development of a serious, independent character having thus been tacitly ruled out of court for one-half the population, the so-called "popular romances" of the nineteenth century could only hinge on what amounted to an obligatory manhunt, its wild success or furious failure. Strategic scheming, tactical artifice, the clinching of a satisfactory marriage and the production of heirs were what filled the empty existence of young ladies in a culture that offered few and limited alternatives.

The readying of girls to fit the preestablished mold was a full-time occupation that left no margin for serious reading and study. All energies were absorbed by the obligatory instruction in how to smile, how to show the right kind of love for a man, how to cook, set a table, wash, iron, and mend—everything, in short, that would be needed to care for the future husband and children. Inevitably, the product of this wholly onesided education was a weak woman who could only take refuge in dependence on the male. Passive and lethargic, she sought incarnation in the "other"; her inner void reflected the ennui and stagnation of her own home. Italian popular romances are almost exclusively concerned with the experience of girls who scour the horizon in search of love and, more especially, of the status that can be gained only through marriage—for the social structure in which they are confined will accord them no valid identity save through the husband.

Almost without exception, tales of romantic love, whether fulfilled, betrayed, or desperate, hinge upon this unvarying ideal of female domesticity as the only road to acceptance and respect. Daydreaming heroines, obsessed with thoughts of the ideal marriage that guarantees security, may marry men they scarcely know, solely to gain a sense of "family." Psychologically and emotionally, such unions represent more of a power struggle than an experience of love.

With marriage—essentially, her conquest of social position and self-respect—the heroine has only begun her journey. As long as she becomes a respected mother and fills the role demanded by society, all will be well; so all her yearnings are concentrated on the gestation of the male child desired by her husband and his family. Should she fail to become pregnant in due season, she may resort to the most unedifying propitiatory rituals in hopes of attaining fecundity. Wholly dependent upon the call of nature and the promptings of a society that imperatively insists upon reproduction, maternity, and submission, she is assigned a sex role that removes her from all decisional power.

In addition to her childbearing responsibilities, moreover, she is charged with the further task of fitting her boy and girl children respectively for the roles of lord and vassal, thus carrying her own subordination forward into the next generation (Camaiani, 439).

Marriage and children being the only acceptable outcome of romance, the novels of the era focus mainly on the intimate domain of women: family, fashion, servants, gossip. Dress style itself had ideological significance in the nineteenth century. The voluminous garments of the era disguised the contours of the female body in deference to religious expectations, while their impracticality compelled the woman to lean heavily upon the arm of her powerful, virile husband. That the latter experienced abundant frustration in his relationship with this chaste angel of the hearth is strongly suggested by the proliferation of mistresses and prostitutes so conspicuous in nineteenth-century Italian society—and not only in fiction.

Through the later nineteenth and well into the twentieth century, women's literature was dominated by authors of aggressively conventional outlook and vigorous opposition to divorce or, indeed, to anything that threatened to alleviate the feminine condition. Widely differing in age yet remarkably similar in ideological bent were such writers as "Neera" (Anna Radius Zuccari, 1846-1918), Carolina Invernizio (1858-1916), Annie Vivanti (1868-1942), and "Liala" (Amalia Liana Cambiasi Negretti Odescalchi, 1897-1995).

The self-styled "antifeminist" Neera was nineteenth-century Italy's outstanding champion of the cult and mystique of maternity. Exalting the religion of the domestic hearth, for thirty years she sang what has been called an "uninterrupted hymn to the woman-mother" (Nardi, 89)—an acknowledgment and reaffirmation of woman's supposedly unique destiny of motherhood, closeness to the crib, and joyful performance of domestic and female duties.

Maternity, for Neera, offers rich compensation for any disillusionment in love; it provides the means of escape from the alienation caused by ugly reality. *L'Indomani* (The day after, 1890), for example, tells of a failed marriage that is saved by the conception of a child, and in which the heroine sublimates her inner dissatisfaction in the sentimental importance she attaches to the biological phenomenon that is her unborn baby. The author's poetics of maternity finds its culmination in her late novel *Duello d'anime* (Duel between souls, 1911), in which she lays it down that the destiny of the fecund woman is rebirth; that of the sterile woman, death (Nardi, 91).

Neera's antifeminism found definitive expression in her book of essays entitled *Le idee di una donna* (A woman's ideas, 1903). In it, she declared that George Eliot and George Sand gave little to humanity as compared with such women as the obscure mothers of Leonardo da Vinci and Dante Alighieri. The mothering of a just man, she asserted, is the greatest feminine achievement imaginable. Convinced that the sexes are not only diverse but unequal, she nevertheless perceived the woman as the unique repository of a fecundating power that is eternally renewed in "ideal maternity."

Ten years younger than Neera, the astonishingly prolific Carolina Invernizio offered her countrywomen what amounted to an unrivaled course of continuing education through the medium of no fewer than 130 sentimental, pathetic, melodramatic novels, replete with cautionary images of sin, crime, and perdition. Whatever educational value such works possessed lay in the identification of the many kinds of conduct that do *not* conform to the precepts handed down by mothers for their daughters' happiness.

Writing at a time when many young unmarried women were beginning to devote themselves to badly paid, extradomestic labor, Invernizio warned tirelessly of the dangers of their situation. An unwanted pregnancy, inevitably followed by abandonment on the part of the father, could result, she admonished, either in infanticide or in lifelong abjection that must be endured as a form of expiation. Meting out due punishment and rewards to the protagonists of her terrifying tales, Invernizio held in thrall a reading public that was vast by Italian standards.

Annie Vivanti's almost 400-page novel *The Devourers* (1910) offers another variant of the nineteenth-century monument to maternity. For Vivanti, unselfish motherhood is the exclusive justification for a woman's life. In a work that revolves entirely around the conflict between sacrificial maternal love and female self-realization, the author unequivocally subordinates the mother's individuation to the overriding requirements of society. Vivanti's later novel, *Vae victis!* (Latin for Woe to the conquered, 1917), celebrates maternal rites and rituals in all their sacredness and shouts hosannas to "the sublime and triumphant instinct of Maternity" (263).

Last of this quartet is "Liala," whose life belongs almost entirely to the twentieth century but who continued to insist, in over eighty popular romances, that the single recipe for happiness is a good marriage. As with her older contemporaries, her works exalt the concepts of female purity, devoted wifehood and motherhood, and accommodation to the type of the "decorative" model imposed by male ideology. As in all these works, the key assumption is that motherhood is the woman's supreme act of self-definition.

Turning momentarily from fiction to poetry, it is not surprising that *Maternità* should be the title of Ada Negri's 1904 book of exuberant verses inspired by the birth of a daughter. Though their author was an "emancipated" figure committed to populist and socialist ideas, Negri's verses illustrate how deeply engraved was the maternity cult even in nominally emancipated circles. Her poems abound in concepts that might have been considered outmoded even at that time: joy and mystery in the eyes of the pregnant woman, the dreaming baby in its cradle, the ecstatic mother's lullabies.

Allegedly Mussolini's favorite woman poet, Negri deemed maternity to be self-justifying and sufficient unto itself. With her, the concept of motherhood is carried beyond the familiar ethical and juridical categories (family and marriage) into the domain of the old fertility goddesses—"la sacra Natura immortale," as she herself calls it (*Maternità*, 3)—and is forced into what one writer has called parameters of primordial and cosmic functions (Nozzoli, 31).

Dissentient voices

In spite of literary insistence on the maternal mystique, some writers did allow their heroines to manifest a degree of uneasiness in their maternal straitjacket. Not all Italian women were so weighed down and crushed by the dominant ideology as to lose sight of what was happening to them or to surrender all aspirations to a selfhood beyond maternity.

The sadness and loneliness of the feminine condition, the lack of female self-determination, the impossibility of finding alternative life styles did inspire occasional feeble attempts to break through the crust of socially approved sex roles. Most often, the heroines of such works fall short of achieving the identities they seek; ironically, they usually end up as victims of their own and others' ideas of what they should be. Yet, softly, they do begin to voice their dissatisfaction with the male-dominated society that had kept women under oppression for centuries, even though for the moment they can only hint at the reasons for women's feelings of alienation in their unbalanced world.

A sensitive ear can catch occasional murmurs of dissent from the very beginning of the nineteenth-century maternity cult. Notable is the case of Elisabetta Caracciolo Forino (1817-?), who targeted the injustices perpetrated against women destined by their parents for convent life even in the absence of anything like a religious vocation. Herself an ex-nun, Caracciolo in her memoirs takes up the cudgels for these victims of Church and family interests. Her bitter criticism of power, religion, and the law employs the convent emblematically as the closed space and institutionalized place for the oppression of women.

She even goes so far as to condone the conduct of a nun who becomes pregnant and is spurned by a hypocritical Church and society. Failing in a suicide attempt and finding no forgiving Virgin Mary to whom she may turn, the nun curses the Madonna and all the saints: "go to the devil and don't talk to me about Heaven and the Madonna. If it's true that the Madonna helps those in need, why doesn't she come to help me and the creature stirring inside me?"[4]

A better-known figure is that of Cristina Trivulzio di Belgioioso (1808-1871), one of the many women who worked for Italian unity during the

Risorgimento—in her case even to the point of raising her own militiamen and leading them into Milan during the 1848 revolution in Lombardy. In addition to her indefatigable revolutionary activity, Princess Belgioioso produced a brilliant satirical portrait of Turkish society as seen through the eyes of an Italian traveler.

If the convent symbolized the oppression of Italian women for Elisabetta Caracciolo Forino, Belgioioso's Turkish harem represents no less powerfully the workings of sexual oppression, and not only in Turkish society. Among the painful humiliations and insults suffered by women in this milieu is the deep disdain directed against the sterile one. "[S]corned, despised, and rejected in the Orient," this unfortunate must "grovel in the mud." "[T]he lowliest female slave, so long as she is pregnant, is authorized to trample" on the woman who has failed to produce offspring.[5]

As the century progressed, women novelists employed new strategies in an attempt to break out of the traditional mold. "Marchesa Colombi" (pseudonym of Maria Antonietta Torelli-Vollier, or Torriani, 1846-1920) confronted in her writing such burning late nineteenth-century feminist issues as divorce, abortion, and prostitution. It is true that her books were generally seen as inculcating the need for young girls to subordinate their individuality and will and become good wives and mothers through acquiescence, chastity, and self-sacrifice. But, at the same time, her works are tinged with new elements of satire and irony.

In her noted book of rules of etiquette, for instance, Colombi writes satirically that if a man should mention women's intimate apparel in the presence of a young girl, the latter would be expected to faint on the spot! (*La gente per bene* [Well-bred people, 1877], quoted in Camaiani, 439). Irony heightens her depiction of the joylessness of motherhood in *Un matrimonio in provincia* (A country wedding, 1885), whose heroine, deprived of any mental stimulation whatsoever and no more than a vessel for fertility, is dedicated exclusively to her daily chores and her family's respectability: "Now I have three children. Daddy says...that the Madonna has been a good inspiration for me.... But the truth is that I'm getting fat" (103).

Another dissident woman writer is Regina di Luanto (ca. 1862-1914), author of *Un martirio* (A martyrdom, 1894), a novel in diary form that describes a humiliated, downtrodden woman's ongoing battle with her husband for at least partial release from domestic life. To her protests that she would like to study and make something of herself, her husband—a university professor—contemptuously replies that studies do not provide useful recipes for making soup for babies. This loathsome pedant condemns his wife's aspirations outright: "A woman will never find her place outside the circle of domestic life…. A woman of good social standing must stay at home, manage the household, take care of her children…. That is her true mission" (quoted in Morandini, 184). The heroine does not rebel; she bows to what is, after all, the traditional division of responsibility. But the resentment she feels at the sight of her husband out in the world—and, of course, guilt-free—translates itself into deeply negative feelings toward her home and babies.

With the twentieth century, a new boldness begins to characterize the incipient revolt against the female condition. Remarkable for its time is the work of the comparatively little known Anna Franchi (1866-1954), which dwells upon the physical realities of childbirth as well as her psychological reactions to maternity. *Avanti il divorzio!* (Ahead with divorce!, 1902), which is autobiographical in content even though written in the third person, recounts the author's battle during her married life for liberation both as a woman and as a writer.

Having gone through her first pregnancy "without feeling the slightest bit enthusiastic," she describes her delivery as "supreme uninterrupted pain…stimulated and prolonged by the doctor." Feeling "something big and soft oozing out of her body in a gush of blood," she knew that the child was born—and all around her "she felt a void." Pregnant once again, "the unpleasantness of the fact made her even sadder than before" (quoted in Morandini, 252-54). This bitter work concludes with an indictment of the children who uttered no word in defense of their unjustly accused mother. Resignedly, the author concludes that a woman, to be acceptable to society, must throttle every expression of her own individuality.

An equally striking account of the burdens of motherhood is that of Carola Prosperi (1883-?), whose *La paura di amare* (Fear of loving, 1911) describes the heroine's lassitude as she gives birth to and then breastfeeds four awkward, ungainly, clumsy boys. "Her freshness grew stale, all her beauty seemed to tarnish." Each new pregnancy and birth left indelible traces: "…her entire body grew flaccid and flabby." The little time she found for reading plunged her into sadness, if not despair. "Marriage, motherhood, family, home… Woman needs nothing more, they all said…and now…in her withered and weary state, she had a feeling of nausea, her body having already been mangled too many times."

But when a pretty baby girl is born to her, Prosperi describes in glowing passages the pride the heroine takes in her maternity, in seeing her own past beauty reborn in the baby girl. To this child, the author perspicaciously assures us, the heroine will devote the "blind, absolute, exclusive and jealous adoration of all fanatical mothers." None the less, the book ends with gray descriptions of a stillbirth and of an assortment of guilt-ridden women plunged in postpartum depression and schizophrenia (quoted in Morandini, 324, 325, 327), victims of an education that had promised them a life of fulfillment and transcendence through motherhood.

The incipient revolt against existing conditions took many different forms. Encroaching on what had hitherto been considered male territory, the anarchist and revolutionary Leda Rafanelli (1880-1971) raised her voice against "il *potere*, la *religione*, la *legge*" (power, religion, law) (*Seme nuovo*, quoted in Morandini, 307) in her depiction of strikes, political meetings, arrests, deportations, inquisitions, and all other forms of institutional oppression.

At the opposite extreme was the highly charged response of at least some women to new European literary and artistic trends like Symbolism and Decadence. Rather than sniping at the complacency of the self-satisfied male, they sought relief from current norms in an exaggerated sense of esthetic refinement, often accompanied by heightened erotic sensibility. The sensual, decadent heroine clad in billowing veils—the femme fatale of D'Annunzian stamp—impressed her own image on the meretricious opulence of Italian high society. Poisonous flowers and forbidden fruits lured readers into a voluptuous world of passion and romance. Yet behind a facade of liberation and dangerous living, many such women nurtured a vulnerable psyche that longed for a more traditional, conventional, and emotionally fulfilling existence (Russell, xv-xxiv).

An example of such creeping emotional emptiness is that of the frankly sensual and erotic Amalia Guglielmetti (1885-1941), who had never married and who acknowledged late in life a lack of maternal feeling that she herself found "hopelessly sad"—since, she said, if she had loved children, her life would have had a "reason" (quoted in Turoff, 164). Such a confession highlights the extent to which Italian women had internalized the dicta of the Roman Catholic culture with its idealization of motherhood as woman's supreme raison d'être.

Chapter 4
℘〇℆
The Twentieth-Century Revolt against Maternity

The Italian nineteenth century, particularly after the realization of Italian unity in 1860-1870, can now be seen as a period of transition between the unthinking, automatic acceptance of the maternity cult by the vast majority of the population and the questioning, even the outright repudiation of such an outlook as we see it today, not only in the work of such writers as Rita Levi Montalcini and Dacia Maraini but in the lives of an appreciable cohort of Italian women.

We cannot emphasize too strongly that women in the literature of the nineteenth century existed at most as relative beings, as instruments of a particular generative function rather than as fully developed personalities. History had reduced the power and importance of female sexuality to a point where the typical Italian woman had little choice but to attempt to play the ideal wife and perfect mother, cost what it might.

Yet this ostensibly happy wife/mother figure was not without a secret sense of victimization, of being smothered and devoured by the family relationships in which she was inextricably entangled. Side by side with her normal maternal feelings, she could not fail to feel irritated and invaded by her children's presence and behavior. Dimly she experienced a need to craft for herself some kind of existence outside of and beyond the family. By the

close of the century, women writers and their fictional heroines were
beginning to grope for an identity distinct from the outworn clichés of
heterosexual romance, marriage, and motherhood.

Stealthily and *sotto voce* but in ever greater numbers, the Italian woman
began to acknowledge the oppressive nature of her daily existence. Slowly
she opened her eyes to the inherent contradictions of the husband/mother/
child relationship. Warily she admitted the possibility, even the need to direct
her life toward some higher, more ideal goal outside of the dreary cycle of
childbearing and child-rearing.

Now, for the first time, Italian women writers began to call attention to
the tensions and restrictions inseparable from the national concept of
domesticity—the conflict between the urge to independence and the reality
of enforced dependence, between the need for self-assertion and the
requirement of self-abnegation. Italian heroines began to plot rebellion
against the prevailing, severely limited concept of what was "proper" for
mothers in family and social relationships. They began to reject the sense of
guilt when failing to live up to cultural expectations that had become
impossibly onerous.

Still saddled with all the paraphernalia of the traditional maternity cult,
Italian fictional heroines began to see in it a kind of ghetto, a form of
household slavery, and the home itself as a place haunted by the ghosts of
"good" and "bad" mothers (*Maria, Medea*, 57). Family ties were beginning
to be felt as fetters and prison bars. There was a dawning belief that the
female self must undergo a separation from the family if it was ever to
recreate itself from within.

Heroines who possessed a sense of being "different" from the oppressed
mass of their suffering sisters began to reject, in thought and sometimes
even in fact, the customary physical, biological and physiological
exploitation based on male authoritarianism and the accompanying familial
norms. But the "different" woman who chose to assert her individuality
faced painful isolation and rejection, not only by the family group but by
external society as well. Only as she learned to heal her tormenting self-
division would she experience a growth toward new possibilities, toward
being "at home" in the external world.

Sibilla Aleramo's Bid for Freedom

Such was the message communicated in 1906 by Sibilla Aleramo in
her autobiographical novel, *A Woman*, the foundation stone of twentieth-
century Italian feminism and our best introduction to that century's open

revolt against traditional maternity. *A Woman at Bay*, to use the book's alternative English title, suggests the desperate but not the less heroic position of the woman who, unable to retreat, bravely confronts the consequences of her own bid for freedom.

At a stroke, this novel subverted the nineteenth-century model of conventional womanhood. Describing her struggle to escape the bonds of an inferior social position and a stultifying family situation, Aleramo dared to speak in this book of having glimpsed "a higher human destiny [for women], distant but none the less attainable" (114). In justifying her claim to existence as an autonomous being, she fought to affirm her own identity rather than submit to a familial system she found oppressive, depersonalizing, and dehumanizing.

Aleramo's heroine had initially chosen the relative independence of a factory wage-earner, one who unequivocally vowed that she could "never be happy unless [she] could go on working" (29-30). But her resolve was brought to naught when she was raped and then forced to marry a fellow worker. The reparatory marriage deprived her of her freedom to wander, and entrapped and submerged her in the matrimonial abyss.

At first, she eagerly awaits the birth of her child, having been led to believe that she would thereby "acquire a new dignity" (61). Intent on rising above the "barbaric practices" of her own family, she resolutely refuses amulets for the baby's cradle, swaddling clothes, magic spells to ward off the evil eye, and similar precautions (59, 69).

Once the child is born, the ambiguity of the heroine's feelings finds reflection in her simultaneous experience of "heaven" and a "sense of overflowing goodness" as she presses her lips against her small son's head (62), and, at the same time, the "grandeur of her images" as she reflects upon her future role as teacher and companion to the child and as author of a book that will give "artistic expression to a torrent of new emotions" (63-64).

She willingly endures the pain of breastfeeding, experiencing fresh moments of "unutterable excitement" at the sight of his "little red mouth sucking avidly" and the sound of "his throat gulping down the liquid" (63). She scorns the doctor's assertion that the baby's smile is only "a muscular contraction...produced by physiological pleasure in that moment of satiety." Steeped in the Italian tradition of mother-child "*compenetrazione*" or interpenetration, she prefers to think there is already a current of sympathy between the two and that her child is "charmed by the sight of [her] loving face."

For her, she later recalled, the baby's smile was only "a prologue to the bliss he would bring me as he grew up" (64). As time went on, her total obsession with the child obliterated all reality; she loved him "more and more extravagantly, and felt that everything that was of value…was contained…in his small body" (66). The smallness of that obsessional body may be interpreted as antonymous to the repressed "grand images" in the heroine's own psyche.

With the passage of time, however, she begins to experience feelings of dissatisfaction and frustration. She becomes aware that there is a fundamental deficiency in her life: "That rosy, breathing infant gave me pleasures and anxieties which…seemed constantly at odds with a sense of instability, a strange oscillation between lethargy and excitement, desire and indifference. I couldn't explain where this instability came from, but the result was that I began to see myself as an unbalanced, incomplete person" (67).

It finally dawns upon her that the elements of her dual role are incompatible—that "the mother and the woman in me couldn't live together," (67) and that, though the bond of maternity is still strong and commanding, she must separate from her son.[1]

Incredibly, this early twentieth-century provincial Italian mother abandons home, husband, and beloved son in an effort to throw off the maternal yoke and assert her inalienable right to develop her own role as a woman and a writer. Revolting against the oppressive culture of Mediterranean marriage and maternity, she attempts to break the "monstrous chain" that has fettered women like her through the ages.

Undeterred by the certainty of her classification in the ranks of so-called "bad" mothers, Aleramo—for it is she herself who addresses us through the medium of her heroine—had plotted not only her personal escape from the traditional Italian home, but also the dealing of a blow to the maternal mystique as such. She was prepared to welcome any employment outside the home, and connected with writing, as a blessed release from husband and child.

In reclaiming her own body and demanding her own space, in separating herself from her role as mother, Aleramo was seeking to reintegrate the conflicting aspects of herself as a woman. Proclaiming her potential as a creative writer, she turned her back on her past and began her journey of self-exploration (Nozzoli, 37, 40). In the struggle between family and career, her aggression and sheer determination had resulted in liberation—but only at the price of permanent separation from her family.

For Aleramo, her act of individual liberation gained significance from its impact on what she saw as a multigenerational process. Early in the novel, the woman had accepted the pattern of women's duties and roles which she had inherited from her mother, a procreator like herself (Pickering-Iazzi, 328). Her own mothering was merely part of an "umbilical lineage," connecting the baby backward to her mother and, through her, to her maternal grandmother and great-grandmother—and, at the same time, forward to her unborn daughter (Joan Raphael-Leff, cited in Parker, 256).

Aleramo thus experiences in her own person aspects of her relationship with her mother, and it would be the normal expectation that she in turn will pass on to her daughter the accumulated heritage of self-denial and self-denigration. But while continuing to voice expressions of love for her child, in the end she breaks the cycle and develops her self-identity in such a way that her desertion becomes a proud, fulfilling alternative to the expected self-sacrifice.

An obstinate and solitary dissident, Aleramo challenged the distinction of gender roles at the heart of Italian society, and has continued to shock the historiographers of Italian motherhood by presenting her heroine as a woman to be emulated. She endured opprobrium and at the same time offered herself as a controversial mother/writer struggling against tradition.

Her novel vividly reflects her lack of faith in the judicial process. As the novel proceeds, the father of her child has become both "criminally indifferent" and riddled with venereal disease. But she knows the meaning of Italian "justice": "the law insist[s] that my son be bound to his father" (210). She must give up her son, and she is willing to pay the price.

In this supreme sacrifice, she is acting not in willful abandonment but because she believes she is conferring more dignity on her child by choosing "real human feeling" in preference to the conventional, clinging maternal love (98). "A good mother must not be simply a victim of self-sacrifice, as mine has been: she must be *a woman*, a human individual" (113). She must set an example.

A "new woman" thus emerges from Aleramo's novel. She has rejected the concept of passive sexual submission, and with it the stifling sterility of the family hearth. The family was the fixed place of her alienation and inferiorization; she rejects the so-called maternal function which holds women in slavish subjugation. Not for her was what has been aptly called the "captive, subservient, but utterly loyal subgroup [of women who] are relied upon to do the job of nurturing, and to do it well" (Helen Franks, quoted in Parker, 127).

In her later novel *Amo dunque sono* (I love therefore I am, 1927) she prophesied that the "new woman" would be a "liberated hermaphrodite…inviolable…never entirely possessed by a man" (66).

More than anyone else, it was Aleramo who shattered her culture's conventional notion of the "abandoning mother"—a concept which persists to this day, and not only in Italy. "It is easier to regard women who leave their children as selfish, irresponsible and unnatural," writes Helen Franks, "than to take into account the idea that they might leave but still love them and grieve for them. Once we accept that women can both love and leave, we are into very deep and uncharted waters" (Helen Franks, ibid.).

It cannot be claimed, however, that Aleramo's bold move was crowned by unqualified success on either the personal or the societal plane. She had emancipated herself from the maternal function in order to dedicate herself to poetry and to the endless love affairs that inspired her verses and that may be seen as rites of passage in her life—personal crises followed by artistic and cultural maturation. But she continued to yearn for a child born of love. Unlike the son she had borne for her despised husband, she wanted "a masterpiece of my flesh, my heart and my spirit." "Like an earth mother, her function is creation," writes one critic, perceiving Sibilla Aleramo as an "animist goddess" generating "love and…art…through a transfigured erotic maternity" (Bassanese, 1994, 14).

Disappointed in these late-blooming maternal hopes and no longer perceived as one of the feminist vanguard, the always ambiguous Aleramo fell a victim to Mussolini's propaganda and ended up as a promoter of the very maternity cult she had so bitterly denounced. In praising the Duce for reawakening "the female masses to their precise and sacred function as reproducers of the species,"[2] she had come full circle, consigning women once again to the same "monstrous" chains she had herself so vociferously denounced and, at least for a time, succeeded in breaking.

The Futurist Fiasco

Not less ambivalent in their attitude toward Italy's traditional maternity cult were the Italian Futurists led by Filippo Tommaso Marinetti (1876-1944), whose glorification of dynamic movement, linked with a wide-ranging rejection of inherited values, enlivened the Italian cultural scene in the years just before and after World War I. Glorifying male virility, war, and the machine age, the antibourgeois, nationalist intellectuals who recognized Marinetti as their leader professed disdain for women and for the kind of sentimental love extolled by Sibilla Aleramo. To them, these were nothing more than obstacles in the path of Man's march to outdo himself.

For Marinetti, woman's proper allegiance was "not to the man but to the future and to the development of the race" (quoted in Nozzoli, 57)—an attitude that proved by no means incompatible with the Fascist worship of female fecundity and demographic growth. Similarly, women writers of the Futurist persuasion extolled not maternity as such but an ideal—or at least a doctrine—of female vitality.

Outstanding is the example of Enif Robert, whose 1919 novel coauthored with Marinetti, *Un ventre di donna. Romanzo chirurgico* (A woman's womb: surgical novel), purported to demystify the womb and divest it of its sacral qualities. Rejecting the sentimental, decadent literature of the nineteenth century, she proposed a female archetype consistent with Futurist ideology.

Unlike Anne Sexton, who sang of the "sweet weight" of the womb in her 1969 poem "In Celebration of My Uterus,"[3] Robert revolted against that organ: "Today I received [Marinetti's] greetings from the battlefront...How disgusting to be a suffering uterus when all the men are out there fighting!" (*Un ventre di donna*, 25). The personified uterus of Enif Robert's novel thus becomes the symbol of woman's natural fragility, and the cause of the ugliness that the author discerns in the mother who has borne too many children, her flabby folds of flesh strapped into her corset cuirass.

Despite this revolt against her woman's body, Robert submits at last to male supremacy in the person of Marinetti, and, like Sibilla Aleramo, executes an astonishing volte-face that ends in reassigning woman to her ancient biological role. After first cursing her uterus for blocking her mental development, she turns inexplicably to glorifying the fecund womb as it thrills to receive the "warm masculine gift" (205). In a radical shift of sociopolitical viewpoints, the originally misogynous Marinetti becomes an apologist for the Fascist myth of the exemplary Mother, while the wavering Enif Robert returns to upholding "honest family life" along with other "female role" commonplaces.

Other Futurist women writers found equally bizarre ways of vaunting woman's reproductive function. Valentine de Saint Point, in *I Manifesti del Futurismo* (1914), excuses rape by victorious Italian soldiers on the grounds that it "recreates life." "Benedetta" (the pseudonym of Benedetta Cappa Marinetti, wife of the Futurist leader), in mystical-spiritual vein, saw woman's reproductive function as a sublimating force: the Woman-Creator, she maintained, is the vital principle that generates not only human beings but ideas and passions as well. And where would Italy be, asked Maria Ginanni in "Cannoni d'Italia!" (1917), without the women factory workers who contribute their cannons for war and their children for the fatherland! (quoted in Nozzoli, 52).

A somewhat different emphasis pervades the work of Rosa Rosà (Edith von Haynau, 1884-1978?), which belongs mainly to the post-World War I years of national malaise and incipient Fascism. Taking an evolutionary view of biological sex roles, she held that not Nature but cultural development accounts for changes in female and male functions and inherent traits. She hailed with enthusiasm the impact of the war on women's lives, the new roles women were assuming in the workplace and at home.

In the pages of the Florentine weekly *L'Italia Futurista*, Rosa Rosà wrote of "le donne di posdomani" (the women of the day after tomorrow), who would supplant the "aged and worn-out mothers...exhausted from having lived their lives for others." Maternal altruism and "usefulness to the family" were not for the new woman, she asserted; the new woman would be "less maternal," but active, virile, energetic—a "free, immortal 'I' who gives herself to no one and to nothing."

But Rosà, too, like most of her contemporaries, fell a prey to ambiguity, eventually yielding to old myths and even heeding the call to motherhood. The novel *Non c'è che te!* (There's no one but you, 1919), while it denounces family institutions, explicitly places the heroine in a situation in which her persona is swallowed up and she is reduced, like so many before her, to a reproductive machine. Her love for the adult male a failure, she has a child instead in the hope that at last her love will be entirely welcome and put to good use. As a reinterpretation of the mother-son relationship, the novel "does not," in the words of one critic, "develop a convincing, alternative option for women" (Della Coletta, 357).

The failure of all such bold initiatives could only be abetted by the realities of Italian life after 1921. The deepening national economic crisis undid the socioeconomic gains of wartime, accelerating the expulsion of women from factory employment and bringing new emphasis to the agricultural sector as the key to national equilibrium. Just when women were beginning to brace themselves to smash old idols—or at least modify them in accordance with their real needs—the ground was cut from beneath their feet by the advent of Mussolini and the foisting upon the nation of a glorified mother/wife syndrome in the name of Italian patriotism.

Grazia Deledda

More straightforward and unequivocal than the Futurists in her rejection of traditional attitudes regarding motherhood was the Sardinian Grazia Deledda, who in 1926 became the second woman, and the first Italian woman, to be awarded the Nobel Prize for Literature. (Giosuè Carducci, the Italian poet, had won the prize in 1906, and Selma Lagerlöf, the Swedish novelist, in 1909.) Explicit both in her rejection of marriage and motherhood and in her refusal to bow to outmoded prejudices, Deledda divined her own talent as a writer and embarked upon a literary career at a time when no Sardinian woman could write fiction and still be considerd a lady. She bypassed the primitive social expectation that she bear many children and identified a variety of other outlets for female creativity. When she eventually married, it was simply to escape the paralyzing traditionalism of her backward countrymen. But becoming a wife and a mother in no way changed her life of learning and the intensity of her literary production.

She casts no favorable light upon the archaic, agropastoral society into which she had been born, and in which she was initially compelled to live. It was a society whose defining concepts reached far back into antiquity, one in which women saw themselves either as heiresses of the prolific "Great Mother" or as guardians of the family lares and penates, custodians of the hearth on which a few coals of the "sacred fire" had to be kept burning at all times.

Grazia Deledda scorned such outmoded ideas and practices, which she attributed in large measure to an antiquated educational system. In her autobiographical novel *Cosima* (1936), she took issue with the time-honored double standard whereby female education ceased with the fourth grade while boys could continue upward. The highest literary function conceded to the weaker sex was the telling of stories and singing of lullabies, activities firmly associated with the ruling maternal image.

In the teeth of this tradition, Grazia Deledda discovered the great classics and herself began writing at a very early age, although she avowed no taste for the "many volumes in Latin, and ascetic books, the lives of saints, the Bible, religious monographs: these didn't attract me," she writes (*Il paese del vento*, 832-33).

Her family and kindred were not merely indifferent but actively hostile to her literary interests, not only for "moral" reasons but out of fear that they would preclude a good marriage. Her mother would later look in horror upon her first payment for the translation rights of her novels, considering it "the fruit of a mortal sin" (*Cosima*, 135). Her two illiterate aunts burned the pages of the magazine which had published her early work, *Sangue sardo*.

Even her brother, who had originally encouraged her writing, disapproved of the lifestyle she had adopted along with it. But Deledda resolutely followed her own path, though even in erotic matters it lay far outside the parameters set for "girls from good families" (92).

Deledda hated the islanders' savage, guilt-ridden form of religiosity, a combination of devout Catholicism, atavistic superstition, witchcraft and pantheism. The Church did scarcely anything to alleviate the hopelessness of poverty, she noted. So-called Christians offered merely verbal support to poor peasants and shepherds, who lived in subhuman conditions, and found nothing but opprobrium for transgressive lovers and unwed mothers.

Grazia abhorred the example of her own mother, a somber, austere *mater dolorosa* type obsessed with rearing her six children and seeing them all married "cristianamente." A deeply religious but self-blaming woman, wrapped in secret worries and without strength or will to combat them, she confessed at times that she could "no longer believe in God" (117). Grazia, fearful of developing in her mother's image, was all the more determined to eschew the Mediterranean female type the older woman represented. She was determined to seek joy in her writing, not sorrow in her children.

"Sweetness and light" was not to be her genre, however. Her writings abound in starkly realistic images, many of them centering in the experience of childbirth as she had observed it in this primitive setting.[4] She lingers over the stenchful pool of black, fetid blood in which her pregnant sister has died after a miscarriage (56): "She closed [her sister's] large, vitreous eyes, washed the body, carried it on a little bed…to the matrimonial bedroom. She perfumed her; she arranged her beautiful chestnut-colored hair around her transparent face, and finally dressed her in her modest white wedding dress and even put on her little satin shoes. She acted under the impulse of an almost supernatural power…" (56).

After this experience, Deledda was overcome by religious terror and the "ancient, involuntary guilt" that befalls "all men again and again" (56-7). Only her union with the obscure and mysterious presences in nature could dissipate the tensions that arose in her, too, from a rigid obsession with original sin that she had been unable entirely to shake off.

An experience narrated a few pages later seems to strike a happier note. To the mountaintop sanctuary of the Madonna del Monte, where the islanders go to pray, Deledda accompanies them but goes to write rather than to participate in the Novena. Taking pen, paper and ink to the blessed rendezvous, she fashions a writing table in a sacred niche and dedicates herself to the "mysteries of art" while the crude young pilgrims, having soon finished their devotions, turn to celebrating the underlying pagan festival with flirting and sanguinary combat.

Absorbed in her writing, Deledda is plunged in nature and describes the forest and the mountain rocks as "a net of mystery, an unfolding of surprising things, as though she were floating on a deep ocean, surrounded...by all the marvels of a submarine forest" (76). The uterine symbolism here appears more wholesome than that which accompanied her sister's deathbed. The fullness of an all-enveloping nature's warm embrace contrasts with her sister's empty corpse, drained of every drop of blood.

The ambitious young writer observed with wonder that the islanders' primitive baby cribs "never remained empty." In one of her rare descriptions of babies, she expresses shock and disappointment at the aspect of a newborn sister, whom she had imagined with curly blond hair, as in religious paintings—but who in fact was red and swollen, her mouth wide open to cry, while the mother, drained of life, lay pale and impassive.

Such observations fortified Grazia's resistance to her mother's incessant demand that she seek a good husband and have children, conformably to the time-honored assumption that more births meant more workers and therefore more wealth for the family. Recoiling from such primitive socioeconomic expectations, Deledda told herself that the only way she could offer "some consolation" to her disappointed mother was by leaving the island and becoming a successful writer. She dreamed of becoming for Sardinia what Tolstoy was for Russia—observer and epic singer of the land.

A cruel letter from a critic momentarily dampened her literary ambitions. Bitter and discouraged, she even contemplated giving up her career and following her mother's advice, slight as was the prospect it afforded of ever achieving the immortality for which she thirsted. As with Virginia Woolf, it has been suggested that she looked upon her writing as a specialized, nonphysical form of maternity, one in which the typically female enthusiasm over conception is translated into exaltation at the finding of a creative vein. Developing like the organs of a fetus, we are told, such an epiphany could yield a sensation of being above time and death; but when "nothing churns in the mind," the feeling is comparable to postpartum depression.[5]

In spite of discouragement from every side, Deledda gradually resumed her writing and actually began to have some impact in the Italian literary world, where the critics showed a certain respect analagous to what they felt for her famous male contemporaries, Giovanni Verga and Luigi Capuana. Her feeling of success is crystallized in a metaphor that lifts her soul and carries her far from the dark, limited horizon of her island. "Everything seemed grand and luminous," she writes in *Cosima* (104), and in her personal correspondence she also alludes to "an intimate inner voice" suggesting "something high and pure and very luminous."

By this time Deledda had ceased to rely on anything that might come from outside herself, from "the world agitated by men." She now expected "everything from herself, from the mystery of her inner life" (113). That mystery, to be sure, was not consciously related to the reproductive function, but focused upon artistic production through her own imaginative skill. "You tell me to get myself a husband!" she scolds her male editor. "But don't you know that this is the ugliest, most prosaic thing you could wish me?" (quoted in Miccinesi, 3).

This is not to suggest that Deledda was a prey to any particular squeamishness where sexual relations were concerned. In the end, she did marry and moved promptly to Rome, in fulfillment of a not wholly repressed desire to flee the island and be free to write. Prior to her marriage, however, she had wilfully thrown down the gauntlet to society by deliberately and defiantly seeking a sexual experience with the town's bastard cripple, Fortunio, whom she liked because he wrote poetry but whom she knew she would never marry.

According to her own account, this was no "little love peccadillo" but the deliberate enactment of an erotic magic ritual, "shrewdly, because God had given her an above average intelligence...to be her own guide on the road of truth" (92)—her "truth" being her capacity for intellectual creativity. Her affinity to Fortunio as a poet, mixed with the magical elements of moonlight and murmuring waters, connected her sexual act with ancestral memories of Sardinian fertility rites.

It also occasioned a terrible public scandal. Chastised by her brother's fury, she henceforth made writing her sole focus. Through writing, she discharged her repressed energies; writing became the substitute for erotic-sexual release: "She throws herself into the world of her fantasies and writes, writes, writes out of a physical need, [as] other adolescents run...to a rendezvous of love" (78). Her erotic impulses catalyzed her intellectual creativity and gave substance to her imagination.

The relationship of writing to love is an important theme of the central part of *Cosima*. For Deledda, love between men and women is rarely a pure sentiment. She describes passion-love as a primitive sexual force, which endows the lovers with an animal-like strength—whereas her own energies are discharged not in motherhood but in the physical act of writing. Deledda's erotic tensions served as the energizing source of creativity; her approach to the literary work can be conceived as an ineluctable act of love (De Giovanni, 29-31).

In the end, we cannot hope to dispel the ambiguity that permeates Deledda's life and writing. Beginning as a talented woman writer handicapped by her provincialism, she overcame the limitations of her origin by vigorously opposing the antifeminist traditions of an island that denied women the right of self-expression through literature. At times she seemed to affirm maternity, both in her own marriage and motherhood and in those pages where the beauty of nature is clothed in mother-child imagery: "Life was beautiful...among the things created by God for the joy of the heart that is close to Him, close [as] the child's heart is to the mother's" (112).

Yet her stories, filled as they are with dying mothers and aborted children (Migiel, 114), are very far from a wholehearted endorsement of maternity. Her concept of the "new woman" was touched with the demonic and the fantastic. Her ideal, her perfect model, was not the Virgin Mary but rather her actress friend, the inimitable (and childless) Eleonora Duse. She could have found no more perfect embodiment of the attributes she cherished—courage, freedom to love, and freedom to express herself through art (De Giovanni, 67).

The Age of Impatience

What had been called the "bourgeois feminism" of Italy's early twentieth century was superseded in the later 1960s and 1970s by a new wave of literary and ideological debate on the "Woman Question," now viewed in the context of the revolutionary manifestations of students and workers at the same period. Having gained the vote in 1945, Italian women for the first time found themselves in a position where they could demand a part in the historical process from which they had hitherto been excluded.

If divorce was established by law in 1970, four years later a popular referendum was required to protect it against papal and Christian-Democrat attempts to have it annulled; if the voluntary interruption of pregnancy was legalized in 1978, risky clandestine abortions continued to mark the Italian sociomedical scene. Desperate pregnant women, as late as the 1970s, continued to risk pain, infection, and even death, because the country's birth control clinics and maternity hospitals, especially in the South, were—and still are—manipulated by Catholic "objectors" who refuse to apply the abortion law.

Italian women's writings of the 1970s had radical content and made revolutionary claims. In addition to bringing to light the cultural and religious roots of women's oppression and their treatment as objects of consumption in a capitalist society, writers reconceptualized maternity and fought for full abortion rights, making the woman's personal choice central to their demands. Young women in the mainstream rejected maternity openly—lest it place them "within the norm" and diminish their revolutionary fervor.

A series of case studies published by Alice Oxman under the title *Lager maternità. Libro-documentario sulle donne e i bambini in venti storie italiane* (Maternity concentration camp. Documentary of women and children in twenty Italian stories [Milano: Bompiani],1974) decried the horrors of childbirth in Rome's maternity wards, and challenged the psychological and cultural conditioning that literally drives Italian women to pregnancy. Oxman exhorted women to consider maternity a choice, not a duty; she rejected the idea that a woman's self-realization lies exclusively in the role of mother; and she underscored the humiliation of the "fat and swollen pregnant woman who after delivery feels emptied out and useless" but is afraid to reveal her feelings "for fear of seeming strange, or, as they say, 'perverted'" (58). Oxman's work found resonance in the fiction of numerous aggressive women writers, some of whom were also political activists in the 1970s.

New views of women's writings also took shape. The output of women writers was now more clearly recognized as a reflection of specifically feminine biological and psychological traits, differences, and needs. There now seemed to be no longer any limit to the positions a woman could occupy. Whereas in the past the mother/wife had been there for domestic and affective needs, the career woman of the 1970s refused to be defined by her family role, however much her "egotism" might still be derided in more conservative quarters.

Yet Italian working mothers, despite their newfound freedom, were still unable to cast off the fetters of the maternal mystique, to reconcile the conflict between "public" and "private," between "political" and "personal" claims. There was still an ineluctable opposition between the demands of the family and those of a career. A mother who returned to work after having a baby felt the disapproval of a public who remained convinced that her absence must be detrimental to the child. The old idealization of the mother-child relationship was still in the air, sustaining the doctrine that the mother, by her mere presence, minimized the infant's experience of conflict (Neiger, 10).

The Italian working woman was everywhere confronted by a glaring contrast between theory and practice, between law and reality. She was in effect three separate people: wife, mother, and employee, and had to keep shifting her persona accordingly. Sharing with her husband the parity of decision granted to parents in a series of Italian laws of 1962-63, she still remained highly vulnerable emotionally to her children's revolt against parental control, not to mention the problems that might be posed by an unreconstructed husband.

Such difficulties may be dwindling to some extent under the increasingly aggressive stance adopted since the 1970s by Italian women as a group. Less fragmented and more integrated psychically to withstand the male's demands, many women may marry to please their families but reject having children and refuse to stifle their own needs. What they want, in the popular phrase, is to be "free birds."

The increasing prevalence of such attitudes has changed the substance of Italian marriages almost beyond recognition. Women appear to be achieving their own selfhood, seizing control of the home situation and experimenting with alternative ways of dealing with their reproductive function. Rebuffing prejudices against non-motherhood, they insist that propagation of the species should *not* be their principal role. Even if they marry and become mothers, they reject the restrictions of wifehood and the maternal symbol of the all-good Mother. While a part of society still condemns such attitudes as "deviant" and even "criminal," the modern mother is more likely to claim that what would be truly criminal would be the frittering away of her own talents.

While today's women still give power and importance to sexuality, they insist that women's bodies should not be used solely for producing babies. Some go so far as to ask whether reproduction is a biological necessity or merely the fruit of socioreligious "brainwashing" and ingrained conventional habit. They protest the loss of mental freedom that inevitably accompanies maternity. For, as the scholar Marianne Hirsch points out, "Nothing entangles women more firmly in their bodies than pregnancy, birth, lactation, miscarriage, or the inability to conceive" (*The Mother/Daughter Plot*, 166).

It is from such entanglements that the "new Italian woman" is depicted as seeking to escape. Refusing atavistic identification with the fecund Mother Earth, her partisans allege, she cultivates involvement in the things of the mind. Her desire is to explore the world, read women's history, probe her own psychic heights and depths, pursue knowledge, and seek self-mastery. She is now fighting back, we are told, against the feelings of helplessness and the depression that were inevitable concomitants of motherhood. Believing that childbearing and the "mindless" dispensing of affection limit her potentialities for growth, she is now said to dismiss them as "irrational" (*Maria, Medea*, 71; Cattaneo and Pisa, 11).

Italian women authors of today are not easily contented with the commonplace assumption that maternity automatically moves humanity forward. They are now in a mood to reinterpret not only motherhood as such but the ethical standards that conventionally accompany it (Neiger, 157). Their heroines—typically "bad mothers," unencumbered by traditional concepts of maternal obligation—believe they have many functions in the making and remaking of society, quite apart from the basic responsibility of caring for their own progeny. Today's writers claim to be seeking answers to fundamental questions: how to find meaning in life, how to balance one's obligation to oneself with the need for connection. From amidst the difficulties besetting any sensitive and thoughtful woman in the modern world, they speak eloquently, if not always convincingly, of what a woman can make of those difficulties if she really cares to do so.

No single view of pregnancy and motherhood prevails among contemporary woman writers, though few can be said to view these familiar conditions in anything like an affirmative spirit. Their heroines no longer have to kill or hide their unwanted children, since abortion offers a convenient, less burdensome alternative. Others, less resolute, may decide to bear children but resent the accompanying physical deformity, which they see as a kind of unsought expiation for sexual taint. Readers will also meet with many "single" women who are not only pregnant but show a new sensitivity toward the maternal role (cf. Oriana Fallaci's *Letter to an Unborn Child* and Lidia Ravera's *Bambino mio*, below).

Anna Banti

As a writer whose primary concern was the analysis of the "different woman," the woman who escapes inclusion in any of the conventional social, intellectual, and artistic categories, Anna Banti (1895-1985) also made muffled protest against maternity. With her, however, it was not so much a primary target as an aspect of her concern with the painful predicament of the modern woman who wishes to engage in a free and original endeavor but confronts the challenge of a society that has devised innumerable pretexts to deny her the time, space, and other requisites for the development of her talent.

In a career that spanned some forty-six years, Banti constructed a unique identity as a writer of fiction who focused again and again on women's militant quest to develop their talents and pursue their careers with freedom and dignity. Maternity, for her, was but one of the factors contributing to the creative woman's entrapment in the toils of domesticity, societal oppression, and the devastation of war (Ballaro, 36-7). Typical in this regard is one of her short stories contained in the 1940 collection *Il coraggio delle donne* (Women's courage). It tells of three independent, unmarried women whose involvement in intellectual and artistic pursuits entails their social ostracism amid the suspicion and even fear they inspire in the surrounding community.

Banti's post-World War II novel, *Artemisia* (1947), reexamines this dominant concern in an historical setting that centers upon the seventeenth-century artist Artemisia Gentileschi, daughter of the more famous Orazio Gentileschi, whom Van Dyck included in his portraits of one hundred illustrious men. Raped at thirteen years of age, Artemisia courageously denounced her attacker—who, however, was exonerated—and was forced into a hastily arranged marriage with an older man, who subsequently dissolved the bond.

The young woman's admitted failure as a mother is contrasted with her success as a baroque portrait painter, who, despite the hostility of the period, succeeded in obtaining commissions from the Florentine court, established an art school in Naples, and was even invited to paint at the "heretical" Court of England. Art became her entire life, her home and family in a society where women were entitled to procreate but not to create. "A woman," Banti calls her heroine, "who would like to be a man in order to escape herself" (140).

In another of her short stories, "Lavinia fuggita" (Runaway Lavinia, 1951), Banti draws a perplexing parallel between an image of the infant Christ and the musical compositions of her heroine, again the victim of a patriarchal society where women are denied the right to be creative. The heroine's even less fortunate friend, a "mother and grandmother of insolent children," venerates a sheaf of her music "as much as the wax figure of Baby Jesus opposite her nuptial bed" ("Lavinia fuggita", in *Le donne muoiono* [Women die], 88). The mental process that juxtaposes two such disparate values may be read as an unvoiced revolt against motherhood on the part of the envious friend. It also offers a hint of the new attitudes toward traditional religious symbolism that would culminate in the outright sacrilegiousness of some writing of the 1970s.

A variant among these explorations of the problems of female creativity is another bit of historical fiction, *La camicia bruciata* (The burned nightgown, 1973). Two royal princesses, Marguerite Louise d'Orléans of France and Beatrice Violante of Bavaria, are the protagonists, unhappily wedded to the father and son, respectively, of the expiring line of Medici princes. Not content with defying and scandalizing their seventeenth-century Italian entourage, the two discuss their situation directly with their twentieth-century author in such a way as to highlight the latter's own endurance of impediments, inhibitions and frustrations in her writing career.

Princess Marguerite and Princess Beatrice are fully exposed to the injustice and hypocrisy of a society in which women are "always wrong" (141), and, as Banti scornfully puts it, "negligible objects that courts exchange as necessary instruments for obtaining offspring" (207). In a violent protest against her arranged marriage to Cosimo III de' Medici, Marguerite sets fire to her nuptial nightgown, thus providing both a title for the novel and a form of exorcism of the matrimonial and maternal mystique (Nozzoli, 111).

Both Marguerite and her alter ego, Princess Beatrice, insist on claiming their right to social equality and spiritual and cultural parity between the sexes despite their painful ostracism and psychological laceration. They symbolize a human condition that must be defined and defended against obsolete conventions (Peritore, 215).

Lalla Romano

The complexity and arduousness of mothering at a more advanced stage in life were explored by Lalla Romano, herself a mature writer and artist, in her autobiographical novel *Le parole tra noi leggere* (The words between us weightless, 1969). This fine analysis of the discordant yet tender relationship between a mother and her adolescent son echoes the devastating disappointment of a woman who had believed the mother/child relationship would yield her the experience of unshadowed love.

Instead, this symbiotic union had resolved itself into a slave/master relationship in which the mother was the slave. The sources of her enslavement are primarily internal: she needs to protect her sense of herself as a "good mother"; to protect the child whose loss she fears; to assuage her feelings of guilt at not having given enough of herself to the creature who has become her master. Though a conciliatory gesture on his part would suffice to restore the relationship to a manageable form, the son instead goes on erecting barriers against his own mother, responding perhaps to an adolescent need to avoid regression into a primitive form of object-love.

The mother's indulgence, solicitude and enthusiasm for her offspring are counterpoised by resentment, aversion and doubt. Her very ambivalence highlights an honest admission that mother and son both attract and repel each other, each striving to gain the dominant position. His "subversiveness" and disruptiveness sometimes give her covert pleasure, sometimes a sense of shame and helplessness. She idealizes this creature who continuously upsets her life, exulting in his "uniqueness" and justifying his quirks. Subconsciously, this very idealization may be her way of denying a desire to be rid of him; yet when she openly denounces his incommunicability, untidiness and erratic behavior, she may be trying to ease her guilt feelings by justifying that very desire.

The mother's outbursts of anger against her son play a crucial role in the assertion of separateness demanded by adolescence. At the same time, his very anger imbues her with a feeling of hopeless culpability (Parker, 119), a sense of inadequacy and guilt at having caused anguish to the son she loves. She who poured out an excess of love, painstakingly nurturing their visceral bonds, cannot forgive his too obvious view of her as a "bad mother." Watching her son change from a happy, carefree, imaginative child into a somber, preoccupied adolescent, the mother feels that she has failed in what was to have been her life's endeavor.

Her innumerable attempts to communicate with him are rewarded only by increasing withdrawal on his side. Aggression and anxiety accompany his growing independence. He flings accusations against her, spewing out his faults and failures and blaming them on her "irresponsibility." Thus indicted, and faced with the loss of her own self-worth, the mother confesses her defeat.

Here, Romano's adult perspective becomes submerged. By continuing to analyze the blind love which elicits such ferocity, she becomes equally useless to herself and to her son. She has not acknowledged his separate reality; she has not transcended the infant-as-object. Only when the child has been placed outside the area of maternal control will she be able to regain her sense of self as a separate individual, securing space to think and time to begin realigning the mother/child relationship.

Tragicomically, the discord cannot be resolved until the son decides to marry—at the ripe age of twenty-nine! Romano's confession is moderated by humor and as well as rationality, but beneath the surface lies an abyss of suffering, regret and remorse. If the novel has its hilarious pages, most are desolate and heartbreaking. Fundamentally, the tragedy lies in the mother's error in treating her son as part and parcel of her own life, denying him the separate individuality essential to the integrity and growth of both persons.

Lalla Romano combines in her own person the two antithetic parental styles that have been severally imputed to "those who idealise their children and those who just moan about them" (Alan Shuttleworth, quoted in Parker, 120). Her relationship with her own child, to use Natalia Ginzburg's words, is too much the product of a "dark and visceral love…which has nothing to do with reason and judgment" (*Never Must You Ask Me*, 150).

Rita Levi Montalcini

The most conspicuous of Italian career women to have declared her decision *not* to become a mother is Rita Levi Montalcini (1909-   ), co-winner of the 1986 Nobel Prize in Medicine for having identified the proteinaceous substance able to stimulate nerve fiber growth (NGF).[6] Her autobiography, *Elogio dell'imperfezione* (In praise of imperfection, 1987), describing the struggle that ultimately brought her success, tells how she and her artist twin sister, Paola, early in life rejected the idea of raising children—a decision never regretted by either of them, since both considered the role of mothers incompatible with full-time dedication to the activities of their choice (18).

This decision was the easier because both sisters had been indifferent to the interests conventional in children of their sex. "Newborn babies didn't attract me at all," Rita recalls, "and I was completely without that maternal feeling which is so developed in little girls and adolescents. This feeling was lacking in Paola, too…" (41). The difficulties experienced by the two sisters in initiating careers in Italy's male-dominated intellectual establishment could only strengthen the conviction that they were not cut out to be wives and mothers. Their father had decided that they should attend the girls' high school, which at that time did not give entree to the university. (His own two sisters had pursued higher studies in literature and mathematics, only to find that they could not reconcile their intellectual goals with the demands of married life.) Fortunately, he accepted Rita's announcement that she intended to study medicine since she felt no vocation for motherhood.

A marriage proposal from a fellow medical student caused her to waver momentarily, but her personal dilemma was resolved by the enactment in 1938 of Mussolini's anti-Semitic laws, which, among other things, forbade marriage between Jews and non-Jews. Needless to say, this racist prohibition enraged her even while it put an end to her personal problem.

Her studies completed, she continued her research in the United States after World War II. At Washington University in St. Louis, she sensed the frustration of some of the professors' wives, unable either to pursue careers of their own or to find other ways of realizing their potentialitites. She speaks, for example, of one extreme case involving the wife of a professor, an intelligent and cultured woman with capabilities as a sociologist, who became so frustrated by the housewifely obligations of a faculty wife that she ultimately had to be institutionalized.

Levi Montalcini herself, having no such cares, was free to dedicate her life to promoting what she conceived as the betterment of humanity, notwithstanding the admitted "imperfection" of the human species. Envisaging her life as a process of conscious movement toward a higher ideal, she does undoubtedly provide a stunning demonstration of the effective channeling of female energy. No seeker after what others might have coveted under the guise of "female empowerment," she looked on creativity and study as instruments of knowledge, not domination.

Levi Montalcini's autobiography constitutes a sort of "final report" on her personal efforts to move herself and the rest of humanity toward the higher goals which, she feels, are at last within the reach of women. Through knowledge and time, she believes, the human race can eventually be improved. In six arresting pages at the end of her book, she traces the evolution of the human brain over a period of three and one-half million years. Aided by her study of NGF, she concludes that the horrors of the twentieth century must be attributed not to an innate aggressive instinct, but rather to the successful misdirection and perversion of normal thought patterns—in other words, brainwashing—by fanatics and cynics. Levi Montalcini warns her readers to beware of insidious propaganda, instilled religious concepts, dogmatic beliefs, and all the myths that threaten world catastrophe. We may add to her enumeration the demographic explosion, abetted by ecclesiastical pronouncements extolling motherhood and condemning most efforts to regulate it.

Dacia Maraini

In sharpest contrast to the idealism—some might say sentimentality—of Levi Montalcini's hymn to human betterment is the cynicism, aggressiveness, and sheer force of Dacia Maraini's rollicking 1975 fantasy-novel, *Donna in guerra* (*Woman at War*). The focus of this work, by Italy's best-known advocate of all feminist causes, is the perpetual struggle of the married woman against the pressure to have babies—a pressure she equates with nothing less than rape.

Her protagonists are a married but sexually unsatisfied schoolteacher, Vanna, and her husband, Giacinto, and the action centers upon Vanna's evolution from a subservient housewife to a political rebel, committed to social work in superstition-plagued Naples. Married for six years, the couple had lost a son who died at birth, and had thereupon decided to have no more children. But Giacinto, realizing that he had lost the love of his "sweet, shy, so hardworking" wife, had subsequently begun to insist on their "having a child between the two of us," believing this act of magnanimity, as he regards it, to be a cure-all for their painful situation.

His arguments are grotesque: "a married woman without children is just like a cat without kittens, she moans and flings herself about, and bites her own tail in despair"; "we'll even please my boorish mother who keeps on asking: 'When is it due then? When?'," and so forth (259).

In sex, Vanna reports, her husband wanted her "to stay there like a corpse" until he had satisfied himself: "Whether I wanted him or not, felt desire or not, didn't seem to matter to him in the least. I gave in to him, but something inside of me rebelled and made me feel like throwing up" (239).

Although Vanna's dilemma is presented by Maraini in a spirit of serious drama, she descends to out-and-out farce in recounting the contrasting experience of another couple, one whose wealth has failed to bring contentment. Her laughter, in this tale of surrogate motherhood, does not hide the author's deeper protest against the debasement of the woman's body.

The wealthy husband's request for "a son all of my own," from a marriage that has been all too "long and cheerless," permits the author to enumerate with sarcasm the supposed reasons why Italian men feel an "absolute need" for children:

1. A marriage without children is a "disgrace."
2. When the couple is old, who will look after them?
3. To whom will they leave their property, "so large and valuable"?

The author here mocks two conjoined Italian attitudes: the glorification of children, and the lack of support for endowments and humanitarian institutions which would undoubtedly spend the monies more wisely than private legatees.

As to the husband's desire for a son, his spoiled, wealthy consort recoils from the prospect of "having a huge belly, swollen legs and swollen breasts," which would make her look ugly; nor does she fancy "all the pain a child causes when it comes out." Instead, she proposes that the maid be commissioned to bear the child for them (138-9).

The husband, though pleased with the idea, is reluctant to make love to the maid—"I'm not a pig, you know." To obviate this difficulty, his wife promises to put something of herself into it, "so that the child will come from all three of us equally." She then assumes the role of a fertility goddess, ritually collecting her husband's "divine milk" in her mouth and then thrusting the family semen into the maid's womb.

> So the maid got pregnant of the master without his touching her and the mistress goes around saying that the child will come from all three of them because he ejaculated it, she saved it and the maid nourished it (140).

This burlesque tale underscores Maraini's rejection of the identification of woman's personality with reproduction and motherhood. Rather than serving as mere instruments of male supremacy, she wishes women to explore more promising courses for their individuation and fulfillment (Pickering-Iazzi, 334). Unwilling that the female body should serve as a vessel for any extraneous substance, she urges women to turn instead to self-originated, self-transforming activity, be it social or political action, theatrical involvement, or other forms of mental creativity.

Returning to the central personalities of *Woman at War*, we meet the character who is to effect Vanna's escape from the clutches of her insensitive husband. This is the half-English, half-Turkish Suna, whose English mother has run off with a bathing attendant and "now lives in Sorrento, has four children, and starves" (71). Her Turkish father, who yearned for his daughter to have children and thus serves the scathing Maraini as an emblematic patriarch, is a painter of domestic scenes, including "a mother breast-feeding her baby, her arms enclosing him lovingly, her head bent, the whole scene frozen in a syrupy pink" (152). This father had known "women [in Turkey] who'd made love only two or three times in their lives…, didn't have a clue what sexual pleasure was, yet they were healthy, plump, happy" (172).

Suna, the daughter, who acts as Maraini's spokesperson, naturally sees women as martyrs torn to pieces for the "triumph of the great God prick" (274). With a clear perception of woman's role throughout history, she analyzes Vanna's cultural and social discomfort as the product of "thousands

.of years of servitude" (166).

To get a more vivid impression of these past millennia, we are taken to the symbolic island of Addis, whose brutish inhabitants are outrageously dishonest and even "the parish priest steals" (147). The islands serve as ancillaries to Maraini's ideological polemic against violence, religious superstition, primitive instincts and archaisms. She uses irony and mockery to paint the hypocrisy and inanity of the islanders' ceremonies and uncontrollable passions. They climb the steepest mountains to "beg God for grace," and then sell pieces of its rock as holy stone (54). Old women lend themselves to violent expressions of grief, like the Mediterranean wailers of ancient times, lacerating themselves, beating their breasts, and tearing their clothes (55) at the graveside of "Peppino Pizzocane,...cunning as a fox...out to grab and cheat as much as he could" (39).

The principal bootlegger on the island, who counts a family of two hundred members, including cousins, nephews and grandchildren, is also an infanticide: he once killed a three-months-old granddaughter "with a punch on the mouth because she was crying too much" (118). A sick man whose brood lives in one room with no running water and no toilet system spawns a child every year. "Fortunately they die, one of typhus, another of cholera, another of tuberculosis" (119-20). And, irony of ironies, in every grim situation the islanders persist in invoking Holy Mary, Jesus, Lord, and the "holy wafer."

Vanna, our schoolteacher heroine, encounters a similar mindset in her professional life, where she is expected to inculcate the traditional view of maternity and is forced to use a "stupid school book" replete with children "listening to sweet lullabies" of their "calm and madonna-like" mother (268). Maraini is no addict of mother/baby sentimentality: "You can smell that stench of shit, talcum powder and plastic that only babies have," she writes scatologically (138).

Convinced that her teaching is ineffective, Vanna's eyes are opened when her pupils, abetting Maraini's stunning attack on the "innocence of children," act out a rape, two boys holding a little girl by the feet and arms while two others wriggle on top of her, during Vanna's absence from the classroom. She recognizes and seizes upon the perfect moment for an open discussion of sex roles and rape, subjects already uppermost in her unconscious mind. The unusual lesson fills her with "a fever of happiness and fulfillment" as, for the first time, she is able to feel satisfaction with her own teaching.

The headmaster of the school has noticed Vanna's propensity to observation and study, and is sensitive to her aspirations toward something above and beyond her humdrum existence. He openly challenges her and her uterus: "You never dare to take a risk, to dream…. Women's…drives always have their roots in the uterus" (244-5).

It is indeed the uterus that will spur Vanna to decisive action. "Raped" by her husband, she becomes pregnant. Her desire "to take a risk, to dream" finds symbolic expression in the weight of her sleeping husband, pressed against her from behind "like a child astride my back" (276). She knows, like Sibilla Aleramo, that she will have to shake off the weight of both husband and child. Defiantly, she has an abortion, leaves home and begins a new life as the book ends.

Oriana Fallaci

Another "woman at war"—in this case literally—is Oriana Fallaci, a writer and journalist who not only received gunshot wounds during the 1968 riots in Mexico City, but has reported from the scene of wars in Vietnam, Lebanon, Greece, Palestine and Argentina. Clearly not cut out to be a mother and never resigning herself to her own female birth, Fallaci early in life declared, in a play on the word *uomo* (man), that she intended to become at least a *uoma* (female man). She did, however, experience a three-month pregnancy which ended spontaneously after a journalistic assignment requiring a ten-day automobile trip. The fruit of that experience was her novel, *Lettera a un bambino mai nato* (*Letter to an Unborn Child*, 1975), published at the height of the abortion debates in Italy.

Whereas Grazia Deledda and Rita Levi Montalcini were explicit in their rejection of motherhood, Fallaci, herself an unwanted child, is ambivalent: she transcends the limitations of the maternal body without, however, denying the possibility of motherhood. Her novel is an intimate confession of her problems of unsuccessful motherhood, and an analysis of her complex feelings toward the fetus. Deemed blasphemous by some, the book examines all sides of the abortion issue in a lengthy monologue addressed to the protagonist's captive audience—the unborn child.

Fallaci regards maternity not as a duty but rather as a personal choice. Rejecting the ties of maternity and consanguinity, she suggests that a child can be raised just as well by the father or by a surrogate mother, and, in a recurring image, she evokes those exceptional mother hens that do not brood their eggs. She desecrates the Holy Family, calling Mary *"una screanzata"* (unmannerly woman) who, like herself, became pregnant without a husband;

and she mocks the superfluous Joseph, alluding to the birth of Jesus as "the marvelous lie about an egg fertilized by parthenogenesis" (54).

In her attack on traditional maternity, the author also belabors such patriarchal institutions , ideals and myths as the State, the Church, the family, and gender roles (Pickering-Iazzi, 338). The absent father in the novel, whose language is quoted with irony, offers money—which is indignantly refused—for a clandestine abortion; then, in an about-face, he agrees that she should not "throw the child away," because "a-child-is-a-child-not-a-thing. And other banalities" (53). Similarly, the author replicates the language of her employer, who threatens to give her assignment to a man because "men-are-not-prone-to certain-accidents" (59).

In rejecting the father of her unborn child, the self-sufficient protagonist is convinced that she and her fetus need neither him, Saint Joseph, nor God the Father himself (54-5). Offering no single word of appreciation for the woman-man relationship in marriage or outside of it, she asserts the woman's exclusive right to give or deny life to the fetus.

Although Fallaci does wax poetic about the mother-child relationship, she doubts the rightness of sacrificing her own freedom and developed life-style for the sake of a life yet to be. Guilt, fear, and resentment assert themselves as she contemplates surrendering of control over her own life; her thoughts seesaw between love and hate, tenderness and hostility. Voices of reason around her, countering her sentimental proclivities, urge her not to renounce her career. In her dilemma, she challenges not only the "right-to-lifers" but also the fetus that seeks to condition her existence. "What is this respect for you which steals away respect for me?" she asks. "What is this right of yours to exist, which does not take into account *my* right to exist?" (67).

Her first awareness of her inopportune pregnancy had cast her "into a well where everything was uncertain and terrifying." But she remained ambivalent, avowing that although she had long awaited a child, she was not prepared to receive it (7). Powerless to control her body and its contents even though that body is creating a new life, she hears menacing inner voices which she ascribes to the growing fetus, her "tyrant," her "persecutor." As she vacillates over the decision to abort or not to abort, she suffers nausea, dizziness, and abdominal pain; she ponders in her mind the problems of overpopulation and the birth of monsters; her dreams are haunted by huge families as well as by aborters pursued by police and priests.

But now the protagonist's decision is made: the fetus shall be born. Taking full responsibility for her choice, she also accepts all of its discomforts and the renunciation of her personal and professional commitments. Nor is she even now convinced that her choice is the right one: "I've never been at ease with children....The job of being a mommy doesn't suit me at all" (62). Precisely by acknowledging the extent of her negative feelings toward her unborn child, she is able to take up the challenge of its right to exist.

Her visits to the gynecologist convince her that she has "nothing in common" with the other swollen-bellied woman (56). When anomalies in her pregnancy are ascribed to her worry and psychological trauma, she is advised "not to think so much." Rage and rebellion erupt in the woman whose very existence requires that she think: "I can't unscrew my brain and forbid it to think!...reduce myself to...a physiological machine for procreation!" But then, with humor, she concedes to the fetus her body but not her mind (57-8).

Echoes of Fascism resound when the patient, confined to bed in order to protect the fetus, is reminded of her "fundamental duties as a mother, a woman, and a citizen." Threatening physicians fling accusations of "crime," "premeditated homicide," and "common assassin" against the woman who would dare to leave her bed for the sake of a newspaper assignment (63).

In the end, however, the heroine opts in favor of her career: a ten-day car trip liberates her, transforms her into a "flying seagull" (65). A spontaneous abortion leads, however, to her death. In her final delirious dream she sees herself in confrontation with a society that deems her "criminal" and a jury that pronounces her "guilty." But her last words to the fetus are free of illusion: "In other places of the world thousands, hundreds of thousands of babies and mothers of future babies are being born. Life doesn't need either you or me" (101).

Thus, after much wavering, Fallaci acknowledges the lessons of life and history learned from her wartime and professional experience. "A journalist lives history in the best of ways," she had once said; "lives [and] touches history with his hands, looks at it with his eyes, listens to it with his ears.... I am the judge. I am the one who decides" (quoted in Locher, 134).

Lidia Ravera

Mirroring the ambivalence of Oriana Fallaci in *Lettera a un bambino mai nato* is Lidia Ravera's *Bambino mio* (My child, 1979). Ravera's dilemma is that she both wants and does not want a child. Like Fallaci, she is a "*mamma/uomo*" (mother/man), a "*mamma sbagliata*" (mistaken mother), her androgyny summed up in the phrase, "at night I'm a woman, in the daytime I'm a man" (39). At a loss when called upon to perform maternal acts, she refers to herself as an "animal with a retarded maternal instinct" (94).

The unnamed but clearly autobiographical protagonist of *Bambino mio* had at first eased herself into a decision on motherhood by creating a fantasy baby; when, however, she actually carries a real fetus, she flatly declares that she will not imitate her predecessor (Fallaci), who "prevented her body from bringing the child to full term" (54). At the same time, she hates the "joyless little skeleton" inside her (22), which makes her body feel driven with "barbed wire wrapped around her bones" (44). Up to the end of the novel, the protagonist remains perplexed as to why she allowed her "cursed baby" to be born (40, 121).

Whereas both mother and child die in Oriana Fallaci's novel, the disquieting conclusion of *Bambino mio* is that the two—mother and child— are tragically conflated. In a supreme regression terminating in mother/babe identification, the protagonist, "as a mother [is] a newborn" (100). Telescoped in time, she has lost her place in the adult world: "no one knows we were born together" (103).

Ravera's earlier novel, *Porci con le ali* (Pigs with wings, 1976)[7] was originally confiscated by the Italian Solicitor's Office as pornographic, but then released to become a bestseller among all age groups. It outspokenly treats the phenomena of Italy's sex revolution through the correspondence and sexual fantasies of two adolescent characters. Hailed as a minor masterpiece of militant writing, the novel became, for Italy's restless youth, a *vade mecum* written in obsessively obscene language but summarizing the fears and hopes of an entire generation.

By the late 1970s, when Ravera wrote *Bambino mio*, the women's revolution and the spirit of 1968 had lost momentum and the "counterrevolution" was setting in. The voices of women in the piazzas had been silenced, Ravera observes with tongue in cheek, "so they return[ed] happily to the bed" (37); no fewer than fifteen of her own comilitants had babies during the tenth anniversary year of the 1968 revolution (111).

The protagonist of the novel is a woman without religious taboos, disdainful of the roles offered by patriarchal society (33). She sees no "noble function" in childbirth, repeatedly referring to the woman's body as a "female machine for reproduction," or as a "cow," "bitch," or "female rabbit." She wishes she could "resemble [her] father" because "men can't procreate" (10-11, 43). "Isn't being a woman already a kind of sickness?" she asks rhetorically (93). Recalling her childhood habit of hatefully breaking her dolls' heads, she came to see infanticide as the realization of a mother's most secret and deepest aspiration (12).

Ravera minutely analyzes her protagonist's reasons for not wanting a child. They range from her total unconcern should the globe suddenly become uninhabited to her desire for freedom and revolt against the family—"a nucleus of melancholy. A necrophilic institution rising out of the need for mutual burial" (69).

In matters of religion, she rejects the pope and in fact has embraced atheism from the day of her First Communion. She often jokes about an apparition of the Madonna in a public latrine (45), and mocks the Holy Trinity by describing her own triple makeup—man, woman, fetus—as "three in one" like God in the catechism (64).

Nor has she accepted Fascist teaching about the "sweet and obligatory labor of childbirth" as the "fundamental mission of animals of the female sex," for she easily sees through the Duce's propaganda aimed at raising supplies of cannon-fodder (23, 99).

When, however, distraught mothers complain to the protagonist that they are being driven to distraction by their infants' constant crying, she puts herself on the side of the complaining babies, even though she sees their gaping, craving mouths as epitomes of greediness (99). "A mother [is] a mother," she proclaims, but quickly adds "And a mother is not a person" (17). "Maternity," she will later assert, "is a mad choice" (122).

In the fourth month of her real pregnancy, the protagonist aborts spontaneously, occasioning a description of a maternity ward that corresponds in essence to Alice Oxman's *Lager maternità* (above). She does, however, carry a subsequent pregnancy to term, mocking those who see her as in a "state of grace" (46). With great difficulty she and the fetus (who is personified throughout as listening to and arguing with her) learn to tolerate each other. As it grows, her vital energy is sapped. The fetus robs her of "blood space iron intelligence protein and waking hours" (31). She realizes that she is permitting it to grow at the cost of her own mutilation and mental disorder. Her own "I" is impoverished and silenced by her "super-I" which is the fetus.

Ravera burlesques the entire event of the delivery—"Any peasant woman can do it"—and concludes that its "magic" and "heavenliness" are an illusion (106). After the child's birth, she is neither tender nor radiant, as her doting entourage with its ready-made phrases and beatific smiles expects her to be; rather, she is listless and lethargic, envious of the militants of earlier years who, immediately after giving birth, returned to demonstrate at the factories (96).

Revolted by the physical appearance of the "flesh of her flesh," she refuses to hold it in her arms. Her "incarnated phantasm," with its "little squashed head…covered with thin strands of hair," looks like a "little monkey. Flesh from another planet. Unconscious bundle [without eyes or teeth]. Far from the human race" (93,99).

Satirizing both the milky mammals of yore and the artificial milk of today (109), she derides the model of mothering and the milk mystique: "Smile, breastfeed. Breastfeed, smile, and be present" (102). As for the baby's smile, Sibilla Aleramo had allowed herself to believe that her infant was smiling directly at her. Ravera's modern heroine is too knowledgeable: she has read that babies cannot control their facial muscles. She knows that even if the baby looks at her, she is totally alone; that so-called mother/child love is distinguished by its total lack of reciprocity (104).

One of the protagonist's original reasons for rejecting pregnancy was that her life as a writer was lived out in the medium of language: "With language I exist and I bring into existence," she explained. She complains to the fetus that "you don't have words," just as she had blamed her own mother for expressing her rage not in words but by making an unholy din in the kitchen with her pots and pans, disturbing the future writer in her reading (29-30). It is her commitment to writing that she now defends, attempts to salvage, but in the end surrenders in a spirit of renunciation. An experiment with a room of her own, a desperate attempt to resume her "decorous occupation" as a writer, produces only blank pages. Even when closed, the door remains open in her mind to the distractions of "diapers…odors of urine and talcum powder" (17). Her intelligence is stilled. Her body is an "obedient animal" (143), to whose functions she surrenders. "To be creative," she concludes, "I must not procreate" (142).

Bambino mio is a mother's account, in her own words to her child, of an entire range of expectations and emotions as Ravera ponders the conflict between being an individual and helping to reproduce the species. She believes she has fallen into the category of those women who "make people" rather than "make things"—and that she herself will be swallowed up in the process by her own creature. And yet, in defiance of her own tenets, she persists in a belief that rejection of motherhood is selfish, and that nonmaternity spells egocentric self-concern. Her mind is still unprepared for the idea that even nonmothers can be nurturing, altruistic, generous, like the three emblematic women in Anna Banti's *Il coraggio delle donne* (above).

Ravera's ambivalence with regard to the contraceptive pill—which her protagonist first takes, then suspends as a test of her own fertility—reveals, ironically, fear of sterility in the very same woman who, when she becomes pregnant, derisively compares herself to a female rabbit. Sterility, for her, belongs in the category of the "neurotic, hypochondriac, sterile, dry, buggered" (43). Her preoccupation with bedroom slippers and a warm, comfortable cashmere sweater are telltale indices of the protagonist's nonrevolutionary conformism. They illustrate the difficulty she encounters in shaking off her latent desire for traditional domesticity.

Her metaphor of pregnancy is grotesque: "a trousseau of liquids in the lower body [which] hangs heavily like a hunch on the back" (45). Although she accepts the deformation on the ground that it is "linked to life" (58), that life itself turns out to be a torment of anxieties, contradictions, and renunciations, of disturbed sleep, nightmares, nervousness, of screaming and pulling and tearing at the breast—and, most tragically of all, denial of selfhood.

Irreparably divided between the demands of her mind and body, Lidia Ravera's perplexed protagonist is unable to find her place between the women who rejoice in maternity and those for whom motherhood spells suffocation amid images of death (97).

The Case of Elsa Morante

Elsa Morante yearned to become a mother, yet, not unlike Oriana Fallaci, was conscious of a gender uncertainty and confusion reflected in the epithet "*ragazzo/ragazza*" (girl/boy). All of the main characters of her novels and poetry form a single reciting "I" that embodies both her female and her male characteristics. Admitting to an "incurable desire to be a boy," she acknowledged a sense of incompleteness with which she grappled, in *L'isola di Arturo (Arturo's Island,* 1957),[8] by impersonating herself in the hero. "Arturo," she affirmed, "sono io" (Arturo is myself).[9]

Yet from a reading of her *Diary,*[10] in which the expressive language of her libido is specifically feminine, we know that the childless Morante also hungered for maternity. She dreamed about spermatozoa, unborn babies, newborns and children, in varied images of uterus, water, fruit and flowers. In her unconscious, a fetus may have represented her mother—particularly her maternal superego—or something valuable stolen from her mother. She may have feared her mother's punishment for her own infantile destructiveness; or that her pregnancy might be destroyed by the envious mother desirous of controlling it, taking it over, making it her own (Parker, 203).

Repeatedly Morante sought complicity and identification with her mother, who appears in her dreams as a holy figure walking on the sea (27). Through her, she is linked to archetypes of the feminine as the principle of life and as a power that can respond positively to the passing of time and the pain of physical deterioration.

Morante's mother was herself an ambivalent figure. A Jewess, she not only had all her children baptized, but cultivated the friendship of the powerful Jesuit priest, Father Tacchi Venturi, who was Mussolini's confessor. She has been described by her son as searching constantly for true and complete sexual experience while at the same time deploring the sexual act as nauseating. Affirming that she had accepted marriage and childbearing in a spirit of sacrifice in order to satisfy her husband, she showed open disgust at the sight of ugly children (Marcello Morante, 16-17, 20, 33). Elsa Morante's own religious life was a troubled one, drenched in feelings of sin and guilt which she sought to expiate and exteriorize iconographically. Cathedrals, rituals, formulas and prayers are sprinkled everywhere in her writings as a way of invoking divine intervention.[11] Maternity takes on the approved Catholic meaning of the sweetness of salvation: in her imaginary world, children assume the aspect of redemptive forces (cf. *Il mondo salvato dai ragazzini* [The world saved by little children], 1968).

In one of her dreams, Morante is dejected because her mother has refused to give her one of her many pink flowering plants in exchange for Elsa's own fleshy-leaved plant, which does not bear flowers. She is deeply pained by this "lack of maternal love," an ingrained idea that finds frequent resonance in her writings. Filled with a terrible sense of unrequited love, Elsa's own ambition was to be an entirely loving mother, selfless where, she felt, her own mother had been aloof; forthcoming and available as, in her opinion, her own father had been absent and denying.

In her works, Morante generally paints in tragic colors the condition of women trapped in institutionalized motherhood. Stunted in their inner growth and taking refuge in a world of dreams, her heroines, like herself, seem unable to rebel against the patriarchal principles that are destroying them. She molds their socially conditioned female characteristics toward the performance of maternal tasks (Nozzoli, 146). Notions of maternal instinct hold them in thrall; their vital substance is sapped. Passive sweetness, docility, diligence, and fear of authority combine to create the devoted, servile wives and mothers demanded by Italy's patriarchal, phallocratic culture. Confined to their homes by their gadabout husbands, Morante's oppressed females are unremittingly pregnant or breastfeeding until the end of their fertile years.[12] In many cases, this culturally prescribed maternal role leads to self-annihilating insanity.

Joyless and disturbed motherhood had already been the theme of such earlier works as *Menzogna e sortilegio* (*House of Liars*, 1948), of *L'isola di Arturo*, of *Lo scialle andaluso* (The Andalusian shawl, 1963), and of *Il mondo salvato dai ragazzini* (The world saved by little children, 1968). Morante's 1974 work, *La Storia* (*History: A Novel*), offers a convincing symbol of female victimization: Ida Ramundo, a silent, frustrated, abased mother brutalized by the relentless violence of "History." Enveloped in images of enclosure and confinement, the self-sacrificing Ida embodies a male-authored metaphor of motherhood (Pickering-Iazzi, 329-30), resulting in a lapse into deep insanity that lasts nine vegetative years until her demise.

Ida's first child was the fruit of a conventional mariage; her second, of rape. Both were accepted as gifts of God, a clandestine abortion not even being thought of (Cacciaglia, 145). Exhibiting an underdeveloped sense of self, she doggedly performs her appointed roles as wife and mother. An eternal "child-mother," she is sexually undeveloped and even her features, thoughts and behavior are childlike. Though she has been trained as a schoolteacher, her ineffective teaching, like that of Giuliana Ferri's heroine in *Un quarto di donna* (below), is simply an extension of her maternal role. Selflessly dedicated to the world of children, Ida feels most at ease in the classroom—permeated with "that special smell of dirty children, lice, and snot" (48)—and in her own home, a refuge from the social reality she fears to encounter (Pickering-Iazzi, 331).

One critic writes of Ida Ramundo as the "most complete expression of nature itself" (Cacciaglia, 147). She does indeed possess a kind of animal naturalness; she has a "snout-like face"; she displays a "bestial" tenderness; and she lives on grass and insects, denying herself food so that her child may not go hungry. Playing on myths of maternal instinct, fierce protectiveness, and personal renunciation, Morante makes effective use of the literary devices of animal imagery and the identification of children with small animals. The entire female universe of *La Storia*, in fact, is compared by its author to "the mysterious idiocy of animals, who, not with their mind, but with…their vulnerable bodies [have a] *sense of the sacred:* meaning by *sacred* the universal power that can devour them and annihilate them, for their guilt in being born" (30).

Ida's simpleminded counterpart in *L'isola di Arturo*, busy preparing a "nest" for her baby, also has the "trusting ignorance of animals"(233); while a pregnant peasant woman in *Menzogna e sortilegio* is placed even lower in the scale of creation: she is compared to a "plant that germinates and bears fruit [that plops off] in its season" (334).

The novel *Aracoeli* (1982) tells of the mother who at first experiences an almost animal-like devotion to her small son but later rejects him. In sententiously feminine language, Morante describes how the son, now forty years old, remembers his mouth appended to Aracoeli's breast, the sound of her voice with its "tender taste of throat and saliva," her milk warm "like that of a tropical coconut," and the "fresh plum" perfume of her skin.

The breakup of this edifying duo is precipitated by the birth and early death of a congenitally deformed girl. Frustrated and heartbroken by this experience, the mother now rejects maternity altogether. Thinking to recapture his mother's affection, the already traumatized son steals to Aracoeli's exposed breast as she lies dozing and sucks at the nipple. Awakening, the mother recoils in horror; the boy finds himself on the floor, not knowing whether he has fallen or been hurled from the bed by the woman-become-Fury. This is the prelude to Aracoeli's descent into psychic and physical illness culminating in the transformation of this once all-protecting mother into a mythical monster of uncontrolled sexuality.

The adult son, refusing an autonomous life and fearful of the outside world, tries desperately to reconstruct the earlier paradisaic mother/son dyad. He loses his own identity in a pathological maternal mimesis that continues even after his mother's death. The son is unaware that she had threatened his emerging selfhood and hindered a process of identification with his less accessible father.

Only in the end does he understand the "maternal crimes" committed against him. His mother, he then laments, should have aborted or strangled him "instead of nourishing and raising me with your treacherous love, like a little animal being raised for the slaughterhouse" (100). Over and over again he refers to himself as an "animal," in one simile "sniffing out the odors of his den" (9). Winding through a *regressus ad uterum* in searching for the mother with whom he had lived so happily in almost perfect symbiosis, he recalls the ecstasy he had felt in clinging to what Melanie Klein refers to as the "good" maternal breast, and his hurt when that breast became "bad" (Cacciaglia, 151).

It is only after a desperate battle against his mother's memory that the son is able to exorcise her presence in his life and thus gain release. The heroine of *Menzogna e sortilegio* also suffers from her mother's rejection of her love. Not unlike her male counterpart in *Aracoeli*, she sets out to reconstruct the story of an entire family of insane relatives.

Distraught, oppressed, rejecting, haunted by traumatic dreams, insane— Morante's mothers, cocooned in a maternal context, metamorphose into mythic forces and monsters or pathetic animals and plants. The author's images of these women, blind slaves to maternal functions, have nothing in common with the traditional ideology of motherhood. Their earthiness and physicality, their irrationality and emotionalism, their ambiguities and equivocations, deny them access to the world of the mind and the development of whatever intelligence and creativity they may possess.

Perhaps Morante's own failed maternity has made our century richer. Perhaps motherhood in her case would have undermined her ambitions as a writer. Perhaps, with children to distract her, she might not have become one of the world's outstanding twentieth-century authors.

Teresa Ancona

There is no ambivalence in Teresa Ancona's *Una famiglia normale* (A normal family, 1974). The ironic title underscores the abnormality of all three of the key constituents of a northern Italian middle-class family. The father—nervous, preoccupied, uncommunicative—considers himself an "important man," supplies the family with money, but withholds understanding and affection; he is respected by all, he claims, except by his wife and daughter. (He "would have preferred a boy" [64]). The mother, scolding, ill-tempered and self-centered, gave birth when she herself was "almost a child" (61); her principal concern now seems to be the dirtiness of her thirteen-year-old child's hands. The daughter, Anna, is unloved by both father and mother. Every conversation in this "normal family" is a dialogue of the deaf. Lack of parental love, combined with the devastating effects of inculcated religious precepts, lead to the suicide of the sensitive and alienated child.

Ancona mounts her revolt against maternity and vindicates the right to abortion in an original way. Although the novel is essentially the story of Anna, it also provides a damning portrait of the mother who should never have become one, who "knew beforehand" that children bring "only worry and sorrow" (145), and who transfers the blame for her own deficiencies to her husband and to her child.

Ancona questions the raison d'être of this unfit mother, who has brought into the world a child she cannot love. Not so the mother herself, however.

Since society has inculcated in her the notion that a mother can do nothing but love her child, she conforms to type by repeating all the pat phrases which assure others that there is no love like a mother's love (63, 113, passim).

Spineless, she spouts the patriarchal ethic: "Your father...commands in this house, I don't count" (114). She takes it for granted that Anna will follow in her own footsteps: marriage, maternity, sacrifice, quarrels (88). Her daughter's birth had caused her such ravaging pain that she was virtually forbidden by her doctors to have other pregnancies. The child's arrival was "at the wrong time," she claims, when she had not yet gained control of her marital and household responsibilities. "Months of hell" had ensued, the baby continually crying and uninterruptedly whining, denying the mother sleep and "getting on her nerves" (62). Anna, indeed, is pilloried by the mother as the "cause of all [her] fears" and the shame of the entire family. Endeavoring to evade her daughter's intrusiveness and "exigencies" (66-7), she laments her inability to handle the obstinate creature who does not confide in her.

This mediocre woman of limited intelligence, before her marriage, had entertained vague ideas of some form of professional activity in the field of psychology, but all her projects had come to nought; now her principal mental activity is reading magazines. She is unaware that her "nervous temperament" and frequent attacks of neuralgia are due to her own dissatisfaction and unfulfillment, and that Anna's reverie is caused by the pain of conflictual feelings. The husband heaps blame on his wife for Anna's incommunicability, expecting her to "find out her thoughts. That's a mother's job, isn't it?" (78). But Anna's thoughts are, of course, a closed book to this would-be female psychologist who is oblivious to her child's grave affective disturbances.

The mother's persona is quite different. Others see her as an exemplary mother, "simpaticissima," kind, sensitive, intelligent and deeply attached to her child. Outsiders have difficulty believing that the strange, disturbed, alienated Anna is the offspring of such a mother.

Herself the product of a strict Roman Catholic education, the mother naturally subjects her child to the traditional pattern of religious instruction and association with the "Marian Congregation,...that select body which has the honor of belonging to the Virgin Mary" (153). With the best of intentions, mother and teachers succeed in sowing in Anna's mind a vast confusion as to what is "right" and "clean," and what is "wrong" and "sinful"—so much so that the child is seen making the sign of the cross with her left hand because her right hand is dirty. The nun in charge unsympathetically holds her up to ridicule before the entire class.

The child's religion teacher, a priest, discovers that Anna is actually a highly attentive pupil. Her unusual reasons for loving God, however, are definitely not his: "I love God because he polishes lions' eyes until they shine like gold" (96). Anna in fact loves animals more than she loves humans. Indeed, the novel opens on her brusque awakening when she recalls having neglected her prayer the evening before. Hastily, she makes reparation: "Oh God, protect all the animals of the earth and let them die happy. Amen" (13).

Not only have priest and mother inculcated in Anna the notion of original sin; they have given her a definite sense of her own sinfulness. Sometimes she has the impression of falling into "the inferno that long awaits [her]" (191). Her examinations of conscience, her fear of making a sacrilegious confession, and her deep guilt feelings loom larger and larger in her mind and seem to crush her physically. Ancona denounces the catechism that has formed this complex-ridden child; she mocks the exaggerated Catholic-school discipline which triggers Anna's nausea and disgust for herself. Nor will the attentive reader overlook the author's intention in intermingling "God the Father," Anna's own father, pigs and piglets, and "other animals that are good, warm, and soft to the touch" (71).

Anna's lucubrations, ranging as they do from the blackest despair to a blood-drenched rage for destruction, serve as Ancona's literary device for the annihilation of the unfit mother. The child's dreams (printed throughout as subtext in italics) feature such lurid scenes as her naked parents lying dead in a pool of blood that is being lapped up by a "monstrous being" (52); or about her slaughtered parents hanging in a butchershop (89). In her reverie, Anna carries on a process of fragmentation and decomposition of her mother, whose face disintegrates into pieces of surprise, discomposure, diffidence and uncontrolled fear. Then she ideates the decomposition and decay of the entire maternal body.

Throughout her life, Anna had heard the refrain that her parents had made many sacrifices for her. After having apologized to her mother for being born (89), she symbolically kills her parents and then performs the ritual of self-sacrifice by jumping from a high window. Her suicide must be seen as a preannounced *coup de grâce* for all three members of the family.

Giuliana Ferri

According to the Hindu text known as *Vishnu Parana*, eons succeed each other in a circular trajectory and return periodically: Satya Yuga (age of truth) is followed by Treta Yuga, when truth is diminished by one quarter; Dwapara Yuga is the period in which perfection and imperfection are in a dangerous equilibrium, two quarters in one, two quarters in the other. In our era, Kali Yuga (*kal* meaning contestation, discord), property confers rank, wealth becomes the sole font of virtue, falsity the sole source of success, sex the sole means for joy, and justice has been reduced to one quarter.

The incomplete heroine of Giuliana Ferri's *Un quarto di donna* (A quarter of a woman, 1973) is aware that she is an anachronism. Even her thoughts are "quarter of thoughts," so squelched are they by the stupidities of daily existence (39). Three quarters of her true self are submerged in the husband/child/job syndrome which denies her the respect and the intellectual satisfaction she believes she deserves. This mother of two is only a quarter of a woman.

Her two children seem like ten: "it seems to me that for the past ten years I've done nothing but bear children," she laments (39). A typical day in her life is built up of chapters revealing the darkest aspects of motherhood. Her children give her no sense of completeness; rather, they disorient her by their rough and rude "inhuman ruckus" (10). Each day begins with the usual mother/offspring conflict which exhausts her even before she moves on to her job. Still she courageously juggles her two lives, vowing that her "fatigue must not show any signs of fatigue" (34).

This frustrated wife and mother feels herself entrapped in triangular or circular "geometric space" much like that of a madonna/bambino painting, but in which the baby asserts its sway over the entire canvas. The mother's rebellion is abstract, yet she senses that she must gain possession of her own life and her own identity.

Ferri uses descriptions of mouths and hands as metonymies for the physical body as opposed to abstract mind and intelligence. Recalling Grazia Deledda's contemplation of her baby sister, Ferri's heroine sees with distaste the wide open mouth of her crying baby. Questioning the love she feels for the child, she wonders what value such love has (19), or why parents are so concerned about the raising of children who "invariably...turn out differently" (93).

The heroine's hands—a leitmotiv in the novel—are usually full of objects required for the family's needs; she is at a loss as to where to put her empty hands when she sits on a chair while her baby crawls on the floor and she has no desire to play with it. She personifies her hands, which she desperately seeks to put to good use; she sees them as growing old, deprived of the rejuvenation that only mental creativity can generate (20); and the word "hands" appears no less than four times on a single page (25). So harrowing is the heroine's existence that she feels "one must either live or die" (17), a euphemistic substitute expression for her desire to injure the baby.[13]

Torn by the ambivalences of mother love/mother hate, buffeted by incompatible emotions of love and outrage, she is plagued by feelings of remorse, desperation and guilt whenever she is away from home. Seeing herself as only a "piece of a mother" rather than an entire one, she is also dissatisfied with herself as a wife and feels that she could love her husband more were it not for the children (11). "*Stolta maternità*" (stupid maternity) blocks her on every side.

Unable to impose her mental and spiritual needs on her family, she articulates some of her thoughts "inside herself" and others "outside herself." Never does she enjoy her thought processes in their entirety, interrupted as they are by what she calls her senseless mothering. Competing thoughts "superimpose" themselves in her mind, causing "symptoms of illness" (55-6).

She blames herself for carrying out rote motions of mothering—caressing, washing, cradling the baby—as gestures dictated by the heart but not by the intelligence. The moment she interrupts these routine movements she becomes "whole," her cerebral existence comes to the fore, she thirsts for knowledge and protests that she is "drowning in the instinct [of maternity]" (22). The act of lovemaking seems equally void of intellectual interest: "a hand that reaches out to me…an almost obligatory trajectory…without any conspiring on the part of the intelligence" (38).

Increasingly, the heroine determines that she must go beyond the expected love for her husband and children in order to develop her own potential. As she contemplates her reflection in a mirror, she suddenly realizes her own "intellectual infantilism" (56), which she ascribes to mental deprivation under Fascism. Her education had forced her into ignorance, enclosed her "inside the walls of my female domain" (57). Too late, she repines at having never been taught to "discover the multiplicity of worlds within me," which had remained invisible to her throughout her youth (59). A belated aspirant to a life of the intellect, she is aware that ideas are now churning in her mind. But she is prevented from giving expression to them by her immersion in "householditude."

At length determined to apply her mind in a search for "*l'essenziale*," she powerfully inveighs against the traditionalism and conformism of "my country with its priests, its nuns, its prostitutes" (50). Fascist brainwashing, she realizes, had inculcated "an infinite number of conventional ideas on the inherent need in men and women for a family" (119). But now she will search for new dimensions in the "new space of humanity," whose framework will be higher and broader than her immediate family and her personal circle of friends (59). Now she will seek her personal freedom and the end of her marriage, seizing the occasion of another pregnancy as the springboard for her liberation.

Shabby treatment during a clandestine abortion convinces her that this "quarter of a woman," as she calls herself, has been sufficiently mutilated, dissected and fragmented. For the pregnancy in the uterus she will substitute a *"gravidanza nel cervello"* (pregnancy in the brain), an expression frequently used by Italian women writers in revolt against maternity.

In searching for appropriate and dignified words in which to explain to her husband her own ambitions and her need to separate from him, she is conscious of having acquired a certain mastery of language. Words become crucial to her in describing her own predicament to others. Words also give her a means of escape from that predicament.

Throughout the novel, the heroine had sought to look upward toward the skies, but had been forced to bend downward to where her children were playing on the floor. Ferri's writing style echoes the protagonist's "intellectual birth pangs" (56): each preoccupation, each thrust of despair, each shaft of pain, and each sudden impulse toward creativity is captured in short, staccato sentences. In counterpoint, moments of lucidity and of consciousness locked in battle with unconsciousness are presented in flowing poetic fragments. By the end of the book, Ferri has totally debunked the myth of motherhood as a woman's fulfillment. Her final image is that of the "dawn of a new ideality still in its early light" (122). She foresees a new age when women will have minimized the use of their physical equipment and will exercise their intellectual endowment to the maximum.

Luisella Fiumi

Irony, humor and persiflage run through the two hundred pages of Luisella Fiumi's *Come donna zero* (Zero as in woman, 1974). The protagonist, a woman writer and journalist, describes in the first person the joylessness and stultification of wifehood and motherhood in an unequal union with an inferior man. At the time of her marriage, her husband's concept of "conjugal happiness" had been based on the presupposition that "he being a perfect husband…[it was] inevitable that his setoff be an imperfect wife" (9).

The chapter entitled "My own mother told him not to marry me" focuses wittily on the disputations that raged in Italy during the 1970s on the subjects of *patria potestas* (paternal authority), the propriety of children bearing the father's surname alone, and the assignment of female/male responsibilities in raising them. Faced with the thought that he himself might have to care for babies, the husband of Fiumi's protagonist invokes the name of Herod the Great—whereat his mother-in-law recommends that he refrain from having children with her daughter (57).

Using arguments that fail to impress her traditionalist mother, the protagonist vigorously champions female/male equality in the workplace and at home, including a balance between *patria* and *matria potestas*. Though she owns the house in which she lives—indeed is chained to it—what she really desires is a pair of wings or an office outside her home where she can concentrate on her writing (91).

The birth of her twin daughters has in fact wrought havoc in her life; the only time she is delighted with them is when she can send them out to play at someone else's home (20). Though she had refrained from striking the twins up to the age of three, thereafter she could no longer restrain herself—not for reasons of power, authority and discipline but because she felt "a certain enjoyment, the pleasure of getting rid of my tensions." But then, "smitten with remorse" (145), she invariably repented her shameful loss of control over herself and her offspring. She is, however, quite remorseless in heaping invective on the children; as they grow, so does her moral outrage and her arsenal of epithets, ranging from "*stupida bambina*," "*quella cretina*," to "*idiota*" and "*demente*."

The mother had avoided subjecting her children to the religious education she herself had received. She had scoffed at "G.B." (Gesù Bambino) with his Christmas gifts, and she had mocked the nuns' catechism lessons, which always finished with "descriptions of the black, pitchfork-bearing devil wrapped in flames, luring little children into sin"—but whose disappearance could be guaranteed by a ritual sign of the cross (139-40).

Could the problems posed by Italy's "difficult" children be due to their awareness that they have been duped in matters regarding sin and the devil? This is not the question that Fiumi's protagonist asks. She seeks only to know whether Italian children's rambunctiousness is due to "possessive, anxious, permissive, authoritarian mothers," to "fathers who oppress the mothers? Or jobs that oppress the fathers who oppress the mothers?" (126).

All her questions are rhetorical; all her efforts at concentrating on her writing come to nought. Locked in her own room, she allows the thoughts that maddeningly elude her to fly off "in search of a different existence" (198).

Marina Jarre

What did Marina Jarre read in the eyes of a thirteen-year-old Italian girl during the 1968 students' revolt? Quite unexpectedly, she found there the will to produce the best drawing of her entire class, and to continue her schooling in order to "learn how to draw better" (*Negli occhi di una ragazza* [In a girl's eyes], 220). An artist always has the masters in her eye.

Negli occhi di una ragazza (1971) tells the story of Maria Cristina, whose parents did not love her nor did she love them: "It was as though, after having brought her into the world, there was nothing left to add to what they had done" (49-50). Nor has she any love for her favored older brother, a militant student rebel for whom, she asserts, she had been conceived by her parents as company (52). Maria Cristina's mother is ailing, and she herself is saddled with all the chores in this male-dominated household, to the serious detriment of her own education. So young, she realizes that she has fallen—or been pushed into—the trap of domesticity. Her father and brother treat her as a servant, the latter going so far as to mock her "knowledge of the price of potatoes" (67). Relegated by them to the status of an object, she nonetheless astutely plays their game: "I'm stupid…and so I ask stupid questions" (68).

Maria Cristina refuses any connection either to the developments on the national scene or to the notion of family continuity. Her mother's death she easily takes in stride; but she fiercely derides her father's expectation that she will renounce school, marry and have children. As for the priest's question-and-answer sessions in religion class, she sleeps while the others respond in unison. In a mocking tone the author describes Maria Cristina's "meditation" in an empty church whose vesper services are deserted by its parishioners: "Sitting in an empty church is like praying," the girl reflects. "Praying is asking yourself questions and inside of you, if you are good, Baby Jesus answers. If you're not good, if you're like Maria Cristina who tells lies and ran out of the house instead of staying with her mommy…then Jesus won't give you any answers." Maria Cristina feels reified not only by her father and brother but by Jesus as well: "Perhaps he'll grant you his grace when he has made you into a thing" (107).

The self-centeredness of Maria Cristina's pregnant teenage friend,

Eliana—"only her and her belly and the baby" (197)—fills our heroine with repulsion. The birth announcement offends her esthetic sense: "an ugly stork with a little bundle in its beak" (198). But a visit to her friend is *de rigueur*. She is received by Eliana's mother who, Maria Cristina is quick to notice, wears bedroom slippers—the symbol par excellence of householditude in Italian women's writings—while Eliana in her room cries out in pain as she breastfeeds the newborn child. Eliana is afflicted with rhagades (lesions and fissures around the nipples). Heartlessly her mother shifts the baby from one nipple to the other, pressing the infant's cheeks with her fingers so that it will loosen its grip, goading her daughter on, causing her increasing pain with each change of the baby's position. The pale and exhausted Eliana curses the child (*"maledetto!"*), complains to her friend about her life of seclusion, and announces her intention of going to work in a supermarket and leaving the child to her mother (212-14). This pitiful child-mother understands, however, that the best gift she can receive from Maria Cristina would be one of her drawings, framed, which would constitute her "museum" (215).

In the closing scene of the novel, a defiant Maria Cristina explains to her father with all the strength of her convictions: "I don't want to make children. I want to draw and go to school" (221). Receiving neither encouragement nor support in her aspirations, in effect she goes on strike, leaving all her home duties unfulfilled. Her warning to her brother—that she must not stand alone, just as he, "alone, cannot carry out his revolution" (223)—gains for her a minor victory.

Maria Cristina's small domestic revolution is appealingly presented in *Negli occhi di una ragazza*. Earlier in the novel, the author had narrated a symbolic dream in which Maria Cristina saw her own hand, which she raised toward the darkness; and out of that darkness came another hand that grasped hers. But the other hand was not her mother's, nor her father's, nor her brother's, nor her friend's. It was a warm and strong hand—her own. The dream of course signifies that Maria Cristina knew she would have to make herself rather than wait to be made by others. Her strength lay in herself alone—and in the hand that would serve her in future as an artist, a non-housekeeper, and a non-mother.

Armanda Guiducci

Her father—"may God keep him in glory"—had always told Bettina that a woman who lacks a home and family is a wretch and a misfit (*Due *donne da buttare* [Two disposable women], 11). Guided by such paternal maxims, Bettina is now weighed down with keeping up her home and caring for her children, dispensing "so-called maternal love" (42) while furiously envying "those who do sublime things like singing, Maria Callas for example" (12-13). She herself, a talented soprano for whom a promising career had seemed to open, is now without an identity, caught up in the eternal female cycle of all-consuming marriage and maternity which marginalizes and belittles women.

Bettina had been forced to choose whether to remain "inside or outside of the shell. Inside or outside of the marital bed" (13). Her choice reflected the values her parents had inculcated. Like a female Sisyphus, she is now resignedly condemned to repeat the gestures of washing, cooking, cleaning, and marketing, only to begin her routine tasks afresh with each new day. After twenty-five years of effort, she knows that she is unesteemed and will die unmourned even by her family (15).

In a page of almost unpunctuated narration that reflects the children's goading and harassment of their mother, Guiducci describes Bettina's physical and mental degradation at the hands of these offspring who "sucked the life blood completely out of me milk bones marrow"(27). She feels like a shriveled fruit rind; even worse, she still regrets the "sublime destiny" that awaited her beautiful voice (28). Her intuition and intelligence having been repressed, she is now a frustrated, useless, aging woman with no goal in life—"theatre, or singing, or something else" (24). Guiducci, with acuity and humor, demolishes the traditional norms of family life and demonstrates the inherent inferiority of the female condition.

Dust and dirt, symbolic of death, weave through *Due donne da buttare*, whose bantering style and lightness of tone belie the dark shadow cast by the protagonist. Bettina is haunted by the insane women she had seen in an asylum, one a compulsive cleaner who saw dust and dirt everywhere, another crazed by overflowing washing machines—embodiments of gender roles which become housewives' fixations. With her own attention exclusively on her home and children, Bettina has the impression that she, too, is being driven mad by household paraphernalia and cleaning products that pollute the planet. But thoughts of suicide are out of the question, because "they say You must live for your children's sake mom and dad always used to say that to me" (60).

While it is this longsuffering mother who dominates the first part of the novel, she finds a foil—another "expendable woman"—in the prostitute, Stellina. Her function is to demonstrate that both the "proper woman" and the prostitute are equally degraded females in their culturally determined sexual roles. Stellina sells herself for "independent money" (79), whereas her sister, forced into marriage by their parents, has been "sold for her entire life" (91), whoring it for free.

The husbands to whom Stellina has been forced to listen during the course of her work are seen by her as having used their wives as servants, shattering their bodies with sex and pregnancies yet arranging society in such a way that matrimony still remains on the altar, the prostitute on the sidewalk (97). Guiducci mocks the marriage ceremony as a theatrical production, a put-on show whose very existence guarantees that prostitution will continue. Among animals, she notes with tongue in cheek, there is "neither marriage nor prostitution" (98).

Touching on the themes of frigidity and sterility, which figure prominently in Italian women's writings of the twentieth century, Guiducci glorifies these "gifts of nature" because they liberate the woman from bonds of dependency on the male. The frigid woman, in Guiducci's words, is "blessed, the freest on the face of the earth. Free from [men]" (104).

It is only a matter of course, in this author's outlook, that pregnant women who expel their fetuses, or infanticides who cut their newborns into pieces, should dispose of the waste in the cities' sewage systems (45). Undoubtedly these acts contribute to the universal filth that is choking the planet but for Guiducci they also represent, in terms of her basic thesis that woman's physiology is at the root of her inferiority, a revolt against the reproductive function and against maternity. The polluters are here rejecting the world's perception of themselves as nothing more than nurturers.

Guiducci's documentary *La donna non è gente* (Women aren't people, 1977) tells of a contrasting practice in the Italian South, where women perform the ritual of burying their afterbirth in the ground at a spot remote from water or any source of humidity.[14] Rosa, a Calabrian peasant woman, illustrates this bit of regional folklore in Guiducci's work. To Rosa's mind, there is an analogy between afterbirth and the soft spot of the infant's skull. Like unto like: sogginess of the placenta would produce sogginess of the skull; therefore she buries her afterbirth in a sunny, dry spot.

The earth, in Guiducci's writings, represents both fertility and death. *La donna non è gente* is rich in evocation of rituals that have been practiced in rural Italy since ancient times. It is startling to observe their resemblance to some of the ancient Greek festivals with agrarian components, such as those of Apollo (Carneia, Hyakinthia, Thargelia). In celebrating an expiatory death followed by a revival of vegetation, they suggested that sacrifice was a precondition for fertility in the next year's crops.

Rosa's fertility, ironically, is annually ensured by her husband's ritual rape. "Eighteen times he made me pregnant for his own pleasure and convenience" is Rosa's plaint. "I've had eighteen children—ten are alive, eight are dead." "One was born, the next died," she laments. "I was always pregnant" (270). In addition, she has had "five scrapings...out in the open country, like the animals" (249). Such pregnancies had not been easy for a woman who harvested from three in the morning to midnight, who sometimes had to sleep on a rat-infested bed of straw, and who on occasion breastfed two babies simultaneously—one her own, the other to earn "a piece of bread" (238).

Other women whose milk was less abundant than Rosa's had recourse to the "milk statue of Santa Cristina," located in a grotto in the vicinity, from whose breast flowed beneficent waters. An insufficiently lactating mother would wade barefoot through the grotto's waters "like the Madonna walking toward her son," as Rosa put, to suck the breast of Saint Christina. Then she would put some of the water into a bottle for the baby to drink, and "after two days the mother had milk...Also for cows...they lead the animals to drink and after two days the milk comes" (271-2).

Innumerable Calabrian superstitious, religious, funerary, and necromantic practices, as well as knitting-needle abortions for girls raped by their "*padroni*," are described in Guiducci's interview with Rosa, a mother whose paralyzed deaf-mute daughter she views as a punishment for her own lack of faith (284). Another daughter who "saw the Madonna every day" was lost to a convent of cloistered nuns (258).

Shame—because her other children were already grown—prompted Rosa to go into hiding to deliver her last child; but she hemorrhaged so severely that she had to be brought into full view in a hospital. In a final summing up of her life's perpetual struggle, she deplores the "afflictions" of children, husband, and relatives (285). As a prototype of Italy's oppressed Southern female, Rosa embodies Armanda Guiducci's most eloquent protest against the mindless and continuous childbearing inflicted on a woman by a brutish mate.

Writers of the 1980s

Although Elsa Morante's *Aracoeli* (above) and Clara Sereni's *Manicomio primavera* (below) are notable exceptions, the essay rather than the novel was the literary genre that prevailed in the 1980s as the vehicle of women's thoughts about the ongoing transformation of maternity. The diffuse thinking on the subject in previous decades was now gathered, ordered and encapsulated in a series of essays and articles published as *Maria, Medea e le altre* (Mary, Medea and the others, 1982),[15] while the essays contained in Elena Gianini Belotti's *Non di sola madre* (Not by mother only, 1983) articulated the problems of procreation in an oppressive and conditioning socioreligious context.

The pieces—many of them unsigned—in *Maria, Medea e le altre* run the entire gamut of contemporary Italian views on maternity. The "Maria" of the title naturally stands for compliant motherhood, which is forcefully rejected by all the authors; "Medea" who bore Jason two children whom she then killed to revenge his infidelity, finds a certain acceptance; and "the others" are militant figures who challenge the very concept of procreation in times when women are battling for psychological survival and economic independence (14).

Though most of the essays give voice to women who feel publicly mutilated by the experience of maternity, ample space is given also to writers who deliberately chose motherhood even in the face of ostracism by their militant feminist contemporaries. Italy's social organization at that time did indeed seem to require more debate on family planning and overpopulation.

Most of the writers questioned whether reconciliation between maternity and creativity can ever be achieved. Some advocated new forms of motherhood couched in (for Italy) avant-garde terms (72, 82-3, 211-13), while others denounced ecclesiastical involvement in matters of contraception and abortion (15-16). Still others equated maternity and death in invocations of *mater mortifera* (lethal, deadly, mortal motherhood) (60).

The very titles of the articles and essays—"Maternità: io dico no" (Maternity: I say no), "La rabbia di essere madre" (The anger of being a mother), "Perché non ho figli" (Why I don't have children)—attest to many of the authors' outright rejection of procreation, at least for themselves in view of what they consider its irrationality and its encroachments on personal freedom (99).

One writer (D.V.) clarifies her position in terms of a broader comprehension of the world: "I said no [to the biological fact] and I corrected nature's error, which did not reflect my deepest desire.... I want to try to become a complete human being.... I doubt that maternity [is] a positive path to becoming a woman, [a process] understood less and less in physiological terms and more and more in terms of humanity" (68-9).

Elena Gianini Belotti

One of the contributors to *Maria, Medea* is Elena Gianini Belotti, the author of *Non di sola madre* (Not by mother only, 1983). The Bible tells us that "man doth not live by bread only" (Deuteronomy, VIII, 3); Belotti suggests that a child does not live by mother alone. She poses in essay form one of the burning issues of the 1980s: to what extent can the burdens of maternity be transferred to the male? Why, for millennia, have women persuaded themselves that men, though superior to them in any physical or mental manifestation, are incapable of childrearing?

The ideology of maternal love had fostered, as we have seen, a rigid, all-absorbing, and unsustainable concept of the mother/child relationship, delaying any unbiased consideration of the man's possible capacity to raise children. The heavy responsibility of the mother alone, in the long history of maternity, had by the 1980s produced a situation in which it was widely felt that neither motherhood nor childhood was living up to social and cultural expectations. After millennia of social marginalization, intellectual impoverishment, and wasted talent, women were up in arms and not averse to seeking some form of retaliation.

Gianini Belotti accuses society of having ingrained in women the concept of what feminist Armanda Guiducci (above) calls *Mater Mystica*. Pregnancy, delivery, and breastfeeding, she argues, have been forced into molds that correspond to a societal idea of maternity but not to the real needs, desires, and anxieties of either mother or child. The mother's behavior vis-a-vis her children has become robot-like, conformist, and adaptive.

Gianini Belotti scathingly questions the conventional belief that maternity really represents a state of perennial beatitude induced and sustained by maternal instinct. How then, she asks, can one explain the frequency of postpartum depression and of psychotic disorders in the mothers of small children? (5). The answer, according to her, is that the so-called maternal instinct is really no instinct at all. Many women turn away from their newborn; many are doubtful, ineffective mothers. If the so-called maternal instinct is actually rooted in female biology, how may one explain the way it is influenced by socioeconomic conditions, such as the mother's economic status or education? It is up to us, Gianini Belotti writes, to investigate the determining social conditions under which women are compelled to live out their maternity—and to challenge the conditions themselves, not merely the way in which women react to them.

The relationship between mother and child, Gianini Belotti points out, is codified in strict laws laid down by Church and State. It is sharply defined in terms of sexual roles which effectively exclude the father from the process of raising the child. Paternity, like maternity, is socially defined, but in this case in terms of privilege rather than subordination.

Those "eloquent male voices" (6) that have formulated the accepted theories of the mother/child relationship excluded men from the arduous assignment of children's early education—a ploy, she claims, directed to postponing the redefinition of sexual roles demanded by Italian women in the 1980s. Since society assumes that only the mother is capable of divining and satisfying her offspring's need, her constant presence in a child's early years is deemed indispensable. Fathers, grandparents, nursemaids and child care centers are seen as detrimental to the symbiotic relationship between mother and child—another device for chaining the woman to her nemesis. The psychological theory that children suffer due to "lack of maternal care" has unfortunately invaded the collective conscious and strongly conditioned the way in which mothers behave (7).

Gianini Belotti sees the condition of motherhood as absurdly suspended between the heights of omnipotence and the depths of impotence (6). The mother is idealized and exalted as the savior of humanity for just so long as she dispenses unlimited love. In so doing, however, she ensnares herself in an inferior social status, denied the very right to determine how she should apportion that love. What share to herself? to her art? to her child? to her husband?

The organization of society—with which she has had nothing to do— prescribes norms, values, and sanctions. It legitimizes institutions and social structures—not of her making—whose foundations rest on age-old images of women and maternity. Instead of all this, Gianini Belotti maintains, it should be women themselves who mold the social organization of maternity, defining it according to feminine principles. Yet such is the dominance and exclusivity of the male in this domain that no sooner have women elaborated their own concepts of behavior and their own social modalities for maternity than men appropriate them and assume the right to formulate and impose society's new norms.

Challenging the notion of child formation "by mother only," Gianini Belotti deplores those Italians who are fearful of equal parental responsibility in the raising of children.[16] In the face of the woman's difficult choice between maternity and a personal social and cultural life, the author takes the side of "those who [do] not want to die socially just in order to raise a child" (25).

Clara Sereni

With her highly acclaimed 1987 novel *Casalinghitudine* (Householditude), Clara Sereni had begun her own revolt against maternity, decrying the "illusion" that a mother could ever cut the umbilical cord that ties her to her son. "To deliver him completely will always be impossible for me" (45), declares her tormented protagonist, whose child she sees as merely the extension of her own body and not as an autonomous being.

Other extensions of mothers' bodies figure in Sereni's later collection of short stories, *Manicomio primavera* (Spring insane asylum, 1989). Here they are demented or seriously retarded children. Of all the writings under examination here, this book is perhaps the most arresting and disheartening commentary on ther whole subject of maternity. Its theme, in almost every instance, is the suffering of mothers who are denied a harmonious coexistence with their offspring.

In many of the tales, Sereni focuses upon on the fears, frustrations, and exhaustion of those who try to teach their mentally disordered children. She dwells upon their "useless euphoria" (69) at any slight sign of progress—hopes which, of course, are quickly dashed. The children in the tales are, in the words of the Irish poet Thomas Moore, "a whole dark pile of human mockeries."

Even the title of the collection, "spring insane asylum," is an oxymoron: spring, symbolic of the childbearing age, with its golden sun, silver rain, and budding branches, is incongruously coupled with the dark fears and ghastly, sickening ambiance associated with insanity. If Robert Browning, when the year was at its spring, found God in his heaven and all right with the world ("Pippa Passes"), Sereni inverts his image to focus on the sick, despairing and sometimes panicky young mothers who are unable to discern the harmonies of creation.

"Tutto si impara" (Everything can be learned) is the ironic title of a story describing the "ferocious pain," the feelings of "nothingness" experienced by a primipara or first-time mother, who senses "a tragedy or simply a war" unfolding in her entrails (25). Her newborn child seems a strange "enemy entity" from another planet (26)—"red, wrinkly and ugly, its mouth open and voracious...its head big [and] elongated...its body disharmonious and incompatible" (27). She is filled with "inopportune, nay guilty thoughts" at her abhorrence of the child; she knows she is going against all she has been taught to believe about babies (26). Finally she forces herself to take it close to her own body "so as not to have to see it any more" (27). Sighing, she tells herself, "I'll learn to love him. Everything can be learned" (27). The reader is left with a premonition that the mother's life will be spent in building defenses against her unwanted offspring.

The story "Momenti cruciali" (Crucial moments) evokes, within the small space of an automobile, a mother's maddening mental and physical reactions as she observes in the rearview mirror the movements of her retarded child squirming in the back seat. Sereni poetically describes the woman's construction of a defense mechanism against the "innumerable hours [spent in] silence and shadows" (61).

The psychoneurotic child of "Concerto" raises a mad din among dirty garbage bins in a courtyard until he is taken away by force in an ambulance. The distraught mother, left sitting alone on the child's empty bed, draws her knees to her chest and rocks herself mechanically to the tune of a lullaby (77).

The almost unbelievable extent to which women will sacrifice themselves to calm their disturbed children is poignantly narrated in "Amore," in which a mother makes therapeutic love to her aggressive, violent adolescent son, a victim of masturbatory disorders.

Similarly, in "Anniversario," a mother is bound to her abnormal son by his unpredictable fits of temper (97). She spends her days in cleaning the home that he disrupts and dirties; he kicks and bites her, tears to shreds her early photos. "A piece at a time," Sereni writes, "her son is erasing her past" (91), that is, a past that represents a time of freedom.

Each of the sorrowful mothers in Sereni's dolorous collection has lost her personal identity. She paces behind her child like an inseparable doppelganger, to be displaced entirely by her irreversible error. The murder of the mother in *Una strana follia* (below) seems almost a compassionate punishment compared to that of the tragic figures in Sereni's phantasmagoria.

Writers of the 1990s

Paola Moretti

A caricature[17] of Pope John Paul II pregnant with child reflects a prevalent Italian sentiment with regard to the present pope's position on birth control. Paola Moretti's own reflections on the subject are encapsuled in her one-act play, *Una strana follia* (A strange folly, 1996), in which the figure of a female pope permits her to inveigh figuratively against both maternity and the Church.

The legendary Pope Joan, who supposedly reigned in the ninth century under the title of John VII or VIII, is said to have given birth in public during a procession to the Lateran palace, whereupon she was dragged out of the city by her feet and stoned to death. From that day to this, holy processions have taken a different route from the Vatican to Saint John Lateran, avoiding the spot where Joan gave birth; and, in further response, the Church initiated the ritual of manual verification of the sex of elected popes. The Church first acknowledged, then denied, Joan's existence.[18]

According to the legend that underlies Moretti's drama, Joan was an Englishwoman born in Mainz, the town that became the ecclesiastical center of Germany in the sixth century. It is alleged that she fell in love with a Benedictine monk and, disguising herself as a man, followed her lover to Athens—the city that symbolizes philosophy and learning—where she studied, acquired great learning, and underwent a radical transformation of her perceptions. Moving to Rome, she was received with enthusiasm and admiration for her knowledge. She entered the hierarchy of the Curia and finally was elected pope, never, however, renouncing the pleasures of the flesh. Joan is a composite figure of cultural ambition and love of knowledge, of female sensuality and ecclesiastical power. She is the supreme symbol of the woman of talent trapped and martyred by maternity.

Analogies between Pope Joan and the fifth-century pagan Hypatia will not escape the reader. Hypatia is said to have occupied the chair of Platonic philosophy at Alexandria, as well as to have written mathematical and astronomical commentaries. Her cruel murder in 415 by a mob of Christian enemies seeking to stifle her voice is comparable to Joan's stoning by the fanatical Roman mob—albeit for different reasons.

Paola Moretti presents Joan—pope and woman, but certainly no exemplar of "immaculate fecundation"[19]—hiding her swollen belly under papal raiment. She is unable to rid herself of her fetus, to free herself from the "reality" that binds her to the earth. She recounts her clashes with anti-female social and religious prejudices; she confronts the medical profession's Latin hocus-pocus and exposes its ineffectual sage-leaf brews that have been offered to calm her pains.

The fulcrum of the tragedy is the "debt towards nature"—reproduction, the encumbrance of the female body—which women seem never able to finish paying and which robs them of their freedom. Women having been arbitrarily assigned not to History but to Natural History, their every venture in free choice is frowned upon as "rebellion against the laws of nature" or "intrusion into forbidden territory."[20]

Joan herself, since her youth, had sought an identity free of gender restrictions. "At Mainz," Moretti writes, "there was once a beautiful girl [who] wanted to be a boy" (84).[21] Had she been a male, she would have been child-free and free! Her ideals were limitless: she strove to know and embrace the entire outside world, the harmony and movement of the stars, the seasons' cycles, the mysteries of numbers, the origin and destiny of humankind. Her brothers had been educated under the great philosophers of Naples; she had been denied the privilege. Thus, rebelling against patriarchal reasoning, she had invented her own philosophical disputations and created her own systems of thought, which she then proceeded herself to refute. For the medieval male mentality, hers was indeed a "strange folly."

People in her entourage sought to provide the "hysterical girl" with a husband to divert her mind and occupy her body—forced copulation, which she defines as "the oldest, most violent, most contemptible method" for cutting short the development of a woman's mind (84).[22] For Joan, the body is secondary to the soul: "If the soul weeps," she said, "the body complies" (80). To her family's desire that she prostitute her body in order to temper her intelligence, she was quick to retort that God could not possibly wish a man to "molest [the female body] of one of His own creatures" (85).

Subverting her society's expectation that she take a husband, she fled to Athens, where she spent years of "absolute happiness, filled with beauty, in the highest spheres that human thought can reach." She felt she was living an ideal life "in the great family [of her teachers], free, serene." Had she not gone to Athens, she mused, her life would have been an "empty flow of days without hope" (86).

Separation from her mother was the equivalent of freedom for Joan. But she learned that knowledge is useless "if you're not able to love yourself"; that in order to *know*, one must know and love oneself. Such in fact is the basis for Moretti's concept of individuality. Joan as a thinker and teacher has lost her identity in the pregnant fullness that has made her empty: "Who am I? Nothing…an empty form…unrecognizable to myself" (89).

Her "ideal life" in Athens was shortlived in any case. Papal Rome awaited her; there, under the assumed name of "the philosopher Angelicus," she would teach, and the Romans would flock to hear her. Not for nothing does Moretti ascribe the name of Angelicus to Pope Joan. It designates a spirit essentially inferior to God but superior to humans in natural endowment of intellect and will. Saint Augustine notes that the name Angelicus (from the Greek *angelos* meaning messenger) indicates office or function rather than nature. Thus, Moretti emphasizes not Joan's female nature but rather the function her Athenan teachers had assigned her—that of teacher.

Joan's sole interlocutor throughout the play is the papal surgeon who has observed his illustrious patient's "colic" and prescribed two vomitings a week. Of course he may not palpate the supposed Holy Father, out of respect for his sacred person. He notes, however, the patient's "progressive loss of equilibrium of the body fluids," "heavy gait," "pallor," and "troubled breathing." Not recognizing these symptoms of pregnancy, he ascribes the pope's disturbances to excess liver bile (79-80).

As the surgeon prepares to bleed his tired, sad, listless and indifferent patient, Joan reveals her premonitions of death. The city of Rome, kingdom of the pope, wafts an "odor of death" into her chamber. Its church bells toll like "demons whispering secret words," demanding her soul, luring her into darkness. Moretti creates a scene of highly effective interplay between the surgeon's talk of dissections in his anatomy class and Joan's surrender to visions of blood, passion, sacrifice and subterranean spaces. In language evocative of primitive fertility rites, Moretti describes the sounds of churning waters and the murmuring of the birth process emanating from the earth's womb: "water that flows underground, without origin and without respite, night and day, for eternity" (80-81). Undergoing a systematic purgation in order to penetrate to the very core of her reality, Joan's maternal womb becomes a metaphor for death.

Comic relief—as well as severe critique—marks the ensuing scene, in which the surgeon proposes a variety of male diversions to combat His Holiness's malaise: running, riding, and hunting in the woods with his companions, participation in duels and feasts, and "rollicking in the beds of Rome's most beautiful women," to which Joan pungently replies: "Surgeon, the Pope doesn't rollick" (82).

Finally, Joan lets fall her pontifical garb to reveal the contours of her body in its advanced state of pregnancy—to the stupefaction of the trembling surgeon. The guards knock to announce the beginning of the procession, declaring that all Rome awaits its pope in order to render him homage. The play closes with a stark description of Joan's delivery during the procession, and of the death which delivers her from both pregnancy and papacy.

In this drama, Paola Moretti is obviously attacking the prejudices and false morality in society's institutions at any historical period, especially our own. The imaginary pope is a perfect vehicle for her satire of the Church, its hypocritical purism, its exhortations *ad absurdum* to increase and multiply. The disquieting figure of Joan, a woman searching desperately beyond maternity for absolute feminine beauty, knowledge, and self-realization, helps us to form new ideas for new times—times when what was labeled as "strange folly" in the dark ages can now be seen to deserve more sympathetic consideration. Had Joan been able to expel her fetus clandestinely, or had her inventive surgeon been able to provide her with some kind of artificial womb enabling her to give birth without the burden of carrying the child, Rome's enthusiasm and devotion to its learned pope would have continued; the mob would not have killed her; her "death and transformation" would have been quite different.

But this is not the thrust of Moretti's play. Her imaginative focus on pregnancy and papacy highlights two institutions, both of which, in their different ways, are exceedingly difficult to subvert. She introduces her readers to a heroine who remains unique and whose example is unlikely to be imitated.

Maria Sandias

If the exigencies of the papacy forced Pope Joan, the "philosopher Angelicus," to hide her pregnancy, the exigencies of court life required Queen Maria Sophia to conceal her maternity. For she, the wife of an impotent king, was the mother of an illegitimate daughter whose existence had to remain unknown.

Maria Sandias reconstructs history according to her own particular interests in *Maria Sofia di Borbone, una regina in esilio* (Maria Sophia of the Bourbons, a queen in exile, 1996), in which she presents another facet of rejected maternity—a mother who could neither accept nor totally refuse the birth of a child.

Maria Sophia was the beautiful, vivacious, and intelligent Bavarian duchess who in 1859 became the wife of Francis II, the detested king of the Two Sicilies and last of the Bourbons of Naples. Having gained control of both family and state affairs, this enterprising queen offered a heroic resistance to the Garibaldian and Piedmontese forces of the Risorgimento, participating personally in the defense of the kingdom, encouraging her soldiers, visiting the sick and wounded in hospitals, and gaining the admiration of the other European courts.

After the royal couple's exile to Rome, she plotted in her temporary home at the Palazzo Farnese to regain the lost kingdom with the aid of legitimists and mercenaries. Her days of exile, like Pope Joan's in the Vatican, unfolded in a "languid, viscous, enveloping atmosphere, like that of a spiderweb" (123). But as befitted a queen she protected her husband's image, subordinating her personal life to her role in history.

It was in the holy city of Rome that she, like Pope Joan, incurred the hazards of an illegitimate pregnancy. At the discovery of her predicament she became distraught: "I was confused, desperate, suspended between my role as queen and the role of a mere woman" (125). Willingly would she have "disappeared"; but others decided for her. Sworn to maintain the secrecy of her pregnancy, she gave birth clandestinely; her daughter was taken from her, to be raised incognita in Vienna; and the royal honor was saved (126). She admitted that though the separation of mother and child might have appeared cruel, her love for the child had lasted only during the brief moment of its conception, and that the traits of her lover had also faded quickly enough. She had been willing to view the renunciation of motherhood as the most reasonable course, "the wisest, most balanced decision" (126); thus she achieved a psychologically proper degree of separation from her daughter.

The challenge to the mother's solution is presented by her now-thirty-year-old daughter, Maria Luisa, who takes a more restrictive and conventional view of the mother/child relationship. It is Maria Luisa who considers that it is the natural and unvarying role of the woman to be the breeder and guardian of her offspring.

In the confrontation which constitutes the essence of Sandias's one-act play, the daughter reproaches her "Aunt Sophia," whom she knows full well to be her mother, for having denied her both proximity and guidance. Bitterness and regret gush from her lips in a torrent of negative feelings. The queen's enlightened but hardly satisfying reply is only that she has afforded her daughter a space of her own.

At first the advantage of the dialogue seems equally shared by the two protagonists. Each argues her views logically, expounding reasons that seem as strong as they are incompatible. Maria Sophia, with her public responsibilities, had not been free to act out the role of mother. Quite apart from the impotence of her royal consort, the activities inseparable from her own life had been incompatible with maternity. She had been committed to her people and had cherished dreams of justice for them. Realizing the brutal persecutions and crass unenlightenment under Bourbon rule, she had refused to give up her dreams of a new political order. Loyal and courageous men, hopeful of setting up a liberal regime in the kingdom, had seen her as useful to the cause; herself, indeed, had inspired their actions, while deeming herself more a conspirer than an inspirer (119).

Maria Sophia admits that her feelings of loneliness might have been assuaged by the presence of the child, but her "passion for politics" had peopled her solitude and lent wings to her dreams of returning to the throne (129). Among the higher reasons for concealing her motherhood, she also cites her fidelity to an oath of secrecy. To which her daughter only retorts, "I don't know what it means to have ideals" (128).

A "refused" and "betrayed" child, Maria Luisa has never has felt securely attached. She incriminates the "mother who doesn't stretch out her arms" to her, and calls herself "a little unwanted thing" (121). Her mother is a stranger, an alien to her; nor does the younger woman understand her reasons of state. Psychologically lacking the social mirroring of her reality, Maria Luisa threatens to blackmail her mother: "I could let the whole world know that you're my mother," she cries, "thus shocking all the courts of Europe; journalists would vie for interviews with me" (122). Spectators may be conscious here of something like a power struggle between Maria Luisa, who is seeking to be "mothered," and Maria Sophia who plays the "mother" in her own independent and original way. Emotionally deprived and without creativity of her own, the daughter sees herself darkly in a maternal mirror which does not adequately reflect her own image.

Finally, however, Maria Luisa, in a scene still dominated by the mirror concept, seats herself opposite her mother, conceding that the latter's makeup includes "seeds of intelligence, of generosity, of courage" that are lacking in herself. Her inane role as a chattering lady-in-waiting at the court of Vienna dooms her, she realizes, to an inane destiny (128). Lacking any grounding that would permit her to raise her sights, Maria Luisa recognizes her own inferiority. Rising, she takes leave of the mother she will never see again.

At this crucial moment, Maria Sophia challenges her daughter forcefully: she (Maria Luisa) must learn to walk alone, find her own path, understand the meaning of commitments and shoulder the burdens of secrecy. Moved by this new awareness, Maria Luisa now declares her intention to grow and strive for higher ideals. Why, after all, she asks, should her personal identity be so tied up with her beginnings? Why must our parents' identity be ours? Her own separation from her mother is precisely what gives Maria Luisa her independent identity. Though her first intent was to position herself against her mother, she now seeks an active posture in relation to herself. The play concludes with the daughter conceding victory to the mother who refused her, at the same time thanking her for her legacy and for having helped her child take her first step toward dignity (129).

The dignity of Maria Sophia, not unlike that of the intransigent heroine

Antigone, lies in her devotion to an idea of honor which she has created for herself. Antigone's honor bade her bury her brother and face certain death; Maria Sophia's duty was to renounce her child lest open motherhood entail the breaking of an oath and sure political death. Throughout the dialogue, Maria Sophia is unceasingly resistant to every species of conventionality and conformism. As a paradigm of the lucid, rational rejection of "normal" maternal behavior, the delinquent mother gains in stature as the play progresses until in the end all her reasons prevail.

Grazia Livi

Simone de Beauvoir, Virginia Woolf, Gertrude Stein, Gianna Manzini, Anna Banti are foremost among the women writers who have shaped the intellectual growth of Grazia Livi. In her book of essays entitled *Le lettere del mio nome* (The letters of my name, 1992), in which the essays themselves are interspersed with verses of contemporary poets, Livi paints a fresco of woman-in-the-making, historically and poetically.

For four thousand years, she writes, angry women have been "looking on"; finally their eyes have been opened (159). Their millenarian oppression has, in her opinion, been most forcefully exposed by Simone de Beauvoir, whose thought provides the thrust of the entire book. Challenging the female who entertains a deformed and obscured image of her own physiognomy, Beauvoir, for Livi, represents what all women purportedly can accomplish if they set their minds to it. Through achievement, Beauvoir transcends the limitations hitherto imposed on the female. Livi stresses the French author's aversion to ties of every nature. Unmarried and a nonmother, she knew with certainty that a child could not have strengthened the bonds between her and Sartre; nor did she wish his existence to be reflected and prolonged in the existence of another. He was sufficient unto himself and to her, and she too was sufficient unto herself (18).

Livi condemns the Church for placing Beauvoir's *The Second Sex* and *The Mandarins* on the Index in May 1956. She scorns the opinion of the official Vatican newspaper, *L'Osservatore Romano*, that those works "conceal a subtle poison" and contain "immoral doctrines that trample on good morals and the holiness of the family" (121).

The writers whom Livi chooses to delineate are women who sublimated marriage and maternity into works of greater worth. For them, home, family, and social life were inadequate expressions of themselves. They worked instead to know and control the mysterious forces of existence. Livi offers various examples of women who from their early years rejected the gray reality of family life and took refuge in the written page. She focuses as well on women who fell into marriage as "into a social fatality" (210), but who eventually came to question the ancestral conditioning and male pressure which had constrained them to live as "perfect wife and mother" (153).

Proposed as models for emulation are women who will no longer allow their flesh to be "dismembered" by childbirth, who are no longer disposed to focus their lives on "creatures and objects," will no longer be "married to the home," and no longer pretend to be the mothers that society expects. "No, madre no," she writes (145).

Anna Banti, absorbed in her research and writing, had offered literary guidance to young Grazia Livi, who remembered that she "cared not at all about children" (165); whereas Gertrude Stein, discoverer par excellence of the truth that there is no stereotyped woman, believed that "every existence has its own rhythm, which resembles none other" (67). Emboldened by such examples, Livi champions the woman's right to a consciousness, an awareness, and a knowledge of what she truly is. And this is anything but the archetypal figure of the universal mother. What she proposes is a prototype of another woman, a new woman, a "paper" woman—that is, a woman who writes, who will be "cut out of new patterns…with uncertain scissors" (125).

Virginia Woolf had written to her sister Vanessa, in a moment of crisis and at a time when patriarchal society required girls to be transformed into married women, that she was twenty-nine, not married, a failure, without children, and "not a writer" (143). Yet it was precisely this woman writer, as Livi shows us, who gave to herself and to Everywoman an ineffable quality of completeness. It was she who arduously created around herself a concentrated atmosphere, "all of paper and ink," in which she plumbed "*l'interiorità della donna*" (the inner life of the woman) (54-6). In poetic terms, Livi describes Woolf's inner life as liquefying and spreading to form lakes and rivers. Out of images of overflowing waters, fertilizing floods, and porous clay, Livi extracts the body of a triumphant woman (59).

One of Livi's chapters, constructed in an encapsulating drumbeat style, is a reconstruction of the life of a lesser contemporary writer, Carla Lonzi, art historian, critic, poet, and feminist. Lonzi had married and, "incredibly,…blindly given in to biological imposition" and became a mother. Like an automaton, she pushed the baby carriage "in a paralyzing female way" (210). Inside her, all was dead: her interest in art, her time for study, her plans of independence, her identity: "I was as though submerged in an inner catastrophe," she confided to her diary. "Within me an unknown woman was in the throes of death" (210).

The drowsiness of the baby is counterpoised to the activity of the mother's mind. Even as she rocks the carriage, her diary is open on her knees; she listens to silence, straining her ears to hear; in her concentration on her thoughts, she no longer feels her own body (211).

Her writer-husband had always refused to help in the home; nor would he make a single parental gesture toward the child. In his autobiography, his wife, only a "symbolic creature," a "maternal image," disappears entirely (217, 220). For him, she is "*la donna non nata*" (the unborn woman) (214). What will allow her belatedly to be born is the 1,300-page diary published in 1978, in which she analyzes herself and questions her existence until she discerns her own authenticity. "Everything is clear to me," she then writes. "I am free" (215). The bonds of marriage and motherhood had been broken in order that she might devote all her energies toward achieving recognition as "the conscience of a feminist" peeping out at history (216, 221). The essence of *Le lettere del mio nome* is that writing is the new woman's maternity—what William James might have called the "moral equivalent of maternity."

"I formed the page and at the same time my identity," Livi writes (167). If men had snatched the word from women in the past, the time has now come when the woman gives birth to the word "on the written page, strong as never before" (148). If, in the past, men had disposed freely of their female vessels, women now are reclaiming their bodies, Livi writes—and bodies "no longer sad, obtuse, dulled by pregnancies, but free for play, initiative, eros." Though men once snuffed out feminine gifts of expression, women are now reviving those gifts in their own dancing, singing, and painting (148).

Livi's caveat is a reminder that writing is a solitary, irrevocable calling, one whose successful pursuit requires obstinacy and resolve. The woman writer must ever be on guard against falling into the traps of attachments and conventions (202). But the slate of letters that form her name offers a compelling portrait of the intellectually grown woman, released from primitive urges toward "untamed" maternity, and bent on improving and elevating herself. By refining her goals, tempering the tools of her art and of her language, the creative woman enhances the phylogeny of the race as a whole.

The Short Story

The authors of the twenty short stories contained in the volume entitled *Racconta 2* (Recount 2, 1993) have, as it were, cast to the winds the seeds of maternity and allowed them to take root in some unusual printed pages. At least six of the writers included in the volume touch on the theme of reproduction of the species in a macabre, humorous, or scornful way.

Maternity linked to death is the subject of two stories, one set in the last century, the other in a future one: "Pandora," by Elisabetta Chicco, and Pia Pera's "La mamma di Ramon Garcia," respectively. In the former, inopportune babies and unwanted bastards, treated by society with the same indifference as dead rats flung by their tails into garbage bins, are gathered and embalmed by an eccentric marquis to embellish his lonely garrets. In "La mamma di Ramon Garcia," Pia Pera casts heavy doubts on the supposedly immutable concepts of maternity as she ponders the use of the female body and the worth of children in a world of the future. Civilization, to this satirist, is nothing more than "procreation for the express purpose of killing." In a paradoxical metaphor, she envisages a "more rational breeding of humans" in a production line of female bodies that give birth to babies, producers in their turn of transplant organs. Breakthroughs in palingenesis, Pera tells us, will be a side product of humanity's new endeavors.

Two contributors to the collection ferociously satirize male sexual fantasies as secret dreams revolving around the fecundation of all the women in their harems,[23]—or the enjoyment of the results of "permanent penetration," described in a daring desecration of the language of the "Hail Mary."[24] As for the results, Mara Cini tells us of a certain "inevitable reproduction" filling Italy's homes with "children like bread crumbs strewn over the table after an undigested meal."[25]

An unforgettable embodiment of the dark and sinister aspect of maternity is the huge black form which is seen in a Turkish mosque by the heroine of "A stomaco nudo" (Midriff). Crouched on the ground, this potent mass of one hundred kilos of rolls of fat, round breasts and hidden arms "must be a woman,"[26] she realizes. Slowly the creature performs the rituals of scratching and currying each part of its body, putting its fingers into its mouth one by one, combing and rubbing its hair, much like the endless grooming with which our primate cousins attend to their relationships. Then the "woman" mechanically unravels a piece of woolen cloth—more gestures connoting long, arduous efforts that serve no purpose. The figure represents fullness and futility. We may take it to represent the body.

By way of contrast, and representative perhaps of the head, is the forty-year-old Sara, the heroine, who is unable to shake off the "anatomical fact" of her womanhood. Sara is "pregnant in the brain." Her thoughts cause her nausea, headache, and vomiting. Although she is in Istanbul with a lover, her act of love "lights up like a fire," but only to leave her "deflated like a womb emptied of never-wanted children" (250).

Sara had wished for a child in her youth, when she had naively believed that "pleasure would gush magically from the male body and then a child would be born" (251). Now, however, she knows that pleasure in sex is an "infantile desire" and that in the end the woman is left "fat, swollen, peaceful, and dying" (254). At the thought of her lover's expectation of sexual activity each evening, Sara is consumed by "opaque emptiness." Her brain does battle with her vagina. After the sexual act, she feels she is left with only her head—enormous, resting on a cushion, suspended in a void (250-51).

Now her mind is filled with unpleasant thoughts and memories—of the fat female figure, of her own mother, of her grandmother, all the links in the monstrous chain that fetters women through the ages. She would like to exorcise from her body and her head her mother's haunting, taunting question—"Do you want to wind up with gray hair without even having a child?" (256).

Finally, however, the space in Sara's head expands, swallows up her thoughts, grows heavy, takes on corporeality, and acquires a body, arms, and hands. This new being frees her and gives her the feeling of being a "liberated pregnant womb" (258). Deserting her lover, Sara uses her head to focus her eyes sharply on the fat mother figure whom she had previously seen through a veil darkly, but who now becomes the vehicle for her liberation.

Maria Teresa Di Lascia

Compleanno (Birthday, 1994) by Maria Teresa Di Lascia is an autobiographical short story in the form of a letter, published after the author's early death from cancer. The protagonist is a married woman caught between an indifferent, unfaithful husband and a domineering mother who casts a long shadow over the couple's existence. "I married you," the protagonist reproachfully reminds her absent husband, "so that you could take me away from her" (25).

In this felicitously constructed retrospective letter, she recalls the mixture of fear and desire she had felt on first suspecting she was pregnant. She had shuddered at the thought, yet hoped that the pregnancy might save her marriage. She had believed that her new condition would give her the strength to come to a showdown with her husband. While scorning women who used the power of the uterus to trap a man, she had intended to resort to the maneuver: "I would dare to give you the jolt you needed," she writes; "I would impose my new strength and we would have a child" (27).

Now, after the fact, she can honestly admit that it is only because the pregnancy did not materialize that she can write with such conviction. Nor will she ever again use her uterus as an instrument of retaliation. Her "retrospective courage," as she calls it, she now contemns as the pathetic "stuff of cowards" (27).

In lieu of husband and baby, the protagonist had dedicated herself to reading and study; but her new direction had been cruelly interrupted by a diagnosis of incurable cancer that offered her but a single year of life. Her letter to her husband ends with a reassessment of that life, which she now judges as "less inconclusive" than she had feared, thanks to her studies, and spun with at least "a thread of wisdom" (30), thanks to her avoidance of the maternal trap.

Susanna Tamaro

The voice of a child serves as a death metaphor in Susanna Tamaro's epistolary short story, "Sotto la neve" (Under the snow), in her collection *Per voce sola* (Voice solo, 1991). The protagonist, a mature and sophisticated woman, dreams that she is a tiny prisoner in a doll's house, lying on her tiny bed. She hears a voice, at first soft, then loud, of a child singing. Attempting to rise from the bed, she is suffocated by a sheet of ice that drowns out her screams.[27]

As the story opens, the reader learns that the protagonist is a successful and esteemed translator-interpreter who travels extensively for her profession. In contrast to Clara Sereni's descriptions of the dirty and disorderly homes of retarded and insane children and their slatternly mothers, Tamaro plays upon the comfort, warmth, and orderliness of the single woman's home, to which it is always a pleasure to return. Such a home, in "Sotto la neve," is furnished and decorated in the best of taste, a place of refuge, a frame for the gestures and habits of the occupant, to whom it gives a sense of order and perfection (100).

The letter-writing protagonist describes herself as the "heroine of a novel" (106), the villain being the man she met when she was yet a student.

In the sixth month of their friendship, she had become pregnant, and he had deserted her. When she learned that the father of the child she bore had disappeared, "everything around her crumbled"—but not, she adds bitterly, the fetus (107). In a later letter to her son she would write: "I want you to know you're a child of love. Or at least what I thought was love," admitting that the "love" which had conceived the child lasted only a fraction of a second (108).

The fetus continued to grow and could no longer be hidden, yet she did not seek an abortion. Only later would she realize that this was a wrong decision. Since she was still a minor, her parents decided that she should renounce the child legally even before it was born, and assign it to a "real" family instead (109). This plan remained in effect despite the death of the heroine's mother, whom she hated for having, as it seemed to her, first given her life and then taken it away, day after day, drop by drop (102). Turning now to the Madonna, she prayed for the miracle of the father's return. This miracle being denied, the solitary heroine delivered her child, in extreme pain because she defied the gynecologist's instructions and tightened every muscle in her body as firmly as she could: "I knew this was dangerous for both of us," she writes to her son, but "I wanted that risk. Dead together, at the same instant" (110). Both survived, however, and the mother caught her first and last glimpse of her child.

Each year, on the anniversary of the day the child was conceived, her belly begins to swell; she feels nausea and somnolence after the first month, followed by strong pain after nine months—the same pain as when the child was born (112). She mocks herself for having believed that, like the Madonna, she had conceived as the result of intercession from on high. That was before she had been enlightened on the subject of "hysterical pregnancies" (113).

Eventually the heroine reached the age of menopause. But even now her belly swelled again. This time she understood it as "a punishment, the price I would have to pay for my cowardice until the end of my days" (113). Hers is a self-fulfilling prophecy: the doctor confirms that her womb holds "a tumor almost as big as a baby." No longer life-producing, her womb now hatches death. The deadly, uncontrolled cancer cells, personified as a growing fetus, spread throughout her body, colonizing first her liver, then her brain. At the thought of her imminent death, the heroine feels "euphoria" (114-15).

      *   *   *   *   *   *   *   *

Writers of short stories in the 1990s joined with their counterparts in the fields of essay and drama in looking at maternity from a variety of new viewpoints. This group of Italian women authors, so far from being bemused by the maternal mystique, see creativity as more appealing than procreation. As the century closes, these women of Roman Catholic upbringing seem to have reached a settled conclusion—at least for themselves—that "sacred maternity" is neither an ideal, nor a privilege, nor even an advantage.

From "Donne e Management." Sì Magazine, *January 1998.*
(Courtesy of Sergio Ruzzier)

Conclusion
ℬℭ
Italy Awaits the New Woman

R unning through many of the works of Italian women writers is the theme of the "opening of the woman's eyes." The serpent, tempting Eve in the Garden of Eden, promised that her eyes would be opened to knowledge and to the consciousness of good and evil. God, in punitive response, brought down upon her the pain of childbirth. "I will multiply your pains in childbearing. You shall give birth to your children in pain" (Genesis 3:16). But today's woman rejects the idea of punishment via the reproductive apparatus with which she has been saddled since her origins. She is determined that her eyes shall be opened even though her reproductive channels remain closed.[1]

The blindfolded childbearing women of Italian feminine writing of past centuries attempted to accommodate themselves to—or, in rare cases, break the bonds of—the familiar, socially approved sexual roles. Although the "wanting children syndrome" (Fiumanò, 28) served in some instances as a way of taking revenge on a husband or parents, the average woman desired a child mainly to fulfill social expectations and perhaps to validate her nurturing capabilities. Her aspirations were largely shaped by the pleasure attributed to motherhood and by sensations that involved the body more than the mind (Fiumanò, 8, 34).

Such women lived in a closed circle, too weak to make their escape from primitive fertility preoccupations and too conditioned to question the maternal myth upheld by the rank and file. Only the rare, exceptional woman succeeded in launching a career and demonstrating her creativity outside the fixed parameters of maternity.

The belief that the mother/child relationship would satisfy a woman's longing for union was deeply embedded in Italian culture. Religion offered structured meaning and purpose in terms of the root metaphors of the Holy Family and the powerful but beneficent Mother of God. But the expectations nurtured in such soil inevitably collided with the experiential reality of the powerlessness and hopelessness of the woman caught in the toils of the paradoxical, Mediterranean-Mariolater patriarchal society.

Undoubtedly, the mothers of Leonardo da Vinci and Dante Alighieri, as Neera claimed, contributed enormously, through their offspring, to the progress of humanity. Hope springs eternal in the mother's breast that her child, whether naturally or artificially fecundated, will be born an artist or a genius of some sort. But how many millions of Italian mothers have in reality, in their mindless childbearing, expelled from their wombs more and more functionally impaired children, creating more and more poverty, disease and unemployment, particularly in the conservative, Catholic South? Naples' squalid *"granili"* swarming with wretched, rickety humans are "a demonstration," wrote Italy's eminent neorealist, Anna Maria Ortese, "of the decline of a species" (*Il mare non bagna Napoli*, [1953], 63).

The works we have examined by women writers in revolt against maternity reflect a dramatic change in the way Italian women view themselves and their function. All are aware that the prolonged, intense style of mothering which has hitherto been dictated by Italian culture can only produce daughters who will themselves be eminently fitted to perpetuate the same outworn model. But rather than reiterating the traditional idealization of motherhood, all of these newer writers now focus upon the hatred and chaos that can lie beneath a surface devotion to husband and children.

Indifferent to ecclesiastical censure, today's Italian women authors reject the traditional Mary/mother parallel and allege that the seeming madonna next door may be just as sullied as her prostitute sisters. They show how State and Church, while continuing to pay homage to the archetypal mother-on-a-pedestal, deny her the needed protection against violent husbands, marital rape, sexual abuse, and the poverty that in some cases has been known to drive her to infanticide (Morris, 155).

Some young authors ponder the idea that a baby can be "manufactured" as a consumer product without ever having to be "conceived." Conception (from the Latin *concipere*, to "take together" or "hold together") can in fact be just as well viewed from an intellectual and spiritual as from a biological angle—as we note, for example, at the beginning of the Gospel According to St. John. A woman capable of procreation may also be able to "conceive" an idea, a book or a project (Fiumanò, 18-19).

In seeking an identity distinct from the fertility function, the protagonists of our women writers are striving for fulfillment not through sexual passion and maternity but through self-knowledge and even self-love. Despite limitations and failures, they are groping their way toward a personal vision of moral responsibility and communal obligation which will both enable their survival and dignify their self-awareness.

In their hunger for the kind of intellectual growth that will enable them to change themselves and the world around them, they are reexamining the human condition in quest of a higher consciousness. Rejecting the notion that "the family must go on" in the accustomed way—i.e., through the exploitation of the woman's body to the detriment of her mind (and the closing of her eyes)—they scorn the popular idea that "any normal woman" must wish to become a mother. How can one be sure, they ask, that motherhood itself is "normal" from the standpoint of historical development, or that the expectations of our epoch are consistent with whatever ideas may be governing the wider, immemorial universe?

In overcoming the biases of reactionary ideology, the authors of the works examined in this volume herald a new concept of womanhood. Pregnancy, in the face of modern technical possibilities, is no longer of prime importance as a source of either hope or dread. Keeping pace with their withdrawal from the maternal role is an opening out of professional opportunities for those women who can focus their creative energies in a new type of life built around scholarship, teaching, writing, journalism, art, science, healing, political activism, and so forth.

In 1492, an Italian male explorer from an underpopulated Europe discovered a new world inhabited by hitherto unknown peoples. In our overpopulated world, the twenty-first-century Italian woman seems likely to direct her talents not toward procreation as such but toward the creation of a rational and well-ordered society in demographic equilibrium. National identity in the traditional sense may come to have increasingly less meaning as Italy becomes part of a Europe whose ethnic makeup is changing and whose inhabitants are beginning to regard themselves more as peoples of the Earth than as members of a particular national or even multinational community.

From the point of view of the human species, it matters little who is born and who dies, provided some die to leave room for those being born. Nor, perhaps, does it matter from this wider viewpoint whether humans are reproduced by natural or artificial means (Fiumanò, 16). It is, in any case, high time to discontinue the cult of fertility as an end in itself, at least as far as human beings are concerned.

The new trend away from all-encompassing motherhood may well disturb the sense of continuity in traditional individuals and groups. But the challenge has been deliberately accepted by some Italian women writers. In subverting existing codes and the myth of *italianità* or Italianness, they anticipate a restructuring of meaning and purpose for both the individual and the community. They are even forcing the Italian religious tradition to recast its root metaphors in order to reach compatibility with more universal realities.

As we have suggested, the writers we have looked at seem to be conjuring up a new type of female character as the main protagonist of twenty-first-century literature. The new woman, as her outlines begin to clarify, offers solid proof of her ability to reshape herself dramatically by sheer will power. Taking direct control of the most basic aspects of her biology, she is willing to impose moral restraint upon her own appetites; but she demands in return that she herself shall choose her chains and establish the limits on her maternity, rather than having them imposed by male husbands, priests, or legislators. The Church would have women accept no limits on their maternity, but without limits there can be no freedom, and it is primarily physical and mental freedom that the new woman seeks.

Some observers believe that women may be on the verge of creating a third gender, that of the self-declared "nonmother woman," who, freed from the overriding concern with maternity and motherhood, might constitute a female power base at the center of intellectual life. The "nonmother woman" would transcend the rhythms of woman's biological clock, which have heretofore dominated her from menarche to menopause. She would be a woman in movement toward higher goals, with a new, specifically female world outlook no longer determined by her childbearing function. Most of the contemporary writers we have looked at propose a new, still vaguely delineated feminine archetype—a "woman in progress," as distinguished from the traditional "woman in childbed." New wealth could flow from the opposition and balance between the two, each of them courageous, secure, and free to express herself, the one through Art, the other through maternity.

Procreation does not of course directly undermine a woman's intellectual capacities nor preclude artistic creativity. Women neither expect nor desire to shed their biological-biographical experience or to emerge as strange, asexual, aseptic, improbably neuter animals. Nor can all women be intellectuals, as Anna Banti might have liked (Nozzoli, 94). But woman's knowledge must include the biological, the anatomical, political, economic, and cosmological as well, for all are equally essential if humanity's quality of life is to be significantly improved.

Women undoubtedly carry within themselves a baggage of archetypal echoes strictly dependent on their being sexed. But what endures best, and what helps one to endure, are the values contained in humanity's civilizing impulses, especially the values associated with Art in its broadest sense. The human question for women is whether they want or are able to live forever in the "maternal" phase of their existence, or are prepared to be "dematernalized."

Italy has outlived its era of fertility goddesses. The myths surrounding motherhood may be "the last thing to fade," but, like the smile of the Cheshire cat, "fade they do." Plodding maternity seems to be dissolving into revolutionary new concepts; old frameworks are being quickly torn down and new ones erected. Italian women look forward to possibilities of modification and innovation, the breaking of existing configurations, and the opening of new fields for the release of their energies. Looking forward to a new era, Italy's new myth may be the antitype of the goddesses of fertility who too long remained unchallenged by any other concept of creativity and too long held sway over women's fecundity. Perhaps a new and different "Bona Dea" will soon emerge to symbolize the reorientation.

Mircea Eliade saw women's fertility, eroticism and nudity as centers of "sacred energy" and sources of complex ceremonials.[2] Perhaps the new woman's sacred energy will lie not in her body but in her female mind, as possible source of a complex new cult. It may be that more and more women, turning away from the strictly biological routine of reproduction, will use their bodies in such combination with their minds that the phylogeny of the human female and the entire human race will benefit. Our evolutionary path can certainly be modified through the incorporation of technical advances that can alter the human genetic trajectory.[3]

Homo Sapiens has made a long climb from his mystery-surrounded past to an unknowable future. Perhaps *Virgo Sapiens* will now at length begin her own climb from the queendom of the maternal to a more scientific knowledge of fecundation and reproduction, and ultimately to the noosphere.

How should the new woman direct her mental "sacred energy"? What role should she play as geophysicist, oceanographer, biologist, or planetary scientist? Should she continue merely to aspire toward the replication of traditionally male roles, or should she strike out in new directions where she may enjoy a competitive advantage? Are there activities she might drop—such as maternity—the better to focus her efforts? How can she encourage other women, and women's organizations, to join her? How can she engage her capacity to contemplate the expansion of life in its many forms throughout the universe?

Astronomers and bioastronomers look to the heavens, hoping to decipher the mysterious link between the comets and the first stirrings of life on earth, and searching for tidings of cosmic fertility. Women, in their own quest for the makings of life, may also be breaking through to a new way of thinking that radically transcends traditional intellectual modes.

Notes

Preface

1. The most recent statistics show a decrease of 9.8% between 1990 and 1993 (Istituto Nazionale di Statistica, *Popolazione, Nascite, Caratteristiche demografiche e sociali. Anno 1993.* Roma: Istat), 53.
2. Alice Balint, "Love for the Mother and Mother Love," cited in Roszika Parker, *Mother Love/Mother Hate*, 103-4. An unusual illustration of "civilized maternity," involving a wide divergence of interest between mother and children, may be seen in the case of a woman in England who, after fertility treatment, planned to give birth to octuplets, apparently for publicity and financial gain. Cf. "Mother 'plans to have octuplets'," *The Sunday Times* (London), August 11, 1996, 20.

Chapter 1. Ancient Fertility Goddesses

1. In a parallel case of iconographic borrowing, the figure of Horus harpooning his enemy Setekh, represented in the form of a crocodile, seems to have served as a model for Saint George killing the dragon (Encyc. Brit. XI:738).
2. The chthonic aspects of the Black Demeter, of Isis, and of other black deities of paganism later found an echo in Christianity's so-called Black Madonnas. Cf. Marvin H. Pope, *Song of Songs: A New Translation with Introduction and Commentary* (New York: Doubleday, 1978), 307-18, cited in Jaroslav Pelikan, *Mary Through the Centuries,* 78; Lucia Chiavola Birnbaum, *Black Madonnas: feminism, religion and politics in Italy* (Ithaca, NY: Northeastern University Press, 1993), 23, passim.
3. The sow reproduces by multiple births, farrowing around eight to twelve pigs in the domesticated state. Tradition ascribes the old French family name Porcelet ("piglet") to the multiple births of nine children to one of its early female members. Cf. Paolo Picca, *Fecondità miracolose,* 5.
4. A striking example is that of the Syrian-Canaanite goddess Anat, who, after slaughtering the enemy of her brother and consort, Baal, cut her lifeless victim in pieces and burned, ground, and sowed him in a field, repeating in essence what the farmer routinely does in restoring life to the earth. In destroying and sowing the corpse, Anat encompasses Baal's rebirth (Encyc. Brit. II:942a).
5. A particularly venerated Madonnella, once located under a Roman bridge (formerly known as "Quattro Capi" from the pair of two-headed herms at its farther end), was carried away in one of the Tiber floods, but its candle is claimed to have miraculously remained alight amid the torrential waters, with the result that the image is now preserved and venerated in the nearby church of San Giovanni Calibita on the Tiber Island.

6. In modern Greek literature, the emblematic old woman of Skiathos, although not a divinity, was determined to kill as many baby girls as she could because she saw herself, her daughters, and all the women of the Greek island so full of suffering and misery. Cf. Alexandros Papadiamantis' short novel, *Fonissa.*

7. *Nuraghi* are megalithic towers with a large inner cavity (*nur*). In the Sardinian sanctuaries containing sacred wells, female divinities were worshiped, as evidenced by wall and architrave reliefs of breasts, bovine horns, and lunar crescents (cf. Giani Gallino, 156).

8. One such grotto, in Calabria, is described by Armanda Guiducci in *La donna non è gente* (below). The psychologist Tilde Giani Gallino has seen in the grotto-like niches of mosques (*mihrab*), with their white, breast-shaped decorations and their fountains, a representation of the uterus and bosom of the Great Mother as conceived by Islamic architects through the workings of the collective unconscious (*La ferita e il re*, 191-2).

9. This expansionist procedure recalls the biblical exhortation to the Israelites: "Enlarge the place of thy tent, and let them stretch forth the curtains of thine habitations: spare not, lengthen thy cords, and strengthen thy stakes; for thou shalt break forth on the right hand and on the left; and thy seed shall inherit the Gentiles, and make the desolate cities to be inhabited" (Isaiah 54:2-3).

10. The Roman territory itself had expanded by the fourth century B.C.E. to an area of 4,500 sq.mi., with a population of at least one million (Grant, 57-8).

11. Now preserved in the museum of Bologna. Elsewhere, Thalna appears as a protective maternal figure close to Tinia-Jupiter.

12. The name is associated with words connoting young maturity (e.g. *juvenis*) and so may denote a marriageable woman.

13. The tutelary fairy Mélusine in French romance has been fancifully identified with Juno Lucina. Screams in apprehension of personal pain are referred to in French as "*cris de Mélusine*"

14. Equivalent to a promise when unfastened, the girdle when fastened symbolized negation and has been seen as a specular image of Mary, the virgin bride (Warner, 320).

15. Down to modern times, herdsmen and shepherds of eastern Europe celebrated on April 23 a similar festival dedicated to Saint George, their patron saint of cattle, horses, and wolves (Frazer, II:530).

16. Also of pagan origin are litanies, a form of responsive prayer in which the priest voices invocations or petitions, to each of which the worshipers answer with short, often repeated responses akin to acclamations.

17. For the metaphysical significance of milk, see Warner, Chapter 13, entitled "The Milk of Paradise," pp. 225-39.

18. Tertullian in the third century described an old Christian version of baptism in which milk and honey were administered to the neophytes as a promise of their rebirth in a new world in which they would acquire knowledge (Warner, 227).

19. The feast celebrated in a town near L'Aquila on the first Thursday in May goes

back to a pagan snake-raising ritual which was Christianized and dedicated in the Middle Ages to Saint Dominic of Foligno, who was believed to cure miraculously those bitten by poisonous snakes (Paccosi, 8).

20. The position of the priest on the donkey probably was meant to signify greater enjoyment of divine presence. The Syrian-born emperor Elagabalus (218-222 C.E.) entered Rome walking backwards behind the black conical stone fetish of his local sun-god Baal, whose worship he imposed on the Roman world.

21. Many aspects of the Christian ritual of baptism reflect pagan practices. In ancient Greece, the house door of a newborn was decorated with olive branches if the child was a boy, with bands of wool if a girl. The women who had assisted in the birth washed their hands to purify themselves from a contact considered polluting. Two of these women then lifted the child and carried it rapidly around the hearth. The feast terminated with a banquet at which the guests presented gifts for the child.

A comparable ceremony in ancient Rome took place on the day of purification (*lustratio*, as of the fields), which was celebrated eight days after the birth of a girl, nine days after that of a boy. On that day the child (*pupus*) received its official name and was doused with purifying water in the presence of the parents, relatives, and guests. Sacrifices were made to the gods, especially in honor of Juno and Hercules, the latter being the benevolent *numen* who kept evil spirits away. Around the neck of a freeborn child was hung a *bulla* or amulet, which was laid aside by the girl at matrimony and by the boy when he donned the *toga virilis*.

Chapter 2. The Mutations of Madonna Worship and the Mutability of Motherhood

1. Still other dedicatees were Saints Anne, Bridget, Catherine of Alexandria, Elizabeth, Euphemia, Eurosia, Faustina, Flora, Rita, and Zita (Dini, 79, passim).

2. *Maria lactans*, a type whose earliest image, dating from before the third century C.E., may be seen in the Roman Catacomb of Santa Priscilla. The symbolism of milk and breastfeeding is analyzed by Marilyn Yalom in *A History of the Breast* (1997) and by Warner, 225-39. Milk as Logos in the nuptial symbolism of Christ and his Bride the Church is noted by James, 197-8.

3. The genesis of the *Magnificat* is studied by Warner, 31-33.

4. Elsa Morante, who frequently highlights the superstitious element in southern Italian manners, lends comic effect to the listing of Madonnas invoked by a simple, pious Neapolitan woman in her 1957 novel, *L'isola di Arturo* (p. 93): "Ella non credeva a una sola Madonna, ma a molte: la Madonna di Pompei, la Vergine del Rosario, la Madonna del Carmine e non so quali altre; ma...la più straordinaria, la più miracolosa, la più cortese, era la Madonna di Piedigrotta. Poi, al di là di tutte queste Vergini e dei loro Bambini, c'era Dio."

Roberto Morozzo della Rocca studies the wide variety of Madonnas invoked by Italian soldiers and chaplains during World War I in "Il culto dei santi tra i soldati" (Cult of the saints among soldiers) in Emma Fattorini, ed., *Santi, culti, simboli nell'età della secolarizzazione (1815-1915)*, 225-34.

5. Woman's womb would begin to be demystified and "desacralized" by the Futurists in the early twentieth century (cf. F. T. Marinetti and Enif Robert, *Un ventre di donna. Romanzo chirurgico* [1919]), although Futurism would pave the way for the Fascist ideals of male virility and female fecundity (see below).

6. This "most venerated doll of Rome," Margaret Fuller wrote in the nineteenth century, "has received more splendid gifts than any other idol." Its abode she described as "the church of Aracoeli...near the site of the Temple of Capitoline Jove, which certainly saw nothing more idolatrous" (cited in Joseph Jay Deiss, *The Roman Years of Margaret Fuller*, 122-23).

7. Otto von Simson, *The Gothic Cathedral* (1956), cited in Pelikan, 125.

8. The theory of maternity as a "long moment" in a woman's life is analyzed in *Parto e maternità. Momenti della biografia femminile* (1980). The maternal experience, according to some scholars, provokes a "temporal irradiation" which theoretically explains why women's time references are different from those of men (*Maria, Medea e le altre*, 223).

9. An example is the medieval Madonna with Saints Praxedis and Pudentia in the crypt of the church of San Prassede in Rome. The prominence given to the Virgin's girdle and the gesture of her left hand may be interpreted as alluding to her miraculous maternity, while her jeweled crown suggests the themes of glorification and incorruptibility (Feudale, 17).

10. Two other panels of the seated Virgin are also thought to portray the Madonna of Expectation: one in the Museo dell'Opera del Duomo in Florence, attributed to the atelier of Bernardo Daddi and dated 1334, and the other the so-called "Magnificat" in the Vatican Pinacoteca. Two further fourteenth-century examples of the Madonna del Parto, both in the style of the Orcagna brothers (next note), may be found in the Museo Bandini in Fiesole and in the Vatican Pinacoteca. In addition, Rossello di Jacopo Franchi (ca. 1377-1456) painted a pregnant Mary early in the fifteenth century, while in north Italian painting of the late fourteenth and early fifteenth centuries, one finds in the Verona Gallery a pregnant Madonna in the central panel of the 1428 polyptych attributed to the school of Stefano da Verona, and, in the Academy of Venice, a variously attributed Madonna del Parto from the Venetian church of Santa Caterina (Feudale, 11-12).

11. Nardo di Cione was the brother of Andrea Orcagna, author of the large sculptural relief of the Dormition and Assumption of the Virgin (1359) in the guild oratory of Or San Michele. This piece of devotional imagery, focused upon Mary's eternal glory and incorruptibility, is one of the most notable surviving examples of the expressive art that sprang up in Tuscany in the wake of the Black Death (1347-48), symbol *par excellence* of physical corruptibility. Cf. Millard Meiss, *Painting in Florence and Siena after the Black Death* (1964).

12. Other biblical passages having to do with the fertilization of the earth and lending themselves to a Marian earth symbolism are Psalms 72:6, Hosea 6:3 and 14:6, and Ecclesiasticus 24:42 (Cassee, 96). Later reflections of a related line of thought are found in the works of the nineteenth-century moralistic painter Giovanni Segantini, whose "Il castigo delle lussuriose" (The Punishment of the Wanton Women, 1891) and "Le cattive madri" (The Unnatural Mothers, 1894) feature hovering weightless women who have refused to become mothers. Unborn babies gnaw at the breasts of these deviates who are denied rootedness in the earth, Goddess-Mother par excellence. In "La fonte del male" (The Fountain of Evil, 1897), Segantini chastises female perversity in the figure of a naked woman (Eve?) gazing at her reflection in a uterus-shaped fountain where "knowledge" writhes among primeval serpents, familiar sexual symbols (Bram Dijkstra, *Idoli di perversità. La donna nell'immaginario artistico*, 213).

13. A pale reflection of this attitude is the still not wholly extinct practice of pregnant women in concealing themselves and their condition out of "*pudore*" (modesty, decency, reserve, shame). Related to the hiding of pregnancy was the disqualification of gravid women to serve as godmothers, a function presupposing a sinlessness thought to be inconsistent with the gravid state (Neiger, 22-3).

14. The well-known, deeply venerated statue of the Mother and Child by Jacopo Sansovino (1486-1570) in the church of Sant'Agostino in Rome is called the "Madonna del Parto" not because she is herself pregnant but because she is frequently invoked by pregnant women seeking a safe delivery as well as by married couples desiring a child.

15. Warner (*Sola fra le donne,* 33-34, 215) analyzes the popular version of Christ's birth as well as the influence on fifteenth-century paintings of Saint Bridget's vision in which Mary "gave birth on her knees and immediately adored Him."

   Nativity and Epiphany scenes were special favorites not only of the Renaissance painters but of the designers of creches, popular three-dimensional representations with carefully modeled figures of the Holy Family, angels, Magi, shepherds, and farm animals that were set up in homes, churches, even in ancient pagan monuments. Garry Wills studies the artistic, theological, and political roots, as well as the propaganda value of creches in Italy in "The Art & Politics of the Nativity," *New York Review of Books*, December 19, 1996, 75-82. Not until Christmas 1996 did Italians begin to question the propriety of installing Catholic creches in the public schools.

16. By devoting an entire page of titles to the subjects of "Maternity," "Maternal affection," "Maternal caress," "Maternal duty," etc., the *World Painting Index* (Patricia Pate Havlice, ed., II, 1693) shows how many artists have portrayed this archaic, idealized mother-child relationship, inspired by what has been called the fantasy of "infantile bliss and plenitude within the mother-child fusion" (Parker, 35). "[T]he paintings of Madonna and Child have been so frequent," another writer affirms, "that it would be possible to write a history of the idea of children on the basis of them" (Pelikan, 222-23).

17. Correggio in the sixteenth century accentuated the note of intimacy and domesticity with an astonishing softness and beauty of painterly texture in such masterpieces as the "Madonna of the Basket" (National Gallery, London), the "Virgin Adoring the Child" (Uffizi Gallery), and the altarpiece of the "Madonna of Saint Francis" (Dresden Gallery).

18. Jean de La Bruyère and Thomas Mann, *inter alios*, were not to be misled by such fictions. The former wrote in *Les Caractères* XI, 50: "Children are haughty, disdainful, irascible, envious, indiscreet, self-seeking, lazy, fickle, cowardly, intemperate, untruthful, secretive; they laugh and they cry easily; they experience inordinate joy and bitter affliction over the slightest matter; they don't want to suffer hurt but are quick to inflict it: they are already men" (quoted in Morris Bishop, ed., *A Survey of French Literature* I, 275).

　　　　"For small children are to that extent 'innocent' in that they are unconscious," Mann wrote in *Felix Krull*; "but that they are so in the sense of angelic purity is without doubt a sentimental superstition which would not stand the test of an objective examination" (*Stories of Three Decades*, 370-71).

19. The imagery of the *Stabat Mater* has continued to inspire composers throughout the ages, having been set to choral and instrumental music by Giovanni Battista Pergolesi, Franz Joseph Haydn, Gioacchino Rossini, and Antonin Dvorak. Giuseppe Verdi's *Quattro pezzi sacri* (1898) include a *Stabat Mater* as well as a Te Deum, the *Laudi alla Vergine Maria* on a text of Dante, and an *Ave Maria*. (Charles-François Gounod's *Ave Maria* [Meditation] in the sentimental manner was adapted from Bach's C Major Prelude.)

20. The Italian Jesuit Anton Francesco Bellati published an 88-page volume entitled *Le obbligazioni del marito verso la moglie* (The obligations of the husband toward the wife, 1711), while his posthumous *Le obbligazioni della donna verso il marito* (The obligations of the woman toward the husband, 1757) is 256 pages in length (Pier Giorgio Camaiani, "L'immagine femminile," 434).

21. Thus, inferiorization of the woman is found in her maternity. Veneration for motherhood brought about no corresponding rise in her social status. Contemporary Italian women researchers have linked the medical profession with the Church as institutions which on pretexts of morality and science have notably contributed to the undermining of woman's position in Italian society (*Parto e maternità*, 223).

22. Cf. Oliver Wendell Holmes, *The contagiousness of Puerperal Fever* (1843) and Ignaz Semmelweiss, *Die Ätiologie, der Begriff und die Prophylaxis des Kindbettfiebers* (1861).

23. The contemporary historian Anne Glyn-Jones has pointed out that the late Romans suffered from some mysterious, sexually transmitted malaise and that they, like Western peoples today, suffered from a decline in fertility (*Holding Up a Mirror: How Civilizations Decline* [1966], cited in Bryan Appleyard, "How we rise, decline and fall," *The Sunday Times, Books* [London], 11 Aug.

1996, p. 7). Other authorities dispute the contention that reduced population was a major factor in the decline of Rome, as argued by A.E.R. Boak in *Manpower Shortage and the Fall of the Roman Empire* (1955). Professors Cary and Scullard (*A History of Rome*, 553) conclude that the decrease in population probably resulted from excessive governmental demands rather than natural causes.

24. The extent to which Italians today belittle the Mary cult is suggested by a current advertisement that plays on the *Ave Maria* to promote a brand of mozzarella. Depicting tomatoes snuggled in the soft moist white breast-shaped cheese, it bears the words and symbols (printed in pseudomedieval script): AVE VALLE-LATTE I POMODORI †E SALUTANT. A small statue of a Madonna in a glass-covered shrine has been taken as a target by sportshooters in Rome's Via Trionfale.

25. Cf. Rossana Campo, "La volta che Mina mi ha baciata" (That time that Mina kissed me) in Rosaria Guacci and Bruna Miorelli, eds., *Racconta 2* (Milano: La Tartaruga, 1993), 54.

26. Jaroslav Pelikan lists ten apparitions of Mary which have been acknowledged as worthy of pious belief. The number of miracles attributed to Mary, he reports, increased after the Middle Ages and reached something of a peak in the nineteenth and twentieth centuries (*Mary Through the Centuries*, 178-79, 135).

27. In O'Brien's *Girls in Their Married Bliss* (1964), the heroine has herself sterilized in answer to what she sees as the biological unfairness of God's scheme for women (Magill, 377).

28. At this writing legislation is under consideration to admit Italian women to military service.

29. The number of abortions in Italy was estimated in 1962 at 1.5 million annually, resulting in approximately 20,000 deaths each year and with half of the survivors suffering permanent impairment (*Maria, Medea*, 166).

30. "Maternità: un desiderio impraticabile?" (Maternity: an impracticable desire?), "Maternità: io dico no" (Maternity: I say no), "La rabbia di essere madre" (The anger of being a mother), etc. (*Maria, Medea*, 13, 70, 88, passim).

31. Child exposure was accepted by the ancient Romans until late imperial times: in the Forum Olitorium stood a "milk column" at whose base abandoned children allegedly received fresh milk brought to them daily (Magaldi, 17). Only at the end of the nineteenth century did Italian legislators begin to consider the psychological dimensions of infanticide and the need for institutions such as the Opera Nazionale Maternità e Infanzia for unwed mothers (Santosuosso, 121).

    Carol Morris analyzes the infanticide constituting the story "Drop Stars Fall in Unmarked Places" by Moy McCrory, in which the mother who kills her infant is seen as a victim of society and Church. Cf. Carol Morris, "Shattering the Silence," in Ada Neiger, ed., *Maternità trasgressiva*, 169-79.

Chapter 3. Literary Manifestations of the Changing Social Scene: The Nineteenth Century and Beyond

1. Lucy Poate Stebbins, *A Victorian Album: Some Lady Novelists of the Period* (New York: Columbia University Press, 1946), p. vii.
2. Both works were written by Lucrezia Marinella (1571-1653). Cf. Paola Malpezzi Price, "Lucrezia Marinella," 236.
3. The curvilinear structure of the megalithic temples (third millennium B.C.E.) on the island of Malta, for example, is thought to represent the breasts, uterus and vulva of the recumbent Great Mother goddess. Cf. Tilde Giani Gallino, *La ferita e il re*, 136-39.
4. *Misteri del chiostro napoletano: Memorie di Elisabetta Caracciolo de' principi Forino ex monaca benedettina* (1864), quoted in Giuliana Morandini, *La voce che è in lei*, 104.
5. *La vita intima e la vita nomade in Oriente*, no date, originally titled *Asie Mineure et Syrie: souvenirs de voyages par Mme la Princesse de Belgiojoso* (1861), quoted in Morandini, 75.

Chapter 4. The Twentieth-Century Revolt against Maternity

1. In the same year that Aleramo published *A Woman* (1906), Willa Cather was analyzing Mary Baker Eddy's fractured personality and lack of maternal interest in her own child. Cf. Caroline Fraser, "Mrs Eddy Builds Her Empire," *New York Review of Books*, July 11, 1996, 59. More recently, Roszika Parker noted the findings of a 1992 survey in which seventy per cent of divorced mothers who had lost custody of their children said they were "extremely happy," while seven per cent were actually "euphoric." *Mother Love/Mother Hate*, 126.
2. Quoted by Richard Drake in introduction to *A Woman*, xxxi.
3. The suicidal Sexton structured as a prayer to the Virgin Mary her poem "For the Year of the Insane" (1966), in which she struggles to escape her mental and physical confinement. Cf. Magill, *Great Woman Writers*, 484.
4. In her novel *Canne al vento* (Reeds in the wind, 1913), Deledda provides a stunning example of a Sardinian girl who flees her tyrannical father only to die tragically in childbirth. In *Elias Portolu* (1903), the child born of Maddalena and Elias is "the fruit of their sin" and therefore will soon die, while in *Cenere* (*Ashes: A Sardinian Story*, 1904), a tormented relationship between a mother and her illegitimate son results in the suicide of the "superfluous" mother.
5. Neria De Giovanni, *L'ora di Lilith*, 17-18. This critic similarly discerns in Maria Teresa Giuffrè's *La veglia di Adrasto* (Adrastus's watch, 1986) based on the *Meditations* of Marcus Aurelius, a symbiosis between writing and maternity which links Giuffrè to Woolf. Cf. De Giovanni, op. cit., 118.
6. The prize was shared with Stanley Cohen, who clarified the structure of the nerve growth factor (NGF) identified by Levi Montalcini.

7. Coauthored with Marco Lombardo Radice (Roma: Savelli, 1976).
8. Elsa Morante, "Una lettera inedita del febbraio 1957 a Giacomo Debenedetti," *Corriere della Sera*, 26 November 1985, 3.
9. Jean-Noël Schifano, "Barbara e divina," *L'Espresso*, 2 December 1984, 133.
10. Elsa Morante, *Diario 1938*, edited with a preface by Alba Andreini (Torino: Einaudi, 1989).
11. Alba Andreini, preface to *Diario 1938*, viii.
12. Elsa Morante, *Menzogna e sortilegio* (Torino: Einaudi, 1948), 192. Throughout this and her other novels, Morante satirizes superstitious pregnant women bedecked in amulets and rosaries and beseeching the Lord to make their offsprings male.
13. Luce Irigaray explains that mothers hate their children because their fertility is validated only through literal maternity, which is then culturally devalued. Cf. Parker, 250.
14. This ancient practice, described by Frazer in *The Golden Bough* (I, 182-201) as contagious magic of the placenta, is intended in Guiducci's tale to insure the consolidation of the newborn's fontanel.
15. The compilers pointedly reproduced on the back cover of the volume a series of paintings synthesizing the theme of the collection: grotesque perceptions of the Madonna and maternity by Edvard Munch, Gustav Klimt, Max Ernst, Paul Delvaux, and others.
16. Tilde Giani Gallino, in her discussion of the Sardinian feast of "La Sartiglia" (above) analyzes the gratification felt by men and women alike at the capacities of the allegoric Male Fecondator (*La ferita e il re*, 93).
17. By Giorgio Forattini.
18. Alain Boureau, *La papesse Jeanne* (Paris: Aubier, 1988), 10, 23.
19. The term is borrowed from Marisa Fiumanò, ed., *L'immacolata fecondazione* (Milano: La Tartaruga, 1996), 9.
20. Lidia Menapace, introduction to Patrizia Monaco, ed., *Accadde a Roma. Nove atti unici. Nove protagoniste* (Genova: Costa & Nolan, 1996), 13.
21. Alain Boureau (op. cit., 317-18), alluding to a "nostalgia for androgyny" in the historical continuum, points out the similarities between Joan and Yentl, the heroine of Isaac Bashevis Singer's homonymous short story (1962). Tilde Giani Gallino studies the androgynous archetype in the collective psyche in *La ferita e il re*, 88-97.
22. The Roman Catholic Church saw fit to proclaim Saint Thérèse of Lisieux, alias Saint Thérèse of the Child Jesus, a Doctor of the Church on October 19, 1997. Her doctrine of the "Little Way" teaches spiritual childhood, trust, and absolute surrender.
23. Francesca Avanzini, "Piccola città," 91.
24. Carla Ammannati, "Che siamo noi due?", 65-6.
25. Mara Cini, "Primi esercizi," 193.
26. Nicoletta Vallorani, "A stomaco nudo," 249.

27. Susanna Tamaro, *Per voce solo* (Milano: Baldini & Castoldi, 1994), 98-9. Tamaro's merit as a writer has been publicly recognized by Natalia Ginzburg and Federico Fellini.

Conclusion: Italy Awaits the New Woman

1. A deep symbolic connection between the eyes and the female genital organs has been pointed out by the Italian woman psychologist Tilde Giani Gallino, *La ferita e il re*, 53-4.
2. Mircea Eliade, *Trattato di storia delle religioni* (Torino: Boringhieri, 1946), 346, cited in Giani Gallino, 160.
3. Significant in this regard is the 1931 novel, *Plagued by the Nightingale*, by the American woman writer Kay Boyle. It tells of a heroine who chose to bear a child not by her husband, whose tainted genes would have continued the cycle of a crippling congenital disease, but by a vigorous outsider whose health and vitality promised liberation and autonomy. Cf. Frank N. Magill, ed., *Great Women Writers* (New York: Henry Holt, 1994), 45.

Bibliography

Aleramo, Sibilla. trans. 1980. *A Woman*. Translated by Rosalind Delmar. With an
Introduction by Richard Drake. Berkeley and Los Angeles: University of
California Press. [Originally published in 1906.]

Amoia, Alba della Fazia. 1992. *Women on the Italian Literary Scene: A Panorama*.
Troy, N.Y.: Whitston.

_____.1996. *20th-Century Italian Women Writers. The Feminine Experience*.
Carbondale and Edwardsville: Southern Illinois University Press.

Ancona Teresa. 1974. *Una famiglia normale*. Milano: Il Formichiere.

Anderson, Linda, ed. 1990. *Plotting Change: Contemporary Women's Fiction*.
London, Melbourne, Auckland: Edward Arnold.

Andrews, Lori B. 1985. *La cicogna del Duemila*. Milano: SugarCo.

Appleyard, Brian. 1996. "How we rise, decline and fall." *The Sunday Times. Books*.
[London] (11 August): 6-7.

Aricò, Santo L., ed. 1990. *Contemporary Women Writers in Italy. A Modern
Renaissance*. Amherst: The University of Massachusetts Press.

Armstrong, Karen. 1993. *A History of God: The 4000-Year Quest of Judaism,
Christianity and Islam*. New York: Alfred A. Knopf.

Augustine, Saint. trans. 1950. *The City of God*. New York: Modern Library.

Auhagen Stephanos, Ute. 1995. *Il desiderio di maternità*. Torino: Boringhieri.

Badinter, Elizabeth. 1981. *L'amore in più. Storia dell'amore materno*. Translated
by Rosetta Loy. Milano: Longanesi.

_____. 1986. *L'un est l'autre. Des relations entre hommes et femmes*. Paris:
Editions Odile.

Ballaro, Beverly. 1994. "Anna Banti (Lucia Lopresti Longhi) (1895-1985)." In
Rinaldina Russell, ed. *Italian Women Writers. A Bio-Bibliographical
Sourcebook*. Westport, Connecticut and London: Greenwood Press, 35-43.

Banti, Anna. 1940. *Il coraggio delle donne*. Firenze: Le Monnier.

_____. 1951. *Le donne muoiono*. Milano: Mondadori.

_____. 1953. *Artemisia*. Firenze: Sansoni. [Reprint Milano: Mondadori, 1974.]

_____. 1973. *La camicia bruciata*. Milano: Mondadori.

Bassanese, Fiora A. 1990. "Armanda Guiducci's Disposable Women." In Santo L.
Aricò, ed. *Contemporary Women Writers in Italy. A Modern Renaissance*.
Amherst: The University of Massachusetts Press, 153-69.

_____. 1994. "Sibilla Aleramo (Rina Faccio) (1876-1960)." In Rinaldina Russell,
ed., *Italian Women Writers. A Bio-Bibliographical Sourcebook*. Westport,
Connecticut and London: Greenwood Press, 9-17.

_____. 1994. "Armanda Guiducci (1923-1992)." In Rinaldina Russell, ed. *Italian
Women Writers. A Bio-Bibliographical Sourcebook*. Westport, Connecticut

and London: Greenwood Press, 179-88.

Battisti, Carlo and Giovanni Alessio, eds. 1950-57. *Dizionario Etimologico Italiano.* 5 vols. Firenze: Barbera.

Beauvoir, Simone de. 1949. *Le deuxième sexe.* Paris: Gallimard.

Becker, Lucille. 1989. *Twentieth-Century French Women Novelists.* Boston: Twayne.

Bernardini, Enzo. 1983. *L'Italia preistorica.* Roma: Newton Compton.

Bignami, Ernesto. 1965. *Manuale di storia romana.* Milano: Bignami.

Birnbaum, Lucia Chiavola. 1986. *Liberazione della donna. Feminism in Italy.* Middletown, Conn.: Wesleyan University Press.

_____. 1993. *Black Madonnas: feminism, religion and politics in Italy.* Ithaca, N.Y.: Northeastern University Press.

Bishop, Morris, ed. 1965. *A Survey of French Literature.* 2 vols. New York, Chicago, and Burlingame: Harcourt, Brace & World.

Blelloch, Paola. 1987. *Quel mondo dei guanti e delle stoffe.... Profili di scrittrici italiane del '900.* Verona: Essedue.

Bornstein, Daniel and Roberto Rusconi, eds. 1996. *Women and Religion in Medieval and Renaissance Italy.* Chicago: University of Chicago Press.

Boureau, Alain. 1988. *La papesse Jeanne.* Paris: Aubier, 1988.

Brancion Chatel, Marie Magdeleine de. 1995. *Il disagio della procreazione.* Milano: Il Saggiatore.

_____. 1996. "Il punto di oscillazione del rapire." In Luisa Fiumanò, ed. *L'immacolata fecondazione. Perché le donne dicono di sì alla scienza.* Milano: La Tartaruga, 99-115.

Brizio, Flavia. 1990. "Memory and Time in Lalla Romano's Novels, *La penombra che abbiamo attraversato* and *Le parole tra noi leggere.*" In Santo L. Aricò, ed. *Contemporary Women Writers in Italy. A Modern Renaissance.* Amherst: The University of Massachusetts Press, 63-75.

Brown, Peter. 1988. *The Body and Society: Men, Women and Sexual Renunciation in Early Christianity.* New York: Columbia University Press.

Cabibbo, Sara. 1997. "'Dal nido savoiardo al trono d'Italia': i santi di casa Savoia." In Emma Fattorini, ed. *Santi, culti, simboli nell'età della secolarizzazione (1815-1915).* Torino: Rosenberg & Sellier, 331-60.

Cacciaglia, Norberto. 1993. "L'esperienza materna nella narrativa di Elsa Morante (Osservazioni sulla maternità nella *Storia* e in *Aracoeli*)." In Ada Neiger, ed. *Maternità trasgressiva e letteratura.* Napoli: Liguori, 145-52.

Camaiani, Pier Giorgio. 1997. "L'immagine femminile nella letteratura e nella trattatistica dell'Ottocento. La donna 'forte' e la donna 'debole'." In Emma Fattorini, ed. *Santi, culti, simboli nell'età della secolarizzazione (1815-1915).* Torino: Rosenberg & Sellier, 431-47.

Campione, Francesco. 1935. *L'istinto materno.* Milano: Bompiani.

Cary, M. and H.H. Scullard. 1975. *A History of Rome Down to the Reign of Constantine.* 3rd ed. Houndmills, Basingstoke, Hampshire & London: Macmillan.

Cassee, Elly. 1978. "La Madonna del Parto." *Paragone Arte* 29, no. 345: 94-7.

Cattaneo, Angela and Silvana Pisa. 1979. *L'altra mamma. La maternità nel movimento delle donne. Fantasie, desideri, domande e inquietudini.* Milano: Savelli.

Colombi, Marchesa. 1885. *Un matrimonio in provincia.* Milano: Galli.

Confederazione Nazionale Coltivatori Diretti. 1984. *Statistiche Mondo, CEE, Italia.* Roma: R.E.D.A.

Cornini, Guido. 1984. "Il savonarolismo nell'ultimo periodo di Botticelli fra ipotesi e realtà." *Storia dell'arte* 52 (Sept.-Dec.): 171-85.

Cortelazzo, Manlio and Paolo Zolli, eds. 1979-85. *Dizionario etimologico della lingua italiana.* 5 vols. Bologna: Zanichelli.

Corti, Maria. 1989. *Il canto delle sirene.* Preface by Cesare Segre. Milano: Bompiani. Reprint, I Grandi Tascabili, 1992.

Costanzi, Angela. 1995. "Battesimo pasquale a San Giovanni." *Antemnae* XIV (March): 4.

Cutrufelli, Maria Rosa, Rosaria Guacci and Marisa Rusconi, eds. 1993. *Il pozzo segreto. Cinquanta scrittrici italiane.* Firenze: Giunti.

Da Pietremala, Silvana (Maria Sacconi). 1937. *L'inestinguibile fonte d'amore. (Canti della maternità).* Roma: Casa editrice "Roma 900".

De Giorgio, Michela. 1993. *Le italiane dall'unità a oggi: modelli culturali e comportamenti sociali.* 2nd ed. Roma: Laterza.

De Giovanni, Neria. 1987. *L'ora di Lilith. Su Grazia Deledda e la letteratura femminile del secondo Novecento.* Roma: Ellemme.

Deiss, Joseph Jay. 1969. *The Roman Years of Margaret Fuller.* New York: Thomas Y. Crowell.

Deledda, Grazia. compiled 1950-55. *Romanzi e novelle.* 4 vols. Milano: Mondadori.

_____. trans. 1988. *Cosima.* Translated by Martha King. New York: Italica Press. [Originally published in 1937.]

Della Coletta, Cristina. 1994. "Rosa Rosà (Edith Von Haynau) (1884-1978?)." In Rinaldina Russell, ed. *Italian Women Writers. A Bio-Bibliographical Sourcebook.* Westport, Connecticut and London: Greenwood Press, 353-9.

De Martino Rosarol, Adriana. 1937. *Maternità ed infanzia nelle tragedie di Euripide.* Roma: Ausonia.

Devoto, Giacomo. 1968. *Avviamento alla Etimologia italiana.* 2nd ed. Firenze: Felice Le Monnier.

Dijkstra, Bram. 1988. *Idoli di perversità. La donna nell'immaginario artistico.* Milano: Garzanti.

Di Lascia, Maria Teresa. 1994. *Compleanno.* Viterbo: Agorà Millelire Stampa Alternativa.

Dini, Vittorio. 1980. *Il potere delle antiche madri. Fecondità e culti delle acque nella cultura subalterna toscana.* Torino: Boringhieri.

Dizionario enciclopedico Bolaffi dei pittori e degli incisori italiani dall'XI al XX secolo. Vol. 5. 1974. Torino: Giulio Bolaffi.

Donadoni, Mario. 1976. *Poesia di Renata Giambene con particolare riguardo a "Sosta al fiume"*. Pisa: C. Cursi Editore & F.

Donna Paola (Paola Baronchelli Grosson). 1910. *Io e il mio elettore. Propositi e spropositi di una futura Deputata*. Lanciano: Carabba.

Du Plessis, Rachel Blau. 1985. *Writing Beyond the Ending: Narrative Strategies of Twentieth-Century Women Writers*. Bloomington: Indiana University Press.

Eliade, Mircea. 1948. *Trattato di storia delle religioni*. Torino: Boringhieri.

Enciclopedia italiana di scienze, lettere ed arti. 36 vols. 1936. Roma: Istituto dell'Enciclopedia Italiana (Treccani).

Encyclopedia Britannica. 24 vols. 1967. Chicago, London, Toronto, Geneva, Sydney, Tokyo, Manila: William Benton.

Evenou, Jean. 1997. "Liturgia e culto dei santi (1815-1915)." In Emma Fattorini, ed. *Santi, culti, simboli nell'età della secolarizzazione (1815-1915)*. Torino: Rosenberg & Sellier, 43-65.

Falkenburg, Reindert L. 1994. *The Fruit of Devotion. Mysticism and the Imagery of Love in Flemish Paintings of the Virgin and Child, 1450-1550*. Translated from the Dutch by Sammy Herman. Amsterdam and Philadelphia: John Benjamins.

Fallaci, Oriana. 1975. *Lettera a un bambino mai nato*. Milano: Rizzoli.

Fattorini, Emma, ed. 1997. *Santi, culti, simboli nell'età della secolarizzazione (1815-1915)*. Torino: Rosenberg & Sellier.

_____.1997. "Romanticismo religioso e culto mariano." In Emma Fattorini, ed. *Santi, culti, simboli nell'età della secolarizzazione (1815-1915)*. Torino: Rosenberg & Sellier, 213-23.

Ferri, Giuliana. 1973. *Un quarto di donna*. Venezia and Padova: Marsilio.

Feudale, Caroline. 1954-57. "The iconography of the Madonna del Parto." *Marsyas* 7: 8-24.

Fiumanò, Marisa, ed. 1996. *L'immacolata fecondazione. Perché le donne dicono di sì alla scienza*. Milano: La Tartaruga.

_____. 1996. "La maternità tra tecnica e desiderio." In Marisa Fiumanò, ed. *L'immacolata fecondazione. Perché le donne dicono di sì alla scienza*. Milano: La Tartaruga, 11-36.

Fiumi, Luisella. 1974. *Come donna, zero*. Milano: Mondadori.

Fraser, Caroline. 1996. "Mrs. Eddy Builds Her Empire." *The New York Review of Books* (July 11): 53-9.

Frazer, James George. 1911. *The Golden Bough*. 2 vols. London: Macmillan.

Gaspardo, Umberto. 1939. *Maternità cristiana. Istruzioni alle Madri*. Roma: Pia Società Figlie di San Paolo.

Giani Gallino, Tilde. 1986. *La ferita e il re. Gli archetipi femminili della cultura maschile*. Milano: Cortina.

Gianini Belotti, Elena. 1983. *Non sola di madre*. Milano: Rizzoli.

Gimbutas, Marija. 1991. *The Civilization of the Goddess: The World of Old Europe*. San Francisco: Harper San Francisco.

_____. 1997. *Il linguaggio della dea. Mito e culto della Dea madre nell'Europa neolitica.* Vicenza: Neri Pozza.

Ginzburg, Natalia. 1973. *Never Must You Ask Me.* London: Joseph.

Giuffrè, Maria Teresa. 1986. *La veglia d'Adrasto.* Pordenone: Edizioni dello Zibaldone.

Glyn-Jones, Anne. 1996. *Holding up a Mirror: How Civilisations Decline.* London: Century.

Gombrich, E.H. 1996. "The Miracle at Chauvet." *The New York Review of Books* (14 November): 8-12.

Grabar, André. 1969. *Christian Iconography. A Study of Its Origins.* London: Routledge & Kegan Paul.

Grant, Michael. 1978. *History of Rome.* New York: Charles Scribner's Sons.

Grasso, Laura. 1977. *Madre amore donna. Per un'analisi del rapporto madre-figlia.* Rimini-Firenze: Guaraldi.

Graziosi, Paolo. 1965. *L'arte dell'antica età della pietra.* Firenze: Sansoni.

_____. 1973. *L'arte preistorica in Italia.* Firenze: Sansoni.

Grecchi, Ada. 1998. "Donne e Management." *Sì Magazine* (January): 78-9.

Groeber, Corrado. 1927. *La madre. Preparazione, valore e fini della maternità nel concetto cristiano.* Translated by Antonio Masini. Torino: Società Editrice Internazionale.

Guacci, Rosaria and Bruna Miorelli, eds. 1993. *Racconto 2.* Milano: La Tartaruga.

Guicciardi, Elena. 1986. "Mettiamo incinto il maschio." *La Repubblica* (7 May): 26-7.

Guiducci, Armanda. 1974. *La mela e il serpente. Autoanalisi di una donna.* Milano: Rizzoli.

_____. 1976. *Due donne da buttare.* Milano: Rizzoli.

_____. 1977. *La donna non è gente.* Milano: Rizzoli.

_____. 1989. *Perduta nella storia. Storia delle donne dal I al VII secolo d.C.* Firenze: Sansoni.

_____. 1989. *Medioevo inquieto: storie delle donne dall'8. al 15. secolo d.C.* Firenze: Sansoni.

Hall, James. 1974. *Dizionario dei soggetti e dei simboli nell'arte.* Introduction by Kenneth Clark. Translated by Mary Archer. Milano: Longanesi.

Hansen, Elaine Tuttle. 1997. *Mother without Child. Contemporary Fiction and the Crisis of Motherhood.* Berkeley: University of California Press.

Havlice, Patricia Pate, ed. 1977. *World Painting Index.* 2 vols. Metuchen, NJ and London: Metuchen.

Hirsch, Marianne. 1989. *The Mother/Daughter Plot: Narrative, Psychoanalysis, Feminism.* Bloomington: Indiana University Press.

Istituto Nazionale di Statistica. 1996. *Popolazione. Nascite. Caratteristiche demografiche e sociali. Anno 1993.* Roma: Istat.

_____. 1996. *Strutture e produzioni delle aziende agricole. Anno 1993.* Roma: Istat.

James, E.O. 1994. *The Cult of the Mother-Goddess.* New York: Barnes & Noble.

Jarre, Marina. 1971. *Negli occhi di una ragazza.* Torino: Einaudi.

Klass, Perri. 1996. "The Artificial Womb Is Born." *The New York Times Magazine* (September 29): 117-19.

Knapp, Bettina L. 1992. *Images of Chinese Women: A Westerner's View.* Troy, NY: Whitston.

_____. 1992. *Images of Japanese Women: A Westerner's View.* Troy, NY: Whitston.

_____. 1997. *Women in Myth.* Albany: State University of New York Press.

Lazzaro-Weis, Carol. 1988. "Gender and Genre in Italian Feminist Literature in the Seventies." *Italica* 65: 293-307.

Le Coadic, Michele and Laurence Gavarini, eds. 1986. *Maternité en mouvement. Les femmes, la reproduction, et les hommes de sciences.* Paris: Editions Saint Martin.

Levi Montalcini, Rita. 1987. *Elogio dell'imperfezione.* Milano: Garzanti.

Livi, Grazia. 1992. *Le lettere del mio nome.* Milano: La Tartaruga.

Locher, Frances C., ed. 1979. *Contemporary Authors* 77-80. Detroit, Michigan: Gale Research Company.

Lombroso, Cesare and Guglielmo Ferrero. 1892. *La donna delinquente.* Torino: Bocca.

MacCarthy, Fiona. 1996. "The Power of Chastity." *The New York Review of Books* (December 19): 31-3.

McNamara, Jo Ann Kay. 1996. *Sisters in Arms: Catholic Nuns Through Two Millennia.* Cambridge: Harvard University Press.

La Madonna Benois di Leonardo da Vinci a Firenze. Il capolavoro dell'Ermitage in mostra agli Uffizi. 1984. Presentazione di Luciano Berti; testi di Michele Alpatov, Tatiana Kustodieva e Carlo Pedretti. Firenze: Giunti Barbèra.

Magaldi, Emilio. 1939. *Maternità e prima infanzia nel mondo dell'antichità classica.* Napoli: Genovese.

Magill, Frank N., ed. 1994. *Great Women Writers.* New York: Henry Holt.

Malpezzi Price, Paola. 1994. "Lucrezia Marinella (1571-1653)." In Rinaldina Russell, ed., *Italian Women Writers. A Bio-Bibliographical Sourcebook.* Westport, Connecticut and London: Greenwood Press, 234-42.

Mann, Thomas. 1936. *Stories of Three Decades.* New York: Alfred A. Knopf.

Manzini, Gianna. 1928. *Tempo innamorato.* Milano: Corbaccio. Reprint, Milano: Mondadori, 1973.

Maraini, Dacia. trans. 1988. *Woman at War.* Translated by Mara Benetti and Elspeth Spottiswood. New York: Italica Press. [Originally published in 1975.]

Marchesa Colombi. 1885. *Un matrimonio in provincia.* Milano: Galli.

Maria, Medea e le altre. Il materno nelle parole delle donne: rassegna stampa. 1982. Roma: Lerici.

Marinetti, F.T. and Enif Robert. 1919. *Un ventre di donna. Romanzo chirurgico.* Milano: Facchi.

Meiss, Millard. 1964. *Painting in Florence and Siena after the Black Death. The Arts, Religion, and Society in the Mid-Fourteenth Century.* New York: Harper & Row.

Miccinesi, Mario. 1978. *Deledda.* Il Castoro 105. Firenze: La Nuova Italia.

Mieli, Paola. 1996. "Verde: note sulle implicazioni attuali della riproduzione assistita." In Marisa Fiumanò, ed. *L'immacolata fecondazione. Perché le donne dicono di sì alla scienza.* Milano: La Tartaruga, 37-59.

Migiel, Marilyn. 1994. "Grazia Deledda (1871-1936)." In Rinaldina Russell, ed. *Italian Women Writers. A Bio-Bibliographical Sourcebook.* Westport, Connecticut and London: Greenwood Press, 111-18.

Moi, Toril, ed. 1986. *The Kristeva Reader.* Oxford: Basil Blackwell.

Monaco, Patrizia, ed. 1996. *Accadde a Roma. Nove atti unici. Nove protagoniste.* Genova: Costa & Nolan.

Morandini, Giuliana, ed. 1980. *La voce che è in lei. Antologia della narrativa femminile italiana tra '800 e '900.* Milano: Bompiani.

Morante, Elsa. 1948. *Menzogna e sortilegio.* Torino: Einaudi.

_____. 1957. *L'isola di Arturo.* Torino: Einaudi. [*Arturo's Island.* Manchester: Carcanet, 1988.]

_____. 1971. *Il mondo salvato dai ragazzini.* Torino: Einaudi.

_____. 1974. *La Storia.* Torino: Einaudi. [*History: A Novel.* Translated by William Weaver. New York: Knopf, 1977.]

_____. 1985. "Una lettera inedita del febbraio 1957 a Giacomo Debenedetti," *Corriere della Sera* (26 November): 3.

_____. 1989. *Diario 1938.* Edited and with a preface by Alba Andreini. Torino: Einaudi.

Morante, Marcello. 1986. *Maledetta benedetta: Elsa e sua madre.* Milano: Garzanti.

Moretti, Paola. 1996. *Una strana follia.* In Patrizia Monaco, ed. *Accadde a Roma. Nove atti unici. Nove protagoniste.* Genova: Costa & Nolan, 77-90.

Morozzo della Rocca, Roberto. 1997. "Il culto dei santi tra i soldati (1915-1918)." In Emma Fattorini, ed. *Santi, culti, simboli nell'età della secolarizzazione (1815-1915).* Torino: Rosenberg & Sellier, 225-34.

Morris, Carol. 1993. "Shattering the silence: some examples of transgressive motherhood in contemporary Irish women's writing." In Ada Neiger, ed. *Maternità trasgressiva e letteratura.* Napoli: Liguori, 153-82.

Nardi, Isabella. 1993. " Le 'cattive madri': note sul tema della maternità nei romanzi dannunziani e oltre." In Ada Neiger, ed. *Maternità trasgressiva e letteratura.* Napoli: Liguori, 79-97.

Neera. 1903. *Le idee di una donna.* Milano: Libreria Editrice Nazionale.

_____. 1911. *Duello d'anime.* Milano: Treves.

Negri, Ada. 1926. *Maternità.* Milano: Treves. [First edition 1904.]

Neiger, Ada, ed. 1993. *Maternità trasgressiva e letteratura.* Napoli: Liguori.

1994 Demographic Yearbook. Annuaire démographique. 1996. New York: United Nations/Nations Unies.

Nozzoli, Anna. 1978. *Tabù e coscienza. La condizione femminile nella letteratura italiana del Novecento*. Firenze: La Nuova Italia.

Oates, Joyce Carol. 1997. "Troubles I've Seen." *The New York Review of Books* (March 27): 39-40.

Ortese, Anna Maria. 1953. *Il mare non bagna Napoli*. Firenze: Vallecchi. [Edited by Anna Nozzoli. Firenze: La Nuova Italia, 1979.]

Oxman, Alice. 1974. *Lager maternità. Libro-documentario sulle donne e i bambini in venti storie italiane*. Milano: Bompiani.

Paccosi, Omero. 1996. "Il nome segreto di Roma." *Antemnae* XV (May): 7-8.

Pagels, Elaine. trans. 1981. *I Vangeli gnostici*. Translated by Massimo Parizzi. Milano: Mondadori. [Originally published in 1979.]

Palma, Francesco de. 1997. "Il modello laicale di Anna Maria Taigi." In Emma Fattorini, ed. *Santi, culti, simboli nell'età della secolarizzazione (1815-1915)*. Torino: Rosenberg & Sellier, 529-46.

Parker, Roszika. 1995. *Mother Love/Mother Hate. The Power of Maternal Ambivalence*. New York: Basic Books.

Parto e maternità. Momenti della biografia femminile. Quaderni storici 44 (August 1980).

Pelikan, Jaroslav. 1996. *Mary Through the Centuries. Her Place in the History of Culture*. New Haven and London: Yale University Press.

Pennato, Papinio. 1930. *Sacra maternità*. Venezia: Premiate officine grafiche Carlo Ferrari.

Peritore, G.A. 1969. "Anna Banti." In *Letteratura Italiana. I Contemporanei 3*. Milano: Marzorati, 211-34.

Picca, Paolo. 1936. *Fecondità miracolose*. Roma: Fabbrica Romana Prodotti Chimici.

_____. 1937. *Parti straordinari*. Roma: Fabbrica Romana Prodotti Chimici.

Pickering-Iazzi, Robin. 1989. "Designing Mothers: Images of Motherhood in Novels by Aleramo, Morante, Maraini, and Fallaci." *Annali d'Italianistica* 7:325-40.

Pirotte, Jean. 1997. "Le paradis de papier de l'imagerie dévote: Quelle société céleste pour quels chrétiens? (1840-1965)." In Emma Fattorini, ed. *Santi, culti, simboli nell'età della secolarizzazione (1815-1915)*. Torino: Rosenberg & Sellier, 67-104.

Pons, Nicoletta. 1989. *Botticelli*. Milano: Rizzoli.

Ravera, Lidia. 1979. *Bambino mio*. Milano: Bompiani.

Ricci, Giancarlo. 1996. "L'angelo artificiale." In Marisa Fiumanò, ed. *L'immacolata fecondazione.Perché le donne dicono di sì alla scienza*. Milano: La Tartaruga, 61-97.

Rich, Adrienne. 1977. *Of Woman Born: Motherhood as Experience and Institution*. London: Virago.

Rituale romanum Pauli V. P.M. 1625. Roma: Ex Typographia Camera Apostolica. [Originally published in 1614.]

Romaniello, Vito. 1997. "La religiosità nella letteratura popolare: I 'Librettini di storia antiche e moderne' dell'editore Adriano Salani." In Emma Fattorini, ed. *Santi, culti, simboli nell'età della secolarizzazione (1815-1915)*. Torino: Rosenberg & Sellier, 105-15.

Rosà, Rosa. 1917. "Le donne del posdomani." In *L'Italia futurista* (17 June and 7 October).

Rossi, Fiorenzo. 1982. *Indagine sulla fecondità in Italia*. Padova: Istituto di Statistica, Università di Padova.

Rusconi, Roberto. 1997. "Erudizione, devozione, reazione. L'itinerario di una cultura ecclesiastica da Gaetano Moroni a Francesco Lanzoni." In Emma Fattorini, ed. *Santi, culti, simboli nell'età della secolarizzazione (1815-1915)*. Torino: Rosenberg & Sellier, 21-42.

Russell, Rinaldina, ed. 1994. *Italian Women Writers. A Bio-Bibliographical Sourcebook*. Westport, Connecticut and London: Greenwood.

Saadé, Gabriel. 1979. *Ougarit. Métropole Cananéenne*. Beyrouth, Liban: Imprimerie Catholique.

Il sacro e l'Acqua. 1998. Catalog of the exhibition at the Museo Barracca, Rome (23 April-18 October 1998). Roma: Edizioni De Luca.

Sandias, Maria. 1996. *Maria Sofia di Borbone, una regina in esilio*. In Patrizia Monaco, ed. *Accadde a Roma. Nove atti unici. Nove protagoniste*. Genova: Costa & Nolan, 117-29.

Santosuosso, Amedeo. 1996. "Paternità e nuove tecniche di riproduzione." In Marisa Fiumanò, ed. *L'immacolata fecondazione. Perché le donne dicono di sì alla scienza*. Milano: La Tartaruga, 117-50.

Schifano, Jean-Noël. 1984. "Barbara e divina." *L'Espresso* (2 December): 122-33.

Sereni, Clara. 1987. *Casalinghitudine*. Torino: Einaudi.

_____. 1989. *Manicomio primavera*. Firenze: Giunti.

Smyth, Ailbhe, ed. 1989. *Wildish Things: An Anthology of New Irish Women's Writing*. Dublin: Attic Press.

Spretnak, Charlene. 1978. *Lost Goddesses of Early Greece: A Collection of Pre-Hellenic Mythology*. Berkeley, CA: Moon Books.

Stella, Pietro. 1997. "Santi per giovani e santi giovani dell'Ottocento." In Emma Fattorini, ed. *Santi, culti, simboli nell'età della secolarizzazione (1815-1915)*. Torino: Rosenberg & Sellier, 563-86.

Tamaro, Susanna. 1994. *Per voce sola*. Milano: Baldini & Castoldi.

Tortoreto, Walter. 1997. "Da Liszt a Schönberg: musica sacra e sentimento religioso." In Emma Fattorini, ed. *Santi, culti, simboli nell'età della secolarizzazione (1815-1915)*. Torino: Rosenberg & Sellier, 235-45.

Turoff, Barbara. 1994. "Amalia Guglielminetti (1885-1941)." In Rinaldina Russell, ed. *Italian Woman Writers. A Bio-Bibliographical Sourcebook*. Westport, Connecticut and London: Greenwood, 163-70.

Van Buren, Jane Silverman. 1989. *The Modernist Madonna. Semiotics of the Maternal Metaphor*. Bloomington, Indiana and London: Indiana University Press and Karnac Books.

Vegetti Finzi, Silvia. 1990. *Il bambino della notte. Divenire donna divenire madre.* Milano: Mondadori.

Vendler, Helen. 1996. "The Truth Teller." *The New York Review of Books* (19 September): 57-60.

Verucci, Guido. 1997. "I simboli della cultura laica e delle istituzioni civili." In Emma Fattorini, ed. *Santi, culti, simboli nell'età della secolarizzazione (1815-1915).* Torino: Rosenberg & Sellier, 235-45.

Villa, Roberta. 1991. *Leonardo.* Milano: Mondadori Arte.

Villani, Sue Lanci. 1997. *Motherhood at the Crossroads. Meeting the Challenge of a Changing Role.* 1997. New York: Plenum.

Vivanti, Annie. 1928. *Vae victis!* Milano: Mondadori. [Originally published in 1917.]

Warner, Marina. trans. 1980. *Sola fra le donne. Mito e culto di Maria Vergine.* Translated by Attilio Carapezza. Palermo: Sellerio. [Originally published in 1976.]

Welldon, Estela V. 1992. *Mother, Madonna, Whore. The Idealization and Denigration of Motherhood.* New York and London: The Guilford Press.

Welton, Jude. 1994. *Mothers in Art.* London: Studio Editions.

Wiber, Melanie G. 1997. *Undulating Women/Erect Men: The Visual Imagery of Gender, Race and Progress in Reconstructive Illustrations of Human Evolution.* Waterloo, ON, Canada: Wilfred Laurier.

Wills, Garry. 1996. "The Art & Politics of the Nativity." *The New York Review of Books* (19 December): 75-82.

Wood, Sharon. 1995. *Italian Women's Writing, 1860–1994.* London: Athlone.

Woodward, Kenneth L. 1997. "Hail, Mary." *Newsweek* (August 25): 49-55.

Yalom, Marilyn. 1997. *A History of the Breast.* New York: Alfred A. Knopf.

Index

Abeona, 24
Abortion
    Catholic "objectors," 83-84
    legalization of, 54, 83
Adeona, 24
Agrarian cults, 17-24
Alemona, 23
Aleramo, Sibilla, xvii, 72-76, 95
Amaterasu, 10
Ambarvalia, 19
Amo dunque sono (Sibilla Aleramo), 75-76
Anat, 9, 143n.4
Ancona, Teresa, 105-107
Androgyny, 95, 97-98, 101, 151n.21
Anguitia, 21
Antifeminism, 65
Apennine culture, vii
Aphrodite, 5, 8-9
Aracoeli (Elsa Morante), 104-105
Archeological finds, 11-13
Ariadne, 2, 9
Art
    concept of Mary, 36-42
    imagery of the mother-child
        relationship, 40-44
    Neolithic era, 3
    Paleolithic era, 3
Artemis, 5, 8, 9, 11, 20, 29
Artemisia (Anna Banti), 87
Arval brothers, 19
Assumption of the Blessed Virgin, 21, 46

Astarte, 5
Atargatis, 18
Attis, ix, 15, 24-25

Babies. *See* Infants
"Bad mothers," 84-86, 147n.12
Bambino mio (Lidia Ravera), xviii, 97-101
Banti, Anna, 86-88, 129, 141
Baptism, 22, 145n.21
Beauvoir, Simone de, 128, 129
Belgioioso, Cristina Trivulzio di, 67-68
Belotti, Elena Gianini, 118-119
Benedetta, 77-78
Biotechnology, ecclesiastical opposition, xv
Black Madonna, 29, 143n.2
Bona Dea, 21, 141
Boyle, Kay, 152n.3
Bridal allegories, 46
Britomartis, 9

Cabeiri, 7
Cannibalism, 2
"Canzone alla Vergine" (Petrarch), 60
Caracciolo Forino, Elisabetta, 67
Carmenta, 23
Carna, 24
"Catechism" of the Council of Trent, 61
Ceres, x, 7, 18-19
Cerfia, 18
Chastity, 48
Chicco, Elisabetta, 131

Child archetype, 42
Children. *See also* Infants; Motherhood
   abandonment of, 56, 76, 149n.31
   mentally disordered, 120-121
Christianity
   concept of virginity, 9
   emergence of, 27-28, 32
   fertility festivals, 21
   imagery of the mother-child
      relationship, 40-44
   influence of fertility cults, 27-32
   Madonna worship, xv, 33-36
   mother-goddess beliefs, 2-3
   procreation duty, 50
   religious art, 36-42
   responsibilities of marriage, 46-48
   sexual paradox of the Virgin Mary,
      45
Chronology, vii-xii
Chthonia, 7
"Churching of Women," 47
Cini, Mara, 131
Cinxia, 16
Colombi, Marchesa, 68
Colonna, Vittoria, 60
Come donna zero (Luisella Fiumi), 110-
   112
Compenetrazione, xvi, 40-41, 73
Compiuta Donzella, 60
Confarreatio, 22
Cosima (Grazia Deledda), 79-83
Cosmocrates, 6
Council of Constantinople (Second), 33
Council of Ephesus, 33
Council of Nicaea, ix, 32
Council of Trent, 38, 46, 61
Couvade, 2
Creches, 147n.15
Crocefissi, Simone dei, 38
Cults
   influence on Christianity, 26-32
   Roman, 24-25
Cunina, 24
Cupra, 23

Cybele, ix, 6, 15, 24-25
Cyprus, 8-9

da Vinci, Leonardo, 39, 40-41
Dana (Danu), viii, 10
Dea Dia, 19
Dea Syria, 18
Decima, 23
Deledda, Grazia, 79-83
Demeter, 7-8, 11
Diana, 20-21, 23, 29
Diespiter (Jupiter), 23
Di Lascia, Maria Teresa, 132
di Morra, Isabella, 60
Divorce
   legalization of, 54, 83
Duccio di Buoninsegna, 40
Due donne da buttare (Armanda
   Guiducci), 114-115
Dumuzi-abzu, 5
Duse, Eleonora, 83

Earth symbolism, 38, 147n.12
Educa, 23
Egeria, 23
Egypt
   Great Mother, 6
   Isis, 5
Eileithyia, 9, 11, 29
Eliade, Mircea, 141
Eryx, 8-9
Etrusca disciplina, viii
Etruscans, 11
   divinities, 28
   Etrusca disciplina, viii
   fertility goddesses, 15-17
Eudes, Saint John, 52
Euripides, 50

Fallaci, Oriana, 95-97
Fascism
   duties of motherhood, 49-50
   Futurists, 76-78
Fata Scribunda, 23

Fauna, 21
Feast of the Purification (Candlemas), 20
Feminism
    foundation of, 72-76
Feronia, 23
Ferri, Giuliana, 108-110
Fertility goddesses
    divine mothers, 4-6
    Etruscan, 15-17
    the Greek Pantheon, 6-11
    Italian, 11-13
    Magna Mater, xiv
    prehistoric era, 4
    Roman, 17-24
    sanctuaries, 14-15
Festivals, 8
Fiumi, Luisella, 110-112
Flammeum, 22
Flora, 21
Floralia, 21, 22
Fluoria, 23
Fortuna Primigenia, 23
Franchi, Anna, 69
Franco, Veronica, 60
Frey (Freyr), 10
Freyja, 10
Futurists, 76-78, 146n.5

Gaddi, Taddeo, 37
Galli, 6
Gàmbara, Veronica, 60
Geneta Mana, 23
Genetyllides, 8
Gentileschi, Artemisia, 87
Gianini Belotti, Elena, 118-119
Ginanni, Maria, 78
Ginzburg, Natalia, 90, 152n.27
Giotto, 39
Girdle as symbol, 16, 144n.14, 146n.9
Giuffrè, Teresa, 150n.5
Giuturna, 23
Goddesses. *See* Fertility goddesses
Great Mother, xiv, xvii, 4, 6, 11, 14, 15, 24, 150n.3

Greek Pantheon, 6-11
Gregory of Nyssa, 54
Groeber, Corrado, 50
Grotto of the Venuses, 12
Guglielmetti, Amalia, 70
Guiducci, Armanda, 113-116
Gula, 5

Harpocrates, 5, 30
Hathor, 6
Hecate, 7, 20, 29
Helvidius, 36
Hera, 8, 11, 15-16
Hercules, 16
Hirsch, Marianne, 85
History: A Novel (Elsa Morante), 103
Horus, 5
Hunters
    mother-goddess beliefs, 2-3
Hypatia, 122

Iasion, 7
Ibla, 6
Ilithyia, 23
Imago templi, 14, 62
Immaculate Conception, 42-44
Inanna, 5
Infants. *See also* Children
    goddesses of, 23-24
    infanticide, 56
Infertility, 11
Interduca, 16
Invernizio, Carolina, 65-66
Irigaray, Luce, 151n.13
Ishtar, 5, 9
Isis, ix, 5, 25, 33
Italian chronology, vii-xii

Jarre, Marina, 112-113
Juno, 15-17, 23, 30

Key, fertility device, 29
Knapp, Bettina, 32
Kuan Yin, 10

La donna non è gente (Amanda Guiducci), 115-116, 144n.8
La lettere del mio nome (Grazia Livi), 128-131
La Sartiglia, 20, 151n.16
"Lady Chapels," 43
Lamaštou, 11
Lateran treaty, xi
Le lettere del mio nome (Grazia Livi), 128-131
Leonardo da Vinci, 39
Letter to an Unborn Child (Oriana Fallaci), 95-97
Levana, 23
Levi Montalcini, Rita, 71, 90-91, 150n.6
Liala, 65, 66
"Libretti religiosi," 51
Litania maior, x, 19
Litaniae minores, x, 19
Litanies, 144n.16
Livi, Grazia, 128-130
Lonzi, Carla, 129-130
Lorenzetti, Ambrogio, 31
Lorenzo the Magnificent, 60
Luanto, Regina di, 68-69
Lucina, 23
Lucina (Juno), 16-17
Lupercalia, ix, 19-20
Lustratio agrorum, 19

"Madonna del Parto," x, 37-38, 146n.10, 147n.14
Madonnas. *See also* Virgin Mary
   Black Madonna, 29
   influence of fertility goddesses, 27-32
   Milk Madonnas, x, 29-30
Magna Mater, xiv, 19, 27
Magnificat, 33, 145n.3
Maia, 17, 19, 21, 27
Manicomio primavera (Clara Sereni), 120-121
Mansionarii, 22

Maraini, Dacia, 71, 91-95
"Marchesa Colombi," 68
Maria Gravida, 35, 37
Maria lactans, 145n.2
Maria, Medea e le altre, 117-118
Maria in partu, 36
Maria Sofia di Borbone (Maria Sandias), 125-128
Marinetti, Benedetta Cappa, 77-78
Marinetti, Filippo Tommaso, 76-77
Mariolatry, 138
Marriage
   attitudes in modern Italian society, xvii, 54
   as depicted by writers of the 1980s, 116-121
   as depicted by writers of the 1990s, 121-131
   as depicted in nineteenth century literature, 61-70
   motherhood duties, 46-48
   short stories concerning, 131-135
   views of modern Italian writers, 137-142
   the "Woman Question" of the 1960s and 1970s, 83-86
Marriages. *See* Wedding traditions
Mary. *See* Virgin Mary
Mater Dei, 33
Mater Deum Magna, 33
Mater Dolorosa, 36
Mater Ecclesiae, 50
Mater Matuta, 17-18, 23
Mater mortifera, 117
Mater Mystica, 118
Maternal development, xvi
May Queen, 22
Mèlusine, 144n.13
Mens, 24
Middle Ages
   concept of Mary, 36-39
Milk
   milk fountains, vii, 14, 29-30

Milk Madonnas, x, 29-30
   symbolism of, 20, 29
Minoans, 2
Mithra, ix, 25
Moirai, 8
Morality
   chastity, 48
Morante, Elsa, 101-105, 145n.4, 151n.12
Moretti, Paola, 121-125
Mother-goddess symbol, 2-3
Motherhood
   attitudes in modern Italian society,
      53-57
   child abandonment, 56, 76
   as depicted by writers of the 1980s,
      116-121
   as depicted by writers of the 1990s,
      121-131
   as depicted in nineteenth century
      literature, 61-70
   duties of, 46-48
   imagery of the mother-child
      relationship, 40-44
   infanticide, 56
   short stories concerning, 131-135
   in United Italy, 49-52
   views of modern Italian writers,
      137-142
   wanting children syndrome, 137
   the "Woman Question" of the 1960s
      and 1970s, 83-86
   working mothers, 84-85
Mussolini, Benito, 49-50, 66, 76, 78

Nardo di Cione, 37
Naxos, 9
Neera, 65, 138
Negli occhi di una regazza (Marina
   Jarre), 112-113
Negri, Ada, 66-67
Nehalennia, 10
Neolithic era, vii, 3, 14-15
Nerthus, 10

Niccolò da Bologna, 37
Nicene Creed, 32
Ninhursaga, 11
Ninsun, 5, 7
Nobel Prize for Literature, 79
Nobel Prize in Medicine, 90
Nona, 23
Non di sola madre (Elena Gianini
   Belotti), 118-120
Nundina, 23
Nuraghi, 14, 144n.7
Nut, 6

O'Brien, Edna, 51, 149n.27
Ops, 21
Ortese, Anna Maria, 138
Osiris, 5, 25
Ossipagina, 24
Oxman, Alice, 84

Pagels, Elaine, 32, 35
Paleolithic era, vii, 1-3
Paleolithic Venuses, vii, 12-13
Pales, 18
Paradox, sexual, 45
Partula, 23
Per voce sola (Susanna Tamaro), 133-
   135
Pera, Pia, 131
Persephone, 9
Petrarch, 60
Phrygia, 6
Piero della Francesca, 38
Placenta, 115, 151n.14
Pope Joan, 122
Population growth rates, xiii, 56
Potina, 23-24
Poverty, 138
Pregnancy
   Roman goddesses of, 23
   unwanted, 48
Prehistoric era, 1-3
Princess of the Streaked Clouds, 10

Prosperi, Carola, 69-70
Purification of Mary (Candelora), ix, 33-34

Queen Maria Sophia, 125

Racconta 2, 131
Rafanelli, Leda, 70
Ravera, Lidia, 97-101
Renaissance
    concept of Mary, 40-42
Rhea, 6-7
Risorgimento (Italian national revival), 61
Rituale romanum, xi, 42, 46, 47
Robert, Enif, 77
Robigalia, 19
Rogations, 19
Roman Catholic Church. *See* Christianity
Romano, Lalla, 88-90
Rome
    fertility goddesses, 17-24
    mystery religions, 24-25
Rosà, Rosa, 78
Royal House of Savoy, 41
Rumina, 23

Sacrifices, 7
"Sacro Bambino," 36
Saint Point, Valentine de, 77
Saint Thérèse of Lisieux, 151n.22
San Bernardino of Siena, 30
Sanctuaries for fertility worship, 14-15
Sandias, Maria, 125-128
Sarapis, 25
Saturnalia, 32
Segantini, Giovanni, 147n.12
Selene (Luna), 20
Semele, 9
Sereni, Clara, 120-121
Sexton, Anne, 77, 150n.3
Shakti, 10
Short stories, 131-135
Siddieka, 10

"Smadonnare," 52-53
Sospita, 16
Stabat Mater, 43-44, 148n.19
Stampa, Gaspara, 60
Stein, Gertrude, 129
Sterility, 47-48, 68
Stone Age, 1-3, 14-15
Sumeria, 5

Taigi, Anna Maria, 52
Tamaro, Susanna, 133-134, 152n.27
Tellus Mater, 17
Terra, 17
Terracina, Laura, 60
Thalna, 16, 144n.11
Thecla, 41
Theodosius I, 32
Thesmophorizusæ(Aristophanes), 8
Torelli-Vollier, Maria Antonietta, 68
Tornabuoni, Lucrezia, 60
Transgressive mothers, 62-63
Triad (trinity), viii
Tullia d'Aragona, 60

Una famiglia normale (Teresa Ancona), 105-107
Una strana follia (Paola Moretti), 122-125
Uni, viii, 16, 30
Un quarto di donna (Giuliana Ferri), 108-110

Valentinus, 35
Veneziano, Domenico, 40
Venturi, Father Tacchi, 102
Venus of Macomer, 12
Venuses, Paleolithic, 12-13
Ver sacrum, vii, 15
Victorian period, 59
Vierges ovvrantes, 35
Virgin/Child dyad, xiii
Virgin Mary
    attitudes in modern Italian society, 52-53

concept during the Middle Ages, 36-39
concept during the Renaissance, 40-42
development of persona, 33-36
Immaculate Conception, 42-44
influence of fertility goddesses, 27-32
Nicene Council's treatment of, 32
sexual paradox, 45
virtues of, 41-42
Virginity
attitudes in modern Italian society, 53
Christian concept, 9
symbolism related to mythological love goddesses, 9
Vivanti, Annie, 65, 66
Volumna, 24

"Wanting children syndrome," 137
Water
goddesses of, 23
milk fountains, 29-30
sacred waters, 29-30
sanctuaries, 14-15
Wedding traditions, 22-23
A Woman (Sibilla Aleramo), 72-75
Woman at War (Dacia Maraini), 91-95
"The Woman Question," 83-86
Woolf, Virginia, 129, 150n.5
Working mothers, 84-85
Writers. *See also specific writers by name*
dissident women writers, 67-70
early Italian women writers, 60-67
feminism's foundation, 72-76
Futurists, 76-78
nineteenth-century Italian writers, 61-72
Nobel Prize for Literature, 79
of the 1980s, 116-121
of the 1990s, 121-131
of short stories, 131-135

Writers (*cont.*)
Victorian period, 60
views of modern Italian writers, 137-142
the "Woman Question" of the 1960s and 1970s, 83-86